IMAGE AND EXPERIENCE

IMAGE AND EXPERIENCE

Studies in a Literary Revolution

GRAHAM HOUGH

GREENWOOD PRESS, PUBLISHERS
WESTPORT, CONNECTICUT

Library of Congress Cataloging in Publication Data

Hough, Graham Goulden, 1908–
    Image and experience.

    Reprint of ed. published by the University of Nebraska
Press, Lincoln.
    Includes bibliographical references.
    1. English literature--19th century--History and
criticism--Addresses, essays, lectures. 2. English
literature--20th century--History and criticism--Ad-
dresses, essays, lectures. I. Title.
PR453.H58   1978   820'.9'08   78-16733
ISBN 0-8371-9064-9

In reprinting the lengthy prose passage and three complete poems quoted herein, the University of Nebraska Press makes the following grateful acknowledgments:

For the passage from the Introduction by T. S. Eliot to his translation of *Anabase* by St.-John Perse, and for extracts from T. S. Eliot's poems, to Faber and Faber, Ltd. (London); Harcourt, Brace & World, Inc. (New York); and Mr. Eliot himself.

For "To Earthward" by Robert Frost from *Complete Poems of Robert Frost*, copyright 1923 by Holt, Rinehart and Winston, Inc., copyright renewed 1951 by Robert Frost. Reprinted by permission of Holt, Rinehart and Winston, Inc.

For "In a Station of the Metro" and "Fan-Piece, for Her Imperial Lord," both quoted in full, from *Personae* by Ezra Pound, copyright 1926, 1954 by Ezra Pound. Reprinted by permission of New Directions, Publishers.

PREFACE

DURING the last ten years I have been mostly concerned with nineteenth- and twentieth-century literature, and the transitions and the connections between them. This book consists of separate but not unrelated pieces on these subjects. In *The Last Romantics* I tried to trace a way of thinking and feeling from the Victorian aesthetes to Yeats; in *The Romantic Poets* I attempted a straightforward little handbook to the great poets of the earlier part of the nineteenth century; and in *The Dark Sun* I was concerned with the novel, and with a peculiarly modern blending of romanticism and social realism in D. H. Lawrence. As always when one has some definite and limiting jobs on hand, a number of related ideas and topics spring up which cannot be fitted into the main schemes. They get written up as separate papers, but are all more or less linked to a continuing train of thought. This book is the result of such a process, and the best way I can explain its genesis is to risk a slight exhibition of egotism and be merely autobiographical.

For a long time I wanted to continue from *The Last Romantics* and examine the ideas underlying the poetical revolution of the early part of this century. The three lectures called "Reflections on a Literary Revolution" are the consequence of this. It meant thinking a good deal about modern criticism too. Besides the numerous guidebooks to modern poetry, there have been other works on similar lines, and I was confirmed in my intentions by Mr. Frank Kermode's *Romantic Image* and by some of the ideas in Mr. Donald Davie's *Articulate Energy*. "Free Verse" is plainly a part of the same subject, but I was actually impelled to it by considerations arising from the chapter on Lawrence's poetry in *The Dark Sun*. "Psychoanalysis and Literary Interpretation" is also relevant here; it is an attempt to tidy up some ideas that arose in connection both with Lawrence and with the criticism and interpretation of modern poetry.

PREFACE

The two essays in Part Two are both comparisons between the artistic creed of the nineteenth century and that of the twentieth. "Two Exiles" tries to bring out some likenesses and some differences between earlier romanticism and that of our own day. It is a result of writing about Lawrence immediately after writing on the Romantic poets. "Ruskin and Roger Fry" is an offshoot of the Ruskin chapter in *The Last Romantics*, a small part of which it reproduces. I wanted to set Ruskin as a type of the aesthetic outlook of the mid-nineteenth century against a typical spokesman of modern formalism.

In Part Three, I group three essays on novelists; but it has another root too. I was much dissatisfied with the chapter on the *fin-de-siècle* in *The Last Romantics* and knew that I had not dealt at all adequately with the transition from Victorian moral preoccupations to the new formal interests of the nineties. I became interested in George Moore, both as a symptomatic figure of his time, and as an unduly neglected artist of a now unfashionable kind. Of the two essays on him one deals with his literary education and its significance for those years, and the other with his attempt to re-direct the English novel. Conrad is another transitional writer; like George Moore, partly affected by the new formal conceptions of the novel that in France we associate with Flaubert, in England and America with Henry James; and partly by French realism.

This is as honest an account as I can give of how these pieces came to be written, and now that they are together I persuade myself that I see a guiding thread running through them. Most readers of my generation were brought up on what were still the literary ideas of the mid-nineteenth century. Matthew Arnold, whether mentioned or not, was the guardian of the faith in which we were instructed at school. The more seductive ideas of the eighteen-nineties, and some dim notion of their French ancestry, were the discovery of our teens; and before we were well out of them the poetic upheaval of the twenties broke upon us. "Modern poetry" appeared, something quite different from all that we had previously read or heard of, and we began to absorb it without ever understanding how it was connected with what went before. Now, in the fifties of the century and on the

PREFACE

threshold of my own, the desire makes itself felt to go back over the ground, make a sketch-map of it, and see how the road runs from each of our earlier literary halting-places to all the others. Some such impulse lies behind this collection.

"Reflections on a Literary Revolution" formed a series of three lectures given on the Monsignor Dougherty Foundation at the Catholic University of America in the spring of 1959. "Free Verse" was the Warton Lecture of the British Academy for 1957. "Two Exiles" was the Byron Lecture at the University of Nottingham in 1956. "George Moore and the Nineties" was read to the English Institute in New York in the autumn of 1958. The other George Moore piece and the one on Conrad are rather longer versions of centenary broadcasts on the B.B.C. Third Programme. "Ruskin and Roger Fry" was published in *The Cambridge Journal*. My thanks are due to these various bodies and periodicals for permission to reprint.

G. H.

Singapore, 1949
Grantchester, 1959

CONTENTS

Part One

I

REFLECTIONS ON A LITERARY
REVOLUTION

I. IMAGISM AND ITS CONSEQUENCES

LITERATURE, by a fortunate dispensation, does not reflect very accurately the convulsions of the social order. Its revolutions sometimes precede the social ones, sometimes follow them, sometimes, it would seem, overlap them quite pointlessly. In any case the cultural historian has no difficulty in finding the relations he is disposed to find. He deals in large masses of material, the phenomena are so numerous that they can surely be connected in more ways than the ingenuity of a commentator can devise. But as soon as we begin to look closely at a particular patch of literature we are likely to see it developing according to its own principles, which have their own interest, and are likely to be at least partly fortuitous in their relations to the wars, technologies or movements of classes that are their temporal accompaniments. This dispensation is fortunate, for it is a happy instance of what we mean by the freedom of the spirit.

Looked at in a sufficiently apocalyptic light, the extraordinary outbreak of genius and novelty in the literature of the early part of this century can be seen as the response of the imagination to the appalling moral and political history of our age. And so no doubt it is, and all the books with crisis, revolt, dilemma and hazard in their titles are right. But part of the imaginative response has always been to occupy itself with other things than crises and hazards. "I particularly admired your use of the pluperfect subjunctive", as Claudel once remarked to Gide. The imagination has its own procedures and its own stratagems, different for every art in which it expresses itself. In the visual arts and in music the devices may be of international range. In literature they can hardly be that, for each language has its own procedure, never held quite in common with that of any other. The closer we come to a particular literature the more closely its features will be seen to depend on the state of the language at the time, the state of previous writing in it, the prestige or the declining fortune of special forms. In short, a literary revolution must be a *literary* revolution if it is to be anything. It may accompany or be accompanied by almost any other kind of revolution, at almost any distance. But unless we are looking at literature as a symptom of something else (a possibly respectable occupation, but not that of the literary critic) what must be attended to is the behaviour of literature itself.

The years between 1910 and the Second World War saw a revolution in the literature of the English language as momentous as the Romantic one of a century before. It is an Anglo-American development that is itself part of a whole European affair. Beside the names of Yeats, Joyce, Eliot and Pound we should wish to place those of Gide, Valéry and Thomas Mann, perhaps Proust and Rilke from an earlier generation. Here is our identification parade for the modern spirit in letters. But here too we have such a huge and various collective phenomenon that almost anything we care to say about it would be true of sóme part or other; the target is so large that any chance-aimed shot would be sure to hit it somewhere. If we look at it *en masse* we shall soon find ourselves speaking of crisis in Western values, of dissociation of sensibility, of alienation, and disinherited minds. Looking from this vertiginous height we shall surely be able to make many observations that are true, the more easily since they are not liable to the contradictions of particularity. Let us descend and recover balance by observing a fixed spot—London in the years just before 1914. It was there that the English cell of an almost world-wide poetic conspiracy was being incubated—the first plot against the literary establishment for over a hundred years. Of course foreign agents were at work; there had been correspondence with France and the Orient; a person from Idaho and one from St. Louis were actually present.

4

A LITERARY REVOLUTION

So in the next few years "modern poetry" came into being. Strangely, it is still modern poetry, the same article, sold under the same name. The revolution is long past. Of the central revolutionary quartet—Pound, Eliot, Joyce and Wyndham Lewis—"the men of 1914", as Lewis liked to call them (it is characteristic that the turn of phrase should be borrowed from European revolutionary politics), two are dead, one has recently been certified sane by the State Department, and the fourth is happily still with us, the greatest living man of letters. A generation has had to pass to bring about this change of aspect. But nothing has happened to dispute with their productions the title of modern letters. No *avant-garde* has advanced any farther. There is no *avant-garde*. When I was a boy "modern poetry" was to be distinguished from poetry simple. Poetry was inherited from parents and learnt at school; it was the "Ode to a Grecian Urn" and "The Solitary Reaper". Modern poetry was read in a different context; neither one's parents nor anyone at school knew anything about it. Modern poetry is now academically respectable. It is taught in college courses, and the exposition of it gives employment to many worthy persons. But it is still almost as distinct from "poetry" as ever. Distinct in the general imagination, and not only in that; even among those who seriously profess the arts there is a feeling of the discontinuity between the literature of our century and that of any previous one. The singularity of modern poetry, for example, is one of the arguments used by C. S. Lewis to support his hypothesis of a great rift in our culture just before the present age.

This consciousness of modernity is a distinctively modern thing; it is largely the work of the revolutionary generation itself. Pound's essays were called *Make It New*. In the stream of advice and exhortation he offered to young writers there is a continual insistence on novelty and on being up-to-date. "No good poetry is ever written in a manner twenty years old." "The scientist does not claim to be a great scientist till he has *discovered* something."[1] In both his and Eliot's criticism we are always hearing about "what remains to be done", "what is to

[1] *Literary Essays of Ezra Pound* (London, 1954), pp. 6, 11.

be done next". A curious instance of this acute period-consciousness occurs quite recently, in Mr. Eliot's introduction to Pound's *Literary Essays*. He cites as one of the tricks of malevolent critics—"to quote what a writer said twenty or thirty years ago, as if it was something he had said yesterday".[1] It is hard to imagine Johnson or Coleridge or Arnold finding it "malevolent" to quote a twenty-year-old dictum without the appropriate date. Lest I be suspected of malevolence may I add that the date of this remark is 1954, a date far removed from the dust of revolutionary conflict. Plainly the instigators of the late poetic innovation were badly frightened by a Zeitgeist, and the effects have been lasting.

The new poetry was new in the twenties, and it is still new, in the sense that we have nothing newer. As early as 1935 we find Sir Herbert Read, in an essay called *Form in Modern Poetry*, complaining of backsliding, of a decline in revolutionary and experimental ardour. It might be that the new tradition had established itself, that we now have a body of followers working in an accepted mode. But this is not true, or true only in a very restricted area. The revolution of 1914 was quite as momentous as the Romantic one of over a century before, but it was different. The Romantic change was not at all antipathetic to ancient and deep-rooted tendencies. In many ways it was a return to them; the old text-book term is after all the Romantic Revival. The result is that its habits of feeling and expression are a model for the next hundred years. The nineteenth-century shelves are stuffed with Wordsworthian poems, Keatsian poems and Byronic poems. The modern revolution has had a different fate. In one direction, in the establishment of a modern colloquial poetic idiom, the younger writers have certainly learnt the lesson of their elder contemporaries. All that purgation of poetic diction that has been so carefully and beautifully worked out, both in theory and in practice, by Mr. Eliot has become an almost absolute critical rule. The rule has been formulated, with something less than complete approval, in a recent essay by John Crowe Ransom: "That is simply a bad poem whose unfashionable or dated diction the plain reader spots at the first reading."

[1] *Literary Essays of Ezra Pound*, p. xi.

But other parts of the newly conquered territory are being little cultivated. A belated critical posse in full jungle kit still hacks it way through these no longer very forbidding areas, in the pages of the semi-academic reviews; and that is about all. The influence of the generation of 1914 was always of a peculiar kind. On taste, ideas and feelings about literature it was dynamic, radical, and in the end largely triumphant. A diluted version of Mr. Eliot's critical doctrine (and that includes, at one remove, a great deal of the doctrines of Hulme, Pound and Lewis) is by now the possession of undergraduates and school-boys. Mr. Eliot's version of English literary history is as much an orthodoxy as Matthew Arnold's was a generation before. Yet the direct effect on literary practice has been strangely small. There is no other poem of any significance remotely like *The Waste Land*; the metrics and the ordonnance of Pound's *Propertius* have had no successors whatever; no one has ever seriously attempted to emulate Joyce's most characteristic experiments; and the extraordinary bundle of detestations that go to make up Wyndham Lewis are so arbitrary that they are a monument to nothing but himself.

A rich and vigorous body of literature has established itself, but has not established a workable tradition. A possibility (it has been faintly entertained by Mr. Blackmur)[1] is that it is not through this self-consciously "modern" literature that the main road runs; that these writers are not the transmitters of the most vigorous poetic life of our time. Perhaps the authentic torch has been borne by writers of a more traditional cast— shall we say by Robert Frost, Robert Graves and E. M. Forster? But this is not really a possibility. It is not the admirable workers in traditional modes who have given the twentieth century its peculiar kind of vitality. The suggestion is entertained only to be dismissed. As I show it to the door I become aware of one of its relatives faintly demanding admittance. Deep in the folk-memory of English literary critics is the echo of a time when it was possible to speak of something called "the English spirit". Few, in a state of full vigilance, would allow this faded trope to escape their lips now. But I intend to

---

[1] R. P. Blackmur, *Anni Mirabiles*, 1921–25 (Washington, 1956), p. 41.

employ it, not meaning whatever Sir Arthur Quiller-Couch would have meant by it, but meaning something like the spirit of the language, the whole drift and pressure given by the whole body of poetry written in English. The suggestion that knocks at the door is that specifically "modern" poetry is hostile to this spirit and has tried to move against that pressure. A few very powerful talents succeeded in establishing idiosyncratic positions. No one since has been powerful enough to take up the same stance or sufficiently supple and adaptable to go back and take up the old path where it left off. This is at least plausible as far as English is concerned, though in America it may be less so. It need not surprise us when we consider that two of the "men of 1914" were Americans, one an Irishman, and the origins of the other shrouded in mystery.

The suggestion may be allowed to stand in the doorway, for we are not yet in a position to examine its credentials. We have not yet asked what the nature of the twentieth-century revolution is, so we cannot yet know how it is related to the English poetic tradition. It is notable that whatever was happening in those years has not yet acquired a name. Mr. Blackmur has referred to the whole European movement, with which the English one belongs, as Expressionism. I should not be very happy with this as far as our domestic affair is concerned. Expressionism in art has Germanic connotations, and the literature we are considering is Anglo-American profoundly influenced by France. And Expressionism is a name for a kind of critical doctrine, a doctrine of personality and self-expression, that is precisely the one *not* held by our twentieth-century school. I should like to have a name; it is a nuisance not to have one for something one is always discussing; but I should prefer to look nearer home and hope to fare better.

If we look into the archives of the period of revolutionary preparation, the name that is going about is Imagism. A "school of images" is referred to. Ezra Pound announces that as for the future the "Imagistes" have that in their keeping. This was in a note to the complete poetical works of T. E. Hulme (five poems), published at the end of *Ripostes* in 1912. Several forms of an Imagist manifest exist; and Ezra Pound's "A few don'ts

8

by an Imagist" appeared in *Poetry* in 1913. And there are several Imagist anthologies, the first under the auspices of Ezra Pound, others under those of Amy Lowell. In the narrow sense, the name refers to a movement whose history was brief, broken and querulous, whose poetic results were minuscule. The refinement of our numbers was to be accomplished by the introduction of the *haiku*, the Japanese poem of seventeen syllables. The tongue that Milton spake is not easily compressed into seventeen-syllable units; and even in its longer flights Imagism remains a small affair. But as a centre and an influence it is not small. It is the hard irreducible core of a whole cluster of poetic ideas that extend far beyond Imagism as a movement. Imagist ideas are at the centre of the characteristic poetic procedures of our time, and there is a case for giving the word a wider extension.

Imagism sounds like a by-blow from Symbolism. Image and symbol—we have been pestered by both words long enough; often we do not distinguish between them. If we were talking about continental Europe instead of the Anglo-American literary world there would be no need to make much play with Imagism. Symbolism is already there, well established and more or less understood. There have been several attempts to see the new poetry in English simply as a part of this earlier European movement. Edmund Wilson sees it in this way, as a large extension of Symbolism, in *Axel's Castle*. But this justly famous book was written in the middle of the development that it describes, and has been overtaken by the event. Its introductory chapter on Symbolism seems thin to-day, though it was nourishing at the time. Sir Maurice Bowra, largely concerned with Europe, has written of modern literature as the heritage of Symbolism. More recently, Frank Kermode, in a brief, brilliant, unhistorical essay, *Romantic Image*, has conflated Symbolism and Imagism, and even seen both of them as a continuation of the Romantic road. However, there is room for a distinction here, and not only room, but a real need for it.

Though Symbolism is in a sense a late development of Romantic thought it takes a decisively new turn. The great Romantic writers (Wordsworth, Coleridge, Keats) all see literature as deeply rooted in experience. The confessional poem, the truth that has been "proved upon the pulses", the attitude of those "to whom the miseries of the world are misery and will not let them rest"—these are its characteristic expressions. Symbolism moves in the direction of an autonomous art, severed from life and experience by an impassable gulf. The Symbolists share with the Romantics the reliance on the epiphany, the moment of revelation; but they differ sharply about its status in nature and its relation to art. Wordsworth's spiritual life is founded on such moments of illumination, and it is the business of his poetry both to describe them and to relate them to the whole experience of a long ordered lifetime. For the Symbolist poet there is no question of describing an experience; the moment of illumination only occurs in its embodiment in some particular artistic form. There is no question of relating it to the experience of a lifetime, for it is unique, it exists in the poem alone. Rimbaud's *alchimie du verbe* is not a mere phrase, for the poet not only transmits, he creates the revelations that make up his world.

Symbolism therefore has strong transcendental overtones. The poet is a magus, calling reality into existence. Or he is the sole transmitter of a mysterious system of correspondences that actually pervades the universe, but only becomes apparent in art. Or he is capable of evoking from the Anima Mundi symbols of the profoundest import, but strictly unexpoundable, for their content is inseparable from the form of their first expression. At times we seem to be in something like the medieval symbolic universe. But that symbolism has a key, a key given once and for all in revelation. Since the means of grace and some means of instruction are available to all, it was in a sense a joy in widest commonalty spread; while the Symbolist universe reveals itself only in glimpses, only in art, and only to initiates.

Now while modern literature has been afflicted with a persistent hangover from the rich Symbolist symposium, the magical and transcendental pretensions of Symbolism have almost entirely disappeared. It is only in the work of the early Yeats that we can find the Symbolist doctrine in full bloom. Even here it is considerably contaminated with a non-literary occultism—theosophy, spiritualism, Madame Blavatsky and the order of the Golden Dawn. It is doubtful whether we can properly speak of a Symbolist movement in English poetry, in a historical sense. Of course if we like to take Symbolism as a universal, recurrent phenomenon we can rope in such diverse figures as Blake and Herman Melville, and no doubt a dozen others, and make some use of the concept. I am speaking of Symbolism as a more or less datable historical development, as the term is used in French literature. This development several times looks as though it is going to occur in English, but it never comes to much, though relations with the French movement were frequent and beguiling. There was a foreshadowing of French Symbolism in the Pre-Raphaelites; there were many importations of Symbolist doctrine in the nineties; but it is not until the years before the First World War that French doctrines and practice showed signs of giving rise to a new poetry in England.

The history is complicated, and it has still only partly been written. There are probably many reasons that Symbolism took such feeble roots in England. We had a little of it of our own already; English poetry lacks a Baudelaire to stand as *éminence grise* behind the movement; above all, Symbolist influence on sensibility was not paralleled by a close study of Symbolist forms. The *fin-de-siècle*, fertile in sentiments and attitudes that are important for modern literature, was curiously powerless to find forms to match them; and it was not until the years around 1910 that a radically new poetry, and that implies a new poetic form, really begins to appear in English. In those years, when the group that were later to call themselves Imagists were laying their plans, the transcendental pretensions of Symbolism were no longer easy to entertain. The career of Mallarmé had ended in silence and something like despair. *Un coup de dés jamais n'abolira le hasard.* Rimbaud's defection to slave-trading in Africa was itself a symbol of the inefficacy of magical Symbolism; and the innocuous chastities of Japanese poetry in dilute translation were focusing attention on the surface properties rather than on the mystic attributes of the symbol.

Certain aspects of Symbolist doctrine persist, but the nature of the attention is changed. Revelation becomes technique, incantation becomes a code of prohibitions. What emerges is a new phenomenon, to which we rightly give a new name— Imagism. Not to deal in definition at this stage, and in the hope that things will become clearer as we go on, we can describe it roughly as Symbolism without the magic. The symbol, naked and unexplained, trailing no clouds of glory, becomes the image.

Let us clip a few flowers from the imagist's garden of maxims.

> An image is that which presents an intellectual and emotional complex in an instant of time.
>
> Go in fear of abstractions.
>
> The natural object is always the adequate symbol.
>
> I believe that the proper and perfect symbol is the natural object, that if a man uses "symbols" he must use them so that their symbolic function does not obtrude; so that a sense, and the poetic quality of the passage, is not lost to those who do not understand the symbol as such, to whom, for instance, a hawk is a hawk.[1]

Unexceptionable sentiments, according to the canons of much modern poetics; but compare them with some pure symbolist pronouncements.

> A symbol is indeed the only possible expression of some invisible essence, a transparent lamp about a spiritual flame.[2]
>
> Je dis: une fleur! et, hors de l'oubli où ma voix relègue aucun contour, en tant que quelque chose d'autre que les calices sus, musicalement se lève, idée même et suave, l'absente de tous bouquets.[3]

These alone will serve to illustrate the way the symbol has become *opaque* in transforming itself into the image. No transparent envelopes, or mysterious absences, or invisible essences. Direct treatment of the *thing*, we are told, is the great object. T. E. Hulme's early criticism hammers away at accurate description, hardness, clarity. And we know what came of it:

> The apparition of these faces in the crowd
> Petals on a wet black bough.

[1] *Literary Essays of Ezra Pound*, pp. 5, 9.
[2] W. B. Yeats, *Essays* (London, 1924), p. 142.
[3] Mallarmé, *Œuvres complètes* (Pléiade, Paris, 1945), p. 368.

A LITERARY REVOLUTION

Those dozens of little poems in Pound's *Ripostes* and later; clear, limited, without resonance, without transparency. "The natural object is always the adequate symbol"—but of what? Of nothing but itself. A world composed of atomic notations, each image separate from all the others. They neither lead into each other nor to apprehension on any other level. There is in all Pound's practice and theory at this time a positivism, a defiant insistence on the surface of things, and an insistence that the surface of things is all.

Pound writes of Laurent Tailhade:

> I think this sort of clear presentation is of the noblest tradition of our craft. It is surely the scourge of fools. It is what may be called the "prose tradition" of poetry, and by this I mean that it is a practice of speech common to good prose and good verse alike. . . . It means constatation of fact. It presents. It does not comment. . . . It is not a criticism of life. I mean it does not deal in opinion. It washes its hands of theories. It does not attempt to justify anybody's ways to anybody or anything else.[1]

But even Pound could not consistently maintain that the clear presentation of the object was the sole aim of poetry. Though he often talks in T. E. Hulme's terms, as though presentational accuracy was an end in itself, in other places the natural object is seen as the equivalent of an emotion. Poetry is the art of making equations for emotions. But it is an equation of which one side only is to be presented. Imagist convention forbids that most ancient recipe for a poem—the poem in which first a natural object is presented, and then some reflection on human experience that arises from it, or is in some way parallel to it. As a student of Provençal Pound must have been familiar with the *reverdie* and its long history—the spring song, whose first stanza presents "the soote sesoun that bud and bloom forth brings", whose later ones present the happy love that resembles it, or the unhappy love that contrasts with it. By his subsequent lights it is only possible for the poet to say "It is Spring"— and, unspoken, on no account to be uttered, only to be understood—"if you care to make any deductions from this to my

[1] "The Approach to Paris", *The New Age*, Oct. 2, 1913.

state of mind, you may". But since the natural object is always the adequate symbol the poem will not make itself responsible for any of these deductions.

> I leaned against a sturdy oak,
> I thought it was a trusty tree;
> But first it bent and syne it broke.
> Sae did my true love lichtly me.

This is too explicit for true Imagist principles. The proper procedure is to be seen in the "Fan-Piece for her Imperial Lord":

> O fan of white silk,
> Clear as the frost on the grass-blade
> You also are laid aside.

So far, merely a change of rhetorical convention; a laconic novelty of procedure that has its own charm. We know well enough what the Imagists are tired of. They are tired of Arnold's "Dover Beach"; the extended picture of the moonlight, the beach and the tide; and then the inevitable, the too-long expected "The sea of faith was once too at the full . . ."; the melancholy nineteenth-century automatism by which no natural object can appear without trailing its inglorious little cloud of moralising behind it. They were right to be tired. One aspect of the history of poetry is an intermittent warfare against automatisms, clichés of feeling and expression. Only an intermittent warfare, for there are long periods when poetry can rest, contented, healthy and active, within a set of received conventions. But these periods come to an end. This was a time when the battlefront had again become particularly active.

From this point of view Imagism was good tactics, and the skirmish was conducted with vigour and address. But tactics are not principles, and there is always danger when they are erected into principles. Pound was particularly liable to make this transformation. His insistence on procedure and technique is the beginning of this. "A few don'ts"; as though the writing of poetry is the adroit employment of a series of gimmicks; the continual invocation of "the expert"; the deference (in writing that shows little deference) to the progress of the natural sciences.

A LITERARY REVOLUTION

What the expert is tired of to-day the public will be tired of to-morrow.

It is not necessary that a poem should rely on its music, but if it does rely on its music, that music must be such as will delight the expert.

The scientist does not expect to be acclaimed a great scientist until he has *discovered* something. He begins by learning what has been discovered already. He goes from that point onwards.

The best history of poetry would be an anthology in which each poem was chosen . . . because it contained an invention, a definite contribution to the art of verbal expression.[1]

When Imagist doctrine was reinforced by Pound's study (if it can be called study) of Chinese, and his understanding (which was a misunderstanding) of the nature of Chinese ideogram, the gimmicks were well on the way to becoming a principle. When Pound took over Fenollosa's manuscripts he also took over the idea that the originally pictographic nature of the Chinese written character was still a subsistent force, that the reader actually *saw* the image in the complex ideogram. All scholars now agree that this is mistaken; even if they did not, it is on the face of it impossible; as impossible as to suppose that the reader of English resuscitates every dead metaphor as he goes along, thinks of weighing when he ponders, or of the stars when he considers. Even though it was untrue, this way of thinking might have given rise, when applied to an Indo-European language, to some sort of doctrine of radical metaphor—that poetry proceeds by distilling the quintessence of language. This, we have been told, is one of the keys to Mallarmé. But Pound shows no interest in this sort of speculation. His supposed nugget of wisdom from the East is used to provide a cultural foundation for the doctrine of the image. Chinese uses picture-writing and so ought we. A strain of crotchety hostility to the traditions of Western thinking begins to appear. An obscure ideological war is invented in which Confucius knocks out Aristotle and abstraction and discursive thought are left in ruins. Poetry proceeds by the juxtaposition of ideograms, and new ideogram is old image writ large. The unit of poetry is the pictograph, the record of a significant glimpse.

[1] *Literary Essays of Ezra Pound*, pp. 5, 6, 17.

15

IMAGE AND EXPERIENCE

From then on the doctrine burgeons, flourishes, spreads its roots and sends up suckers in every direction. (Many of us have been suckers for it at one time or another.) It connects itself easily with other speculations and manœuvres which start from a different point but begin to converge with Imagism. Joyce's "epiphany", the moment in which the essential nature of an object reveals itself, is presented with a good deal of Thomistic top-dressing; but it is really a survival from magical Symbolism, and our sense of this is confirmed by the *fin-de-siècle* prose in which the earlier Joycean epiphanies are often enshrined. The moment of revelation need not be a revelation of beauty or transcendence. The customs-house clock, Stephen tells Cranly, might suddenly be epiphanised—manifest itself in its essence.[1] Or more frequently, a quotidian object suddenly reveals not only its own nature, but that of the forces that went to make it, or of the whole circumambient situation: "one of those brown brick houses which seem the very incarnation of Irish paralysis". This can become something like a form of Imagist doctrine; more sophisticated, without the pinched prohibitory air that hangs round Imagism. It produces similar technical results—the instantaneous glimpse of a phenomenal object as the basic symbolic counter. *Portrait of the Artist* is built out of a succession of such instants. Compared with the startling technical innovations of Joyce's later work its method is unsurprising. It is nevertheless one of the earliest instances of a narrative, a development, presented by a series of unlinked scenes or shots.

One of the most celebrated offshoots of the Imagist idea is Mr. Eliot's Objective Correlative. We are all heartily sick of the phrase, even Mr. Eliot, so I will only recall briefly its original formulation. "The only way of expressing emotion in the form of art is by finding an 'objective correlative', in other words a set of objects, a situation, a chain of events which shall be the formula of that *particular* emotion; such that when the external facts, which must terminate in sensory experience, are given, the emotion is immediately evoked."[2] Objections have

[1] James Joyce, *Stephen Hero* (New York, 1955), p. 210.
[2] "Hamlet and his Problems", *The Sacred Wood* (London, 1920), p. 100.

been made to the "expressionist" character of this passage—the suggestion that the business of the poet is to find external manifestations for previously determinate emotions. I wish to point to something rather different—the suggestion that the whole natural world offers to the poet a collection of bric-à-brac from which he takes selections to represent emotional states. "Direct presentation of the thing"—the image so produced exists to be one side of an equation the other side of which is an emotion. Plainly an eccentric view of the poet's procedure. We can hardly suppose that either the author of the *Iliad* or the author of

> Christ that my love was in my arms
> And I in my bed again

were collecting *objets trouvés* in this way. Gerard Manley Hopkins wrote "The Wreck of the Deutschland" because he was moved by the account of a shipwreck in which five nuns were drowned; he did not go round looking for a suitable disaster to match an emotion that he already had. This is possibly a position that Mr. Eliot, who wrote of it a long time ago, would not wish to maintain in its full rigour. But we must in some sense hold him to it, for it has consequences in other parts of his thinking about poetry. There is the idea that coherence and validity of thought have nothing to do with poetic worth; Dante made great poetry out of a strong and beautiful philosophy, Shakespeare out of a muddled one, but this does not affect their merit as poets. There is the related idea that poets do not "think", they take over the thought of their time. This would make the poet's activity something like painting flowers on china plates that he had bought ready-made from the factory; and I am sure that this is not what Mr. Eliot means; but it is what he appears to be saying. There is the idea that meaning is a kind of sop thrown to the intellect, like the bit of meat the burglar keeps to give to the dog, while the "poetry" does its work.[1] These are all pervasive ideas in modern, post-symbolist poetic strategy, and they are all related to the root idea that the substance of poetry is the image and its resonances.

[1] *The Use of Poetry and the Use of Criticism* (London, 1933), p. 151.

IMAGE AND EXPERIENCE

The doctrine has its corollary when we come to consider the major structure of poetry; one that is startlingly at variance with the classical view. If poetry is a matching up of images with emotions its underlying framework consists of emotions. Its order is therefore an order of emotions. In classical poetic theory (by classical I mean here one that prevailed generally from the Greeks till some time in the nineteenth century) the order of poetry was an order of events or thoughts. Events are capable of causal connection, thoughts of logical connection; the one is the structure of narrative or dramatic poetry, the other of philosophic or reflective poetry. Only in the briefest lyric can we find an order that is simply that of emotions; and classical poetic theory was not deduced from brief lyrics. One does not insist on an Aristotelian rigour of construction; but even in the looser forms the sense of a syntax of events or a syntax of thoughts is preserved; and criticism insisted on it. Emotions are not capable of such a syntax. A pattern can be made of them, by simple juxtaposition, but it will hardly be an integrated pattern, unless there runs through it the thread of narrative or logic. Imagist poetry has therefore been obliged to invoke *another kind of logic*, a logic of emotions that works in its own way, and is supposed to be especially suitable for poetry. The most compendious expression of this notion is to be found in Mr. Eliot's introduction to St.-John Perse's *Anabase*.

> Any obscurity of the poem, on first readings, is due to the suppression of "links in the chain", of explanatory and connecting matter, and not to incoherence, or to the love of cryptogram. The justification of such abbreviation of method is that the sequence of images coincides and concentrates into one intense impression of barbaric civilisation. The reader has to allow the images to fall into his memory successively without questioning the reasonableness of each at the moment; so that, at the end, a total effect is produced. Such selection of a sequence of images and ideas has nothing chaotic about it. There is a logic of the imagination as well as a logic of concepts. People who do not appreciate poetry always find it difficult to distinguish between order and chaos in the arrangement of images; and even those who are capable of appreciating poetry cannot depend upon first impressions. I was not convinced of Mr. Perse's imaginative order until I had read the poem five or six times. And if, as I

18

suggest, such an arrangement of imagery requires just as much "fundamental brain-work" as the arrangement of an argument, it is to be expected that the reader of a poem should take at least as much trouble as a barrister reading an important decision on a complicated case.

This document is worth examining in some detail. The occasion is particular, but the application is general. What is outlined is the method of a school. Three layers are to be discerned in this ingenious piece of discourse. The first is simply descriptive. We are told of a "sequence of images", of images that fall into the memory successively with no question of reasonableness, of resultant obscurity. This is a general description of Imagist technique; it is the procedure of *Anabase*; it is also the procedure of *The Waste Land* and the *Cantos*. The second layer, interwoven with the first, but we are attempting to separate it, is one of justification. Two justifications of this method are in fact offered. They are not compatible with each other. The first is that any appearance of obscurity is merely due to the suppression of connecting matter: the logic of the poem is like the logic of any other kind of discourse, but it is presented in a concentrated and elliptical form. The second justification, however, is that the poem is constructed according to a "logic of the imagination" which is different from ordinary logic. It requires as much effort as the construction of an argument, but it is evidently of a different kind. And besides these layers, of description and justification, there is a third layer of knock-me-down *argumentum ad hominem*, designed to cause alarm and despondency in the breasts of persons who have not yet accepted the first two. Such persons do not appreciate poetry, cannot distinguish between order and chaos, and, in their benighted triviality, have probably never thought of assimilating the action of a reader of poetry to that of a barrister getting up a brief.

There is much in this sort of argument that arouses suspicion. The device of dismissing one's opponents as unqualified instead of convincing them that they are wrong is one that works only with the very unsophisticated or the very easily scared. It has been greatly overworked by the founding fathers of modern poetics. Only poets can judge poetry; this is a matter for the expert; certificates of culture countersigned by Confucius, Lancelot Andrews and Rémy de Gourmont to be produced on admission—but these minatory gestures have dwindled into a curious historic ritual; and they have been discussed elsewhere. A more serious question is whether the Imagist procedure here described is an ordinary mode of discourse telescoped and abbreviated, or whether some special "logic of the imagination" is involved.

Let us look at the organisation of *The Waste Land*. In detail, and in some places, the first explanation works well enough. The opening twenty lines of the poem can be seen as an elliptical narrative, with fragments of reflection and direct speech. (April is the cruellest month . . . we went on into the Hofgarten . . . and when we were children, staying at the arch-duke's.) In principle it could be expanded, the links could be supplied; what we have is the natural result of the attempt at pruning and concentrating nineteenth-century poetic method. The sense of an existing but not definitely stated plot is still there. It will require a great deal more latitude to apply this argument to the major structure of the poem. We know now that it was of considerably greater length, and attained its present proportions under the direction of Ezra Pound. We have always known that "Death by Water", the Phlebas the Phoenician section, was not originally part of *The Waste Land*, since it is a translation from the French of the last section of an earlier poem "Dans le Restaurant". Its insertion was again due to Pound. We know now too that "Gerontion" was at one time to be included but was in the end left out to become a separate poem.[1] If this is the logic of the imagination it is evidently patient of a good deal of outside influence. There is a curious fortuitousness about it. And mere ellipsis, the omission of connecting links, will not serve as an explanation of the changes of speaker, shifts in time, scene and mode of address, the liberation of the image from all continuity that give the poem its peculiarly coruscating surface.

[1] See *Letters of Ezra Pound* (New York, 1950), pp. 169–72. It is also noteworthy that in John Rodker's circular for Bel Esprit, a proposed literary fund, *The Waste Land* is referred to as "a series of poems". (*Letters of Ezra Pound*, p. 175.)

In the poem as a whole the sense of an unspoken underlying plot has completely disappeared.

I cannot think that the problems raised by the structure of *The Waste Land* have been faced. They have been a party matter, a matter of polemic or defence; they have been a shibboleth; to accept this sort of technique was at one time a sort of touchstone for participation in modern poetry. Above all, the methodological anfractuosities of the piece have fulfilled one of the main economic functions of poetry in this century—they have given employment to a host of scholiasts. But they have hardly been a matter for distinterested inquiry. While the poem was still capable of causing bewilderment it established itself. The brilliance of the imagery, the auditory and incantatory grandeur of its best passages, stole into the consciousness and became a part of our poetical property; it became ungrateful, almost indecent to ask of what sort of continuum these fragments were a part. And we became satisfied with a level of coherence that we should never have found sufficient in any earlier poem. The unity of emotional effect withdrew attention from the logical discontinuity, the extraordinary rhetorical diversity. A poem about frustration, aridity, fear and the perversions of love—these signs were to be read by anyone. They were read, and in combination with the modern urban imagery they instigated the critics who said that the poem expressed "the disillusionment of a generation". For this, some years later, they were sternly reproved by the author; but they were no doubt expressing, in their way, the only sense they had of a unity of purpose in the poem. Meanwhile, prompted by the notes, many persons who had stopped reading *The Golden Bough* looked at it again, and those who had never heard of Miss Jessie Weston read *From Ritual to Romance*. None of them were bold enough to say in public that these studies did little to advance their understanding. Certainly they directed attention to recurring symbolism of death and rebirth, drought and rain. But this was the kind of pattern that in earlier poetry had been only secondary to structure of another kind; it could not be seen as constituting a structure in itself. So we turned to more peripheral matters. We looked up the quotations from Dante and Baudelaire, and our apprehension of isolated lines increased in depth. *Turdus aonalaschkae palasii*, whose water-dripping song is justly celebrated, doubtless afforded satisfaction to many. And the volume of exegesis increased, the explanations that did not explain, the links that connected nothing to nothing. And by the time that the movement of modern poetry had gone far enough for it to be a possible object of contemplation and inquiry, one shrank from asking the real questions, lest what was after all one of the great poetic experiences of our time should be still further buried beneath yet another load of waste paper.

But the questions remain—above all the question of what really makes the poem a totality, if it is one at all. If we can imagine some ideal critic, acquainted with the poetical tradition of Europe, yet innocent of the spirit of our age, and if we can imagine ourselves persuading him to leave the question of total structure in abeyance, "to allow the images to fall into his memory successively without questioning the reasonableness of each"—he would still be struck by the extraordinary rhetorical incongruities. He would find within its four hundred lines passages that are narrative, others that are dramatic, descriptive, lyric, hallucinatory and allusive. The theory of genres was never watertight or exhaustive, but never before was there a poem of this length, or perhaps of any other length, in which the modes were so mixed. Nor is the rhetorical level any more constant than the rhetorical mode. A modern and highly individual elegiac intensity, pastiche Renaissance grandeur, sharp antithetical social comment in the Augustan manner, the low mimetic of public-house conversation—all these and probably several other styles are found side by side. The relation of these is sometimes obvious; it is one of calculated contrast. But it is a question how hard such contrasts of texture can be worked in a relatively short poem without disastrous damage to the unity of surface. It is not so much in the obvious collisions of the high and the low styles that this is felt. That kind of calculated shock action is a limited effect, and the intention of producing the shock itself provides a medium between the two elements. It is the use of language in different and unrelated fashions in different parts of the poem that is disruptive.

A LITERARY REVOLUTION

There is the lovely, romantically evocative manner of the hyacinth girl passage:

> Yet when we came back late from the Hyacinth garden
> Your arms full, and your hair wet, I could not
> Speak, and my eyes failed, I was neither
> Living nor dead, and I knew nothing,
> Looking into the heart of light, the silence.

These lines live unhappily in the same poem with;

> Endeavours to engage her in caresses
> Which still are unreproved if undesired.
> Flushed and decided, he assaults at once;
> Exploring hands encounter no defence;
> His vanity requires no response,
> And makes a welcome of indifference.

The uneasiness does not arise from incompatibility of tone and feeling, but because the two passages are using language in utterly different ways; the first to evoke, by overtones and connotations, the trembling ghost of an intense emotion that is never located or defined; the second to define a situation by precise denotation and intelligent analysis. It is as though a painter were to employ a pointilliste technique in one part of a picture, and the glazes of the high renaissance in another.

When we come to the content of the separate passages the situation is disturbing in another way. It has become fashionable to refer to these contents as "themes", suggesting a vaguely musical analogy; and suggesting, too, I suppose, that the "themes" of a poem are related to each other only as the themes of a musical composition are. But themes in a poem are made of words, and words have meanings; our attention is never arrested at the verbal surface; it proceeds to what the words denote. They denote objects, persons and ideas; and it is very difficult altogether to dispel the notion that the objects, persons and ideas in a single poem should be in some intelligible relation to one another. A very little inspection of the commentaries, or questioning of readers of the poem, will show that this is not the case with *The Waste Land*; there is no certainty either about what is denoted, or how it is related to other denotations. It is sometimes suggested, for example, that the hyacinth girl is or might be the same as the lady who stayed with her cousin the archduke a few lines earlier. To me it has always been obvious that these fragmentary glimpses showed us, and were designed to show us, two different kinds of women and two different kinds of human relationship. Yet I suppose that those who think otherwise have taken at least as much trouble and are no greater fools than I. And I see no means by which the matter could be decided.

We have already remarked that Phlebas the Phoenician had a prior existence in another context and was included by chance or outside suggestion. True, a place is rather arbitrarily prepared for him; Madame Sosostris the clairvoyant, who is supposed to be using a Tarot pack, produces the card of the drowned Phoenician sailor—which is not a member of the Tarot pack—in order to suggest in advance that Phlebas has some part in the structure of the poem. But what his part is remains quite uncertain. Here the commentators for the most part insist on resolutely marking time, for fear of committing themselves to a false step; and we are even bidden to observe that the "currents" which pick the drowned Phlebas's bones have a forerunner in the "currants" in the pocket of Mr. Eugenides the Smyrna merchant. Surely the last refuge of baffled imbecility.

It has been said that the poem adopts a "stream of consciousness" technique;[1] and this sounds reassuring without committing us to anything very much. But it is precisely what the poem does not do. The advantage of the "stream of consciousness" technique is that it allows a flood of images, more or less emancipated from narrative or logical continuity, while still preserving a psychological continuity—the continuity of inhering in a single consciousness. *The Waste Land* conspicuously forgoes this kind of unifying principle. One desperate expedient has been to fasten on Mr. Eliot's note to line 218: "Tiresias, although a mere spectator and not indeed a 'character', is yet the most important personage in the poem, uniting all the rest. . . . What Tiresias *sees*, in fact, is the substance of the poem." In the light of this it can be suggested that

[1] Grover Smith, *T. S. Eliot's Poetry and Plays* (Chicago, 1956), p. 58.

the whole poem is Tiresias's "stream of consciousness".[1] This is probably to give the note more weight than it can bear, and in any case, it does little to the purpose. Who was Tiresias? A man who had also been a woman, who lived for ever and could foretell the future. That is to say, not a single human consciousness, but a mythological catch-all, and as a unifying factor of no effect whatever.

I should like to commit myself to the view that for a poem to exist as a unity more than merely bibliographical, we need the sense of one voice speaking, as in lyric or elegiac verse; or of several voices intelligibly related to each other, as in narrative with dialogue or drama; that what these voices say needs a principle of connection no different from that which would be acceptable in any other kind of discourse; that the collocation of images is not a method at all, but the negation of method. In fact, to expose oneself completely, I want to say that a poem, internally considered, ought to make the same kind of sense as any other discourse.

This should amount to a frontal attack on the main positions of modern poetics. I cannot feel that I have the equipment for this enterprise, nor if I had that it would be the right way to proceed. If the conviction I have baldly stated is just, its justice will be seen, in due time, not by virtue of a puny attack from a single criticaster, but by what Johnson calls the common sense of readers uncorrupted by literary prejudice. So I only wish to press my point in two directions of which I feel fairly certain, neither of them quite central.

For the first I return to the sentence of Johnson I have just quoted. "By the common sense of readers uncorrupted with literary prejudices, after all the refinements of subtlety and the dogmatism of learning, must be finally decided all claim to poetical honours." These are words that no one who cares about poetry in our century can read without a twinge. The appeal to a body of readers who are not specialists or eccentrics, who are merely representative of the common sentiment and intelligence of human kind, is one we feel ourselves so little

[1] Grover Smith, p. 58. See also George Williamson, *A Reader's Guide to T. S. Eliot* (New York, 1957), p. 123.

able to make, one that we know so well, if we are honest, ought to be made—that we can think of it only with a feeling of distress. Where is contemporary poetry read, and where is it written? In the universities. Who is it read by? Students; professional students of literature mostly, and professors, who expect to write papers on it, or to lecture on it— to "explicate" it, in the current technical cant. What has become (not to go back to some pre-lapsarian Eden) of the kind of public that even so recent a poet as Tennyson could enjoy? It has been warned off; it has been treated to sneers, threats and enigmas. It has been told so often that it has no status and no business in the sacred wood, and it has found the business actually being transacted there so remote from its ordinary apprehension, that it has turned away, in indifference, or disgust, or despair. A complex of social reasons is often produced to account for this: no doubt some of them are valid. A covert notion of social determinism is invoked to produce a sensation of comforting hopelessness about almost any undesirable situation to-day. But that is not my business. I am only concerned with what is intrinsic to poetry; and much of the reason for the narrow appeal of modern poetry is in the poetry itself. The wilful Alexandrianism, the allusiveness and multiplicity of reference, above all, the deliberate cultivation of modes of organisation that are utterly at variance with those of ordinary discourse—these are the main reasons for the disappearance of Johnson's common reader. It is hard to say this, for to say it lines one up with the hostile, the malicious and the Philistine, with all those who hate and suspect the exploring sensibility and have never made the attempt to penetrate into the imaginative life of their time. But it is sometimes necessary to risk being put in bad company for the sake of saying what seems to be true. One can only hope that one has better reasons for saying it.

For my second point I hope to produce a better reason. The poem that abandons the syntax of narrative or argument and relies on the interplay of "themes" or the juxtaposition of images according to the mysterious laws of poetic logic is not, so far as it is doing anything positive at all, doing anything that poetry has not done before. Clustered and repeated images, contrasts or echoes among them, a half-heard music of this kind has always been part of poetic effect. We have always partly known it, and modern criticism has done much to make it explicit. But in all poetry before our time this music has been background music. What we have heard with the alert and directed attention has been something different. It has been a story, or an argument, or a meditation, or the direct expression of feeling. Modern criticism has aroused our sense of this second sub-rational layer in our appreciation of poetry. Perhaps the most signal instance of this is the Shakespeare criticism of Wilson Knight, which sees the plays not as patterns made by character in action, but as "expanded metaphors", patterns of "themes" and "images". Modern poetry in the Imagist mode has performed the extraordinary manœuvre of shifting its whole weight to this second level. It has shorn itself of paraphrasable sense, of all narrative or discursive line, and relies on the play of contrasted images alone. In doing so it has achieved a startling concentration and brilliance of the individual image, and a whole new rhetoric of its own, with its own special kind of fascination. I still wish to maintain that it is an inadequate rhetoric, inadequate for anything but very short poems and very special effects—states of madness and dream, for example. I take it that the case of Pound's *Cantos* goes without saying; they are the wreckage of poetry; brilliant passages, sometimes long, sometimes the merest splinters, floating in a turbid sea of stammering and incoherent mumble. But even in *The Waste Land* and the *Four Quartets*, where the level of the individual passages is far more consistent, and where it is just possible to give their arrangement some sort of publicly valid justification, the organising principle is still quite inadequate for poems of this scope. These poems survive, and will survive, not assisted by their structure, but in spite of it.

This is true of much of the work of Pound, Eliot and Wallace Stevens—to name three of the founding fathers of modern poetry. Their poetry suffers, even on the level on which it functions so persuasively and brilliantly, from the lack of any other level, the lack of public, explicit, paraphrasable discourse. We know, of course, about the "heresy of paraphrase" as it has been called—that we ought never to suppose that a paraphrase can tell us what a poem is "about". Perhaps we ought never to paraphrase a poem; but as with many other things that we ought never to do, we ought also to be able to feel that we could do it. The virtue that we exercise in not making a conceptual prose translation of a modern poem is generally a fugitive and cloistered virtue; for it would not be possible to give any such translation if we tried. To attempt to explain to an intelligent person who knows nothing about twentieth-century poetry how *The Waste Land* works is to be overcome with embarrassment at having to justify principles so affected, so perverse, so deliberately removed from the ordinary modes of rational communication. If poetry were to go on in this way it would develop before long into an esoteric entertainment with as much relevance to the experience of the common reader as, say, heraldry or real tennis. The imagist revolution was a sort of spring-cleaning; a much-needed spring-cleaning that got rid of a great deal of the fusty, obstructive and dust-gathering matter that had cluttered up the weaker poetry of the nineteenth century. But the house has not been comfortable to live in ever since. And the clotted rubbish of academic imagist criticism is already beginning to fill it up again. There is no reason to be optimistic about this situation. Poetry can degenerate into a meaningless esoteric exercise, and go on that way for centuries. It has happened. But perhaps it will not happen to us. And we have the example of the greatest poet of the early twentieth century to show that it need not. It is something of a paradox that Yeats, whose beliefs are often supposed to be more fantastic and irrational than those of any other great mind of our time, should never have lost his faith in rational order and the disposing intelligence as the guiding principle of a poem.

II. IMAGIST POETRY AND THE TRADITION

About forty years ago it was possible to be deeply engaged with literature, as a writer or a student, yet to be entirely innocent of any concern with literary theory. This is hardly possible now. One of the minor accompaniments of the Imagist revolution has been, as everybody knows, an immense elaboration of critical thinking. The man of letters (if the word has still any meaning to-day) is almost obliged to have explicit opinions about matters that his predecessors were content to leave to professional aestheticians. This might have led to a general enlightenment and a more general consensus of literary opinion, but a very little examination of current critical journals will show that it has not. No doubt the prophets and the patriarchs, by the time they reached the age of fifty and surveyed the intellectual life of their time, were apt to say that they did not know what the world was coming to; and this precedent has been generally followed ever since; but the sense of uncertainty in judging immediately contemporary literature can hardly ever have been greater than it is to-day; and in current judgments on the work of the past the picture is not much clearer. There is a babel of confused noise; some of it is just the busy hum of academics taking in each other's washing; but some of it arises from quite fundamental disagreement. Wire-drawn discussions, often far removed from the concrete realities of poetic experience, invite an easy scepticism: but debate about what literature is, what it does, about the status of our imaginative experience and its relation to our past history, cannot be unimportant. We can look back with mild regret to a time when such matters were largely settled by custom and unspoken agreement, thus this is not our situation. Once a bundle of experiences has been made the subject of open disputation, there is nothing to do but have it out—unless of course we prefer to pull our coats about our ears and wait till history has it out for us.

A degree of confusion in these matters is not of course unfamiliar. Literary theory has never from the beginning been an orderly affair, with a regular dialectic. Contradictions have been frequent, and mere failures to connect have been more frequent. We should expect judgments of value to differ from one age to another; but they sometimes agree, on quite irreconcilable grounds. Johnson would have been deeply shocked by Wordsworth's poetry, and Wordsworth was entirely hostile to the poetry and principles represented by Johnson; but they both attack Gray's odes for pretty much the same reasons. We might expect a certain agreement in judgments of fact; but we do not find it. Johnson praises Shakespeare because his characters are not individuals but species; and the Romantic critics praise him because each of his characters is so clearly individualised. And so on. It is the business of the historian of literary ideas to explain and disentangle these disorders.

Where however he may expect to find a fair community of thought is in the critical theory of a single period or a single school. Neo-classic criticism has its limitations, but it accounts for most of the features of neo-classic poetry, and gives us some means of seeing it in relation to the poetry of earlier times. Wordsworth's theory of poetic language has many loose ends; he does not always succeed in saying what he means, and Coleridge had to tidy it all up for him; but after all we know what Wordsworth was driving at, and we can see that the massive movement of his poetry is in roughly the same direction. Both neo-classic and Romantic poetic theory could stand a good deal of contradictory detail and imperfect formulation—for each had a philosophy and the movement of a society behind it; the large stream manages to carry the diverse elements along. The remarkable body of critical writing and literary propaganda that accompanied the rise of Imagist poetry does not seem to have the same directing energy. Bating all the possible quibbles about detail, one looks for the underlying consistency, the broad movement of a considerable stream of thought. But it is not there. Imagist poetic theory was inconsistent with itself, and large parts of it were contradicted by the contemporary poetic practice. There could hardly be a better example than the criticism of T. E. Hulme, which makes propaganda for a "hard", "dry" classical art, with weapons taken largely from romantic critics; unless it is the early criticism of Mr. Eliot, which is equally an exaltation of the classic virtues—while he was contemporaneously writing quite revolutionary poetry, of a kind that had deliberately abandoned the prime classical aims and in fact represents the extreme limits of romantic method. But there are other competitors; Ezra Pound recommending the study of traditional Romance versification as a corrective to the laxities of the age, while himself writing in a very refined late-

Victorian style; and a little later evolving a brilliant and novel verse founded on Symbolist *vers libre* and the rhythms of prose. And there is Joyce, primly invoking the firm categories of St. Thomas to justify illuminations expressed in the faint wavering rhythms of Pater and the *fin-de-ciècle*; Wyndham Lewis upholding the virtues of clarity and order in polemical works that are confused, brilliant and explosive packages of insight, prejudice and half-digested philosophy. It is the same story in every case; enormous talent, rising at times to genius of all but the very highest order; heavily armed and brilliantly conducted attacks, dashing sallies, prodigious personal feats, capable of giving more exhilaration, more sheer intellectual delight, than any body of criticism we have known; but no sense of direction; none of that sense of a deeply felt, all-organising human purpose that we cannot fail to notice in the work of the Romantic critics, or even in the earlier literary establishment of Dryden and Pope and Johnson.

Mr. Bateson has referred to this period as "a short reign of terror"[1] which was necessary to discredit once and for all the watery dregs of late nineteenth-century aesthetics, the literary ethos represented by Watts-Dunton, Gosse and Stopford Brooke. Ezra Pound, in a note on T. E. Hulme, concludes that "the bleak and smeary twenties wretchedly needed his guidance, and the pity is that he was not there in person to keep down vermin".[2] A reign of terror, keeping down vermin; both phrases suggest a movement clearer about what it was against than about what it was for. Nobody can read the early critical work of Pound and Eliot without realising that they were against sin. It is much less easy to see what particular virtues they were recommending. In *The Sacred Wood* Mr. Eliot is plainly against "the poetical vagaries of the present age"; he is against literary impressionism; he is against Gilbert Murray's "vulgar debasement of the eminently personal idiom of Swinburne"; against Pater, and the assimilation of poetry to religion. He is against, in short, the late phase of Romanticism in which he finds himself—against Romanticism in general; "there may

[1] *Essays in Criticism*, vol. III, Jan. 1953, p. 2.
[2] Note contributed by Pound to *The Townsman*, Jan. 1938. Quoted in Hugh Kenner, *The Poetry of Ezra Pound*, p. 309.

be a good deal to be said for Romanticism in life, there is no place for it in letters ". But the quality of what we presume to be the classicism that is to take its place is extraordinarily hard to discern. Mr. Eliot at this stage approves of the destructive criticism of Arnold, approves of Aristotle and Dr. Johnson; and this sounds like a decorous English neo-classicism of a familiar kind. Yet the presiding critical influence is that of Rémy de Gourmont, acknowledged—and even if it were not acknowledged it might be suspected—a Symbolist critic of extraordinarily diverse activities and opinions, none of which could be got into the neo-classical box. It is from him that the critical ideal of *The Sacred Wood* is derived, "ériger en lois ses impressions personelles": an admirable and courageous critical ideal, which Mr. Eliot's own best critical work nobly exemplifies —but not a neo-classical one. In fact the neo-classic ideal is precisely the converse of this—to conform one's personal impressions to laws that are conceived of as pre-existing, as part of the natural order. Such positive critical unity as *The Sacred Wood* has is given by a taste—the exquisite personal taste which has always led Mr. Eliot to quote and exemplify so aptly, and thereby to become the most influential critic of his generation. But the taste can cover a multitude of uncertainties—about the relation of personality to the work of art, about the way emotions are expressed in literature, about the relation of poetry to philosophy—all of them matters of importance.

It may be suspected that these uncertainties of direction in early modern criticism are the result of a fundamental spiritual confusion, which we cannot hope to identity clearly, but might be able vaguely to locate. It is in some such area that the criticism of T. E. Hulme seems to originate. I do not want to enter into the question of how great Hulme's personal influence on his contemporaries actually was. Pound tends to play it down, and Eliot had no personal contact with him. But Hulme's ideas, either in his own formulation or in some diffusion, or by pointing back to Hulme's own sources, or to analogues elsewhere, are fundamental to the criticism of this time; and the brash confidence with which he exposes them makes his work a particularly convenient field for inspection.

A LITERARY REVOLUTION

The celebrated essay "Romanticism and Classicism"[1] is both typical and central. Words fail me to record the number of fallacies and contradictions in these twenty pages; or rather, any reasonable number of words fail; it could be done at inordinate length. But the central notion is plain. It is the same idea that was made familiar a little later (Hulme's essay was written about 1914) by Irving Babbit's *Rousseau and Romanticism* (1917)—that Romanticism has a single root, the Rousseauist doctrine "that man was by nature good, that it was only bad laws and customs that had suppressed him". Hulme identifies himself with the opposite; with what he calls the classical point of view, which accepts the finite and limited nature of man; and this, he says, is also the religious view.

> Here is the root of all romanticism: that man, the individual, is an infinite reservoir of possibilities. . . . One can define the classical quite clearly as the exact opposite to this. Man is an extraordinarily fixed and limited animal whose nature is absolutely constant. It is only by tradition and organisation that anything decent can be got out of him. . . . It would be a mistake to identify the classical view with that of materialism. On the contrary it is identical with the normal religious attitude.

The essential of the religious attitude for Hulme is what he calls the sane classical dogma of original sin; and this is the essential of the classical attitude too. I will not pause to wonder at the strange realignment of forces that this alliance of classicism with Christian dogma brought about, though anyone who was following these matters in the twenties will remember it as bewildering. I have only two points to make; one is the extraordinary impoverishment of the religious attitude that would follow from Hulme's formulation; the other is concerned with the literary consequences that he draws from it.

It is not worth wasting much time on Hulme's religious attitude. "Man is an extraordinarily fixed and limited animal whose nature is absolutely constant." "Extraordinarily" can only mean "more than is ordinary with animals". Man is more fixed and limited than the lion or the horse or the duck-billed

[1] T. E. Hulme, *Speculations* (London, 1936), pp. 111–41. The references following are all to this essay.

platypus? This is surely nonsense both culturally and biologically. "It is only by tradition and organisation that anything decent can be got out of him"; and this represents the religious attitude? But all the higher religions have come with the promise of bringing man deliverance from the law. It was not Rousseau, it was the Psalmist who said *Emitte spiritum tuum et creabunter: et renovabis faciem terrae.* It was not Rousseau, it was St. Paul who spoke of Abraham "who against hope believed in hope, that he might become the father of many nations according to that which was spoken. . . . He staggered not at the promise of God through unbelief, but was strong in faith, giving glory to God; and being fully persuaded that what he had promised he was able to perform." And it was not Rousseau who was the witness of the Apocalypse. If religion were a contemplation of the natural world as a closed order—if, that is to say, faith and hope were omitted—Hulme's account of it would be true. But why go on? Anti-Rousseauism may have been a needed tonic, but when it is used to reduce religion to a depressed cosmic Toryism the limited efficacy of this nostrum becomes apparent.

And of course Hulme gives the game away himself. He is not at heart concerned with religion. His version of original sin is a political doctrine, and his performance is a projection of political doctrine into the religious sphere. One cannot accuse him of lacking candour. The names he invokes in the early paragraphs of his essay are those of "Maurras, Laserre and all the group connected with *L'Action Française*". It is they, he says, who have made romanticism and classicism into political catchwords. It is they whose main use for classicism was as a stick to beat the Revolution. As he accurately remarked, the distinction had become a party symbol. "If you asked a man of a certain set whether he preferred the classics or the romantics, you could deduce from that what his politics were." And, though Hulme does not mention this, it was of course Maurras and the *Action Française* group who did notoriously and openly what many have been willing to do covertly—used Catholic Christendom in a purely political sense, were willing to employ Christianity simply as a right-wing political weapon. If Hulme's notion of the religious attitude came to him from this source it is not surprising that it would be an eccentric one.

The literary deductions from this are still more eccentric. Hulme foresees the arrival of a "classical" period in poetry; and this is apparently a straightforward piece of historical prognostication, such as men of letters with their ears to the ground are often liable to make. What are the qualities that the classic-religious attitude will produce in poetry? Since man is a limited creature his verse must also be limited in its aims. The literary vice of romanticism was a continual attempt at commerce with the infinite. This deplorable traffic will now cease. Ruskin wrote, " Those who have so pierced and seen the melancholy deeps of things are filled with intense passion and gentleness and sympathy." But when he did so he was thinking in the corrupt Romantic mode. For the new classical poetry "it is essential to prove that beauty may be in small, dry things": and "the particular poetry we are going to get will be cheerful, dry and sophisticated". Now in the course of developing this argument Hulme, who writes with great liveliness, if not without vulgarity, scores many effective literary hits. And his Imagist propaganda is of great interest from another point of view. But the main drift of his argument is a foolish paradox. The essential of the religious attitude is the dogma of original sin, and this is the essential of the classical attitude too. It is about to become influential again and will produce a kind of verse that is small, dry, cheerful and sophisticated. This is the natural consequence of the religious attitude, which has nothing to do with the infinite—and, I suppose we might add, has produced in the past such small, dry, cheerful and sophisticated words as the *Aeneid, Dies Irae,* the *Paradiso, Piers Plowman* and *Phèdre.* The examples are mine, but they will be enough, I imagine, to indicate the abyss of nonsense into which Hulme would lead us, by a skilful manipulations of half-truths; and into which he did lead a good many literary theorists of the generation succeeding his own.

Now all these operations of Hulme's are conducted in the name of tradition; and tradition, the word and the idea, was to become a spell to conjure with in the coming literary upheaval.

IMAGE AND EXPERIENCE

What we can learn from Hulme's essay is how anomalous, how eccentric, the relation to tradition is. A fragmentary version of the Christian religious tradition is seized on. It is equated with a partial notion of classicism derived from a group of politically-minded Frenchmen. (There is no indication that Hulme has thought about ancient classical literature at all, and if he had cared to look at English classicism he would surely have had to relate it to Deism rather than to traditional Christianity.) And from this mish-mash is drawn a set of literary deductions which are both logically uncompelling and historically false. When we consider the influence that ideas of this sort had, we may suspect that an eccentric and anomalous idea of tradition is generally at work. And this is what we must now try to examine.

Mr. Eliot's essay "Tradition and the Individual Talent" in *The Sacred Wood* is rightly regarded as one of the great critical documents of our time. One part of it contains the most fruitful and, I suspect, the most enduring of all suggestions towards a revised critical neo-classicism—a form of neo-classicism that is workable in the modern literary situation. To think of the existing monuments of literature as forming an ideal order, which is altered, if ever so slightly, by the addition of a really new work to the series; to demand that the new work shall both cohere with the past and alter to that which it coheres— this suggestion both satisfies our sense of an established order and makes novelty possible, as older neo-classicism did not; and it goes far to reconcile historical with aesthetic judgments. If we had to choose a single one of Mr. Eliot's critical principles to preserve and carry away with us, it would be this. But the idea of literary tradition advanced in the essay as a whole arouses doubts and questions. I believe that it suggests a wrong notion of how tradition lives and communicates itself.

The early part of the essay expounds the thesis that not only the best, but the most individual parts of a poet's work may be those parts "where the dead poets, his ancestors, assert their immortality most vigorously". The kind of continuing excellence which constitutes poetic tradition cannot be inherited; it can only be obtained by great labour. It involves the historical sense, and "the historical sense involves a perception, not only of the pastness of the past, but also of its presence; the historical sense compels a man to write not merely with his own generation in his bones, but with a feeling that the literature of Europe from Homer and within it the whole of the literature of his own country has a simultaneous existence and composes a simultaneous order". We see why Mr. Eliot speaks of great labour. Clearly the historical sense involves a great deal of historical knowledge. A little later Eliot anticipates the objection that this seems to require a ridiculous amount of erudition, and that any such demand is contradicted by the educations and careers of many poets in all ages. But he does not really answer it. He suggests that the genius of a special kind can acquire his history by a sort of osmosis, from a very few or very accidental sources; but this is not what he was saying before; it is a contradiction of the plain sense that his earlier words must bear.

For he has already told us that the poet cannot "take the past as a lump, an indiscriminate bolus, nor can he form himself wholly upon one or two private admirations, nor can he form himself wholly upon one preferred period". He must be aware of the mind of Europe, and of the mind of his own country, and be aware that it is much more important than his private mind. An honourable programme, but one reflects that the mind of Europe is a very extensive object of awareness. It includes the Encyclopedists as well as the Fathers of the Church, Spinoza as well as St. Bernard, Nietzsche as well as Dante, Mallarmé as well as the author of *Beowulf* or the *Odyssey*. If we look at the actual operations of the poets they are surely characterised by a highly selective indifference to large parts of this territory.

There is a way of reading this persuasive essay in which it commands an easy, almost unthinking assent. Our minds are prepared for it. Yes, one feels, here is Mr. Eliot saying in his own idiom just the sort of thing that Matthew Arnold said. And of course Arnold was right and was very good for us, and this is right and very good for us too. It is the perpetually needed antidote to Anglo-Saxon laziness and complacency and provincialism. But we have often reflected too that Arnold's programme was a programme for the man of culture rather than a programme for the poet. Of course poets have often been cultured men, and poetry has often been a learned art. But in essence the poet is not coincident with the cultured man; his plan of life is not the same. The cultured man is the transmitter of a tradition of civilisation, the poet is one of its makers. There will always be a need for a body of men with a profound awareness, the kind of awareness that is given only by learning, of our whole cultural tradition. But it is not likely that many of the poets will be of their number.

Behind this whole argument lies the question of whether tradition is something unconsciously inherited or something consciously acquired. And our answer to this will very considerably affect our feeling about the new Anglo-American poetry of the early twentieth century, with its self-consciousness, its acute sensitiveness to both precedent and novelty. Mr. Eliot distinguishes authentic tradition from the mere lazy acquiescence in the habits of our immediate predecessors; and the distinction is important. Perhaps it can be made clearer by analogies from other fields than literature. We have often seen movements, revivals undertaken in the name of tradition, that strike the official bearers of tradition as strange and offensive novelties. Consider the impact of Newman and the Oxford Movement on the old high-and-dry Anglican Church; consider the puzzled scepticism with which Disraeli's Young England movement, its mixture of Carlyle and romantic medievalism, must have affected the old-fashioned county member; or consider in America the Southern literary group, the Fugitives, traditionalist and regionalist in intention, yet with an avowed hostility to the embattled provincialism of the Old South. In each case the young movement claims to be representing a rediscovery of tradition in a purer and more authentic form, while its official representatives stand merely for a debased acquiescence. Something of the same sort seems to be implied in the talk about tradition that accompanied the rise of modern Imagist poetry. In all cases the claims abide our question. Who did really represent English religious tradition, Newman, or, say, Keble? Who did really represent the spirit of English Toryism, Disraeli or the hunting squire? Who is nearer to a central poetic tradition, Ezra Pound or Robert Frost? There is no standard answer to such questions. We can only examine each case on its merits.

Another view of tradition seems to make its appearance in Mr. Eliot's later writings. In *After Strange Gods* (1933) he distinguishes between "tradition"—which is a matter of habit, local association, use and wont, and valuable for that very reason—and "orthodoxy", which is something that must be actively acquired and defended.[1] In *The Idea of a Christian Society* he speaks of the mass of humanity, mainly occupied by their direct relation to their daily duties and pleasures, whose capacity for *thinking* about the objects of their faith must be small. Of these he says "their Christianity may be almost wholly realised in behaviour; both in their customary and periodical religious observances, and in a traditional code of behaviour towards their neighbours".[2] I believe there is an analogical lesson for poetry here. In the sentences just quoted there is an implied contrast between the ordinary wayfaring Christian, whose faith is largely inherited, unconscious and unexplicit, and the theologian or intellectual defender of the faith who needs to be aware of its position in his civilisation as a whole, and of its historic origins. There is also, of course, though Mr. Eliot does not mention him, the saint; and it is possible that the saint may have more in common with the ordinary wayfaring Christian than with the theologian. His sanctity is more likely to reveal itself in behaviour, in his devotional life and in his relation to his neighbour than in speculation or learning. In poetry the analogue to the ordinary Christian is the common reader; the analogue to the theologian is the critic or the man of culture; the analogue to the saint is surely the poet. And both the poet and the saint may dispense with much of the historical consciousness, the acquired deliberate awareness of tradition, which to the theologian or the cultured critic is a necessity.

[1] *After Strange Gods* (London, 1933), p. 3.
[2] *The Idea of a Christian Society* (London, 1940), p. 27.

IMAGE AND EXPERIENCE

If we look at the ways poetic tradition has actually been transmitted I think we shall find that it has been in exactly the ways that Mr. Eliot says it cannot be. Typically, the poet forms himself on one or two private admirations, as Keats did; or on a highly eccentric eclecticism, as Yeats did; or on a single preferred period, as the poets of Augustan England did. Surely the preponderant influence of one or two private admirations is a very noticeable feature of the work of Mr. Eliot himself. The conscientious and laborious taking of all culture as one's province is more characteristic of the scholar-poet, often quite a minor poet, such as Gray.

I believe that a poet's traditional quality, though it may be displayed and expounded by historical scholarship, actually realises itself in his relation to his readers, and in his relation to a certain community of human feeling—what Johnson called the "uniformity of sentiment" that underwrites poetic communication. The traditional poet, or any poet so far as he is traditional, addresses his readers in the confidence that he will be understood; that his rhetoric and his mode of address will be familiar to them from their previous reading of poetry; and he appeals to an order of feeling that he assumes to be common to himself and them, simply as human beings, or as members of a particular civilisation. When Wordsworth speaks in the preface to the *Lyrical Ballads*, not without bitterness, of the expectation that the poet "will gratify known habits of association" in his readers he is aware that he is not writing as a traditional poet, as far as his rhetoric is concerned; though of course he appeals to a very deep-rooted human tradition as far as his material is concerned. But Wordsworth, at this period of his life, is an extreme example of a poet trying to write as though no poetry has ever existed before. This is never possible; but it is necessary from time to time that the attempt should be made. There is always the temptation to equate "traditional" with "good", if we associate poetry with the ancient and enduring in our civilisation; or with "bad", if we associate poetry with revolution and novelty. But both are illegitimate; poetry is good or bad independently of whether it is traditional or not. All that we are concerned with now is to inquire how the traditional quality manifests itself, and to identify it where it occurs.

This is a traditional poem:

> Love at the lips was touch
> As sweet as I could bear;
> And once that seemed too much;
> I lived on air
>
> That crossed me from sweet things
> The flow of—was it musk
> From hidden grapevine springs
> Down hill at dusk?
>
> I had the swirl and ache
> From sprays of honeysuckle
> That when they're gathered shake
> Dew on the knuckle.
>
> I craved strong sweets, but those
> Were strong when I was young;
> The petal of the rose
> It was that stung.
>
> Now no joy but lacks salt
> That is not dashed with pain
> And weariness and fault;
> I crave the stain
>
> Of tears, the aftermark
> Of almost too much love,
> The sweet of bitter bark
> And burning clove.
>
> When stiff and sore and scarred
> I take away my hand
> From leaning on it hard
> In grass and sand,
>
> The hurt is not enough:
> I long for weight and strength
> To feel the earth as rough
> To all my length.[1]

[1] Robert Frost, *Complete Poems* (New York, 1949), p. 279.

IMAGE AND EXPERIENCE

It is traditional in spite of the fact that it has no obvious reference to previous poetry or current awareness of earlier models. It is traditional because it assumes easily and naturally that a reader whose habits have been formed on existing poetry in the same language will be able easily and naturally to respond to it. As Johnson said of some lines in Gray's *Elegy*, "I have never seen the notions in any other place; yet he that reads them here, persuades himself that he has always felt them." With notable originality of turn and image, the poem appeals to a complex of feelings about the love of life in youth, and the approach of old age and death, that can be fairly called universal, that has at any rate often provided material for poetry before, in a great variety of ways. To touch on a detail—the slight, delicate, but quite marked and definite semantic shock given by the lines

> The petal of the rose
> It was that stung

seems to be an eminently traditional way of using language, of combining wit with feeling. I could say much the same thing of many of John Crowe Ransom's poems; but then they are very consciously traditional; he is well aware that he is rewriting "Gather ye rosebuds" or the epitaph on Salathiel Pavy. And my point is that a poem may be traditional simply by virtue of an established rhetoric and an established way of feeling, without any apparent historical reference or learning.

Now let us look at another kind of poem. Mr. C. S. Lewis, in his inaugural lecture at Cambridge a few years ago, posits the idea of a great rift, a break in European culture, somewhere between the battle of Waterloo and our own day. This is not a matter that I wish to argue, it is not our present concern; but he calls in evidence for his contention the nature of much modern poetry. If we eliminate judgments of value and concentrate on the historical fact, he writes, "I do not see how anyone can doubt that modern poetry is not only a greater novelty than any other 'new poetry' but new in a new way, almost in a new dimension. To say that all new poetry was once as difficult as ours is false; to say that any was is an equivocation. Some earlier poetry was difficult, but not in the same way. Alex-

42

andrian poetry was difficult because it presupposed a learned
reader; as you became learned you found the answers to the
puzzles." After citing some other examples he goes on: "I
do not see in any of these the slightest parallel to the state of
affairs disclosed by a recent symposium on Mr. Eliot's *Cooking
Egg*. Here we find seven adults (two of them Cambridge men)
whose lives have been specially devoted to the study of poetry
discussing a very short poem which has been before the world
for thirty-odd years; and there is not the slightest agreement
among them as to what, in any sense of the word, it means."[1]
The symposium in question was conducted in the pages of an
Oxford periodical, *Essays in Criticism*.[2] I should like to add, in
the interests of friendship, local piety and truth, that the correct
and sensible answer seems to me to be given by one of the
Cambridge men, Dr. Tillyard; but what are we among so many?
And the point here is the diversity of opinion among competent
and qualified readers. The poem is very familiar; it is the one
that begins:

> Pipit sate upright in her chair
> Some distance from where I was sitting;
> *Views of the Oxford Colleges*
> Lay on the table, with the knitting.
>
> Daguerrotypes and silhouettes,
> Her grandfather and great-great aunts,
> Supported on the mantelpiece
> An *Invitation to the Dance*.

I will not go into the multiple confusions of the discussion.
Some of them seem to me fatuous, others merely ignorant. To
confine ourselves to one—the question of who Pipit is. It is
variously suggested that she is the speaker's old nurse, a little
girl, a Bloomsbury *demi-vierge*, his mistress, his fiancée, any
femme de trente ans whom he had known as a child. After all, it
makes a difference. I think Mr. Lewis has made his point. This
is a new thing, that a short poem of no verbal intricacy should
leave its contemporary readers in a state of complete uncertainty

---

[1] C. S. Lewis, *De Descriptione Temporum* (Cambridge, 1955), p. 14.
[2] *Essays in Criticism*, vol. III, July, 1953, pp. 345–57.

as to what, in any ordinary sense, it is "about". It is untraditional also in other ways. Not only has the tradition of an easy and immediate communication between writer and reader disappeared; the poem appeals to no permanent and established way of feeling. The rather uneasy superiority of the speaker to Pipit and her décor is not a relation of any depth or importance; and it is not part of any area of feeling with which European poetry has largely dealt. The semantic shock at the end, the contrast between "the eagles and the trumpets" and the weeping multitudes drooping in London tea-shops is mildly startling; but little more than verbally startling, for what is it, after all, but a version of the weak, modern-romantic-ironic contrast between ancient splendour and contemporary vulgarity? The poem is thickly decorated with historical references—Sir Philip Sidney, Coriolanus, Lucrezia Borgia, Madame Blavatsky, Piccarda da Donati; the verse form reminds one vaguely of Gautier, and the tone of Laforgue. But the wealth of cultural references will not persuade us that what we are in contact with here is the mind of Europe.

It is needless, probably, to say that I am not instituting a comparison between the poetical merits of Mr. Eliot and Mr. Frost; and if I were to undertake such an unprofitable task I should not use an early and rather trivial poem of Mr. Eliot's as an example. But though *A Cooking Egg* is not a fair example of achievement, it is a fair example of method, and of a kind of method that extends far beyond the work of Mr. Eliot. Similar illustrations could be drawn from the work of Pound, Wallace Stevens, not to mention younger writers such as Auden and Dylan Thomas. In all of them we find a host of examples where immediate communication between poet and reader fails on two planes; both on the plane of reference, all that is ordinarily called the "sense" of the poem; and on the plane of feeling, the emotional attitude towards the situation presented. Whatever tradition Imagist poetry may have recalled us to, the most important tradition of all, that of a natural community of understanding between poet and reader, has been lost.

In the face of these obscure breakdowns of communication criticism has almost capitulated. Or rather, it has turned with relief to other tasks than judgment. The best modern criticism has made surprisingly little attempt to judge the most challenging contemporary literature, to estimate its value, or what can amount to the same thing, to place it properly in relation to the literature of the past. We are always hearing about this being done, and that it should be done—the existing monuments form an ideal order to which the new work will be seen to attach itself, to form a changed yet continuous pattern. But in fact most of the criticism has concentrated on the novelty rather than the continuity, in panegyric, extenuation, exegesis—everything in fact from log-rolling to what is called explication. The value judgments on the whole have not been made. Modern literature—and modern literature in this context still tends to mean what began in 1914—has become and remained a sort of enclave in the critical tradition, with its own laws and its own ways of interpreting them. Where these writings stand in the general comity of letters has hardly been asked, with any seriousness or pertinacity, still less answered.

There are several reasons for this, some of them entirely generous ones. A novel kind of imaginative writing is commonly exposed to ignorance, abuse and vociferous inertia. When this is going on it is more important to get the new work fairly read than to decide on its ultimate position in a hierarchy. It mattered more in the twenties to get *The Waste Land* read with some degree of sympathy and open-mindedness than to decide on its status in relation to *In Memoriam* or Pope's *Moral Essays*. At such times the most immediately necessary criticism is a kind of propaganda or block-busting for new creative work. If more is attempted it is on a very narrow front. The work is explained on its own terms, and justified by its own standards; but not much attempt is made to apply standards derived from our literary experience as a whole. A symptom of this is the inability to stand outside our own phase of civilisation. The words "plight" and "dilemma" do especially heavy duty. *The Waste Land* (or *Finnegan's Wake* or *Hugh Selwyn Mauberley* or whatever it may be) presents the plight of our time, in the methods of our time. If it seems to be confused, well, so are we. There is an interesting example of this method in the closing pages of that invaluable piece of commentary, the *Skeleton Key to Finnegan's Wake*:

> In some quarters it is the fashion to dismiss Joyce with various charges, all pivoting on the word "decadent". He is a solipsist talking to himself in a nutshell kingdom of his own. He is a sick spirit addicted to pathologic gnawings of no possible interest to those of us with splendid, robust minds. . . . He is a man who has lost his faith and whose world is a living doomsday, a bleak pit of pessimism.
>
> If Joyce is sick, his disease is the neurosis of our age. Lifting our eye from his page we find in every aspect of society the perversion, the decay, and the disintegration of religion, love and morality that he has described in *Finnegan's Wake*. The hypocrisy of political promises, the prurient preoccupation with sex, the fascination of lurid headlines gossip and its effect on a literate but basically ignorant bourgeoisie—all these are mirrored to the life by this liveliest of observers. . . . If Joyce's viewpoint is pathologic, then any rosier lens is sentimental.[1]

The words decadent and sick have not much meaning here without further elucidation; but that is not the point. The point is that the critical argument is a simple *tu quoque*. "Joyce a decadent? Yah, you're another." Joyce is justified, not by showing that he has created out of his material a rational or aesthetically satisfying order, but by the claim that he reproduces faithfully the disorder inherent in his material. By this standard the artist becomes a tape-recorder to the Zeitgeist; his success is in the completeness and finality of his reproduction.

Of course the main object of the *Skeleton Key* is to elucidate, and the passage I have quoted is only incidental to its purpose. And much of the best criticism of modern literature has been of this kind—the providing of readers' guides to difficult works. The guides were needed, and some of them are serious and assiduous to the last degree. The best are probably those that keep most closely to the primary task of smoothing out difficulties of communication, and stick to the informative and demonstrable—do in fact what a good edition of an ancient classic would do.

[1] J. Campbell and H. M. Robinson, *A Skeleton Key to Finnegan's Wake* (London, 1947), p. 295.

A LITERARY REVOLUTION

The danger in commenting on works with such density of reference as much modern poetry is that the immediate impact of the poetry is dulled by the circumambient mass of erudition. The reader is like the hi-fi enthusiast—he is too busy fiddling with the machinery to get the best out of the music.

One of the most striking recent literary developments is the independent emergence of criticism, I will not say as an autonomous art, but as something between a profession and big business. So far as it is a profession, criticism has developed its own standards of expertise and technique; and it has become easy to pass from the useful task of writing guide-books to the elaboration of commentaries, generally ingenious and sometimes of dazzling virtuosity, which still do little or nothing to deepen appreciation of the poetry; and being without standards except those derived internally from the work itself, do little to extend the area of critical order. So far as it is big business, criticism is highly competitive; every interpretation evokes a rival one; and the topic of discussion becomes A's qualification of B's attack on C's elucidation of whatever the original object may have been. Meanwhile the original object has got tacitly taken for granted; the original questions about its value and meaning have slipped out of sight.

There is another reason why explanation of obscure works has been preferred to judgment; and it is a genial one. A consequence of the prevailing Imagist technique and of Joyce's exploitation of multiple verbal ambiguities is that much of modern literature gives great local delight even when its general purport remains obscure. And judgment must be of a work as a whole—ultimately of its whole bearing and direction. Yet it often seems churlish or ungrateful to disturb or question much of the whole foundations of a work that has given intense pleasure in detail. No one sensitive to language (and most modern critics are extremely sensitive to language) can fail to be dazzled, delighted, and sometimes moved by the verbal felicities of *Finnegan's Wake* or the fragmentary fine passages in the *Cantos*, whether or not he has any idea of how they are related to their context, or what the context is. Not only that: the Imagist method, and Joyce's rather different method of

accumulating cartloads of particulars are both profoundly sensual; they make a direct assault on the nerves and the perceptions. They hit the reader between wind and water with
a piercing sensational bombardment, in a way that literature
depending more on logical or narrative connection can never
do. The delight given is more akin to physical pleasure than to
"thoughts more elevate of providence, foreknowledge, will and
fate". I am not referring at all to subject-matter, merely to the
consequences of a poetic method. Prolonged attention to the
works of this school becomes in the end more like an addiction
or a fetishism than an ordinary literary experience, simply because of this concentrated battery of small sensuous shocks.
The quality of addiction or fetishism reveals itself in the inability to consider seriously any other source of literary pleasure; the constant assertions, for example, that in the nineteenth century language was in decay; "Tennyson and Brown-
ing ruminated", "the bankrupt's lavishness with which Morris
and Swinburne dispense their tinfoil counters". The less immediate and sensational literary experiences, if they are present at
all, are decidedly in the background. These shocks of sensuous
recognition, more thickly sown, because of the Imagist method,
in the literature of our century than in any other, are the
sharpest pleasures that poetry has to give; and one who has
felt them does not wish to dull or depreciate their setting
(though he frequently conceals the nature of his appreciation
under a forbiddingly puritan demeanour). And the critic con-
fines himself to providing a minimum framework in which they
can be enjoyed without nagging objections from the discursive
intellect; or, in a justifiable eagerness to make the most of the
parts which have delighted him, plays down the importance of
total communicated meaning—the meaning that can only be
communicated through structure.

The most fantastic example of this procedure is provided (as
one might expect) by Hugh Kenner. He defends Pound's
ideographic method by the following parallel: "Six months
after reading *King Lear* one's memory, one's sense of its vital
reality, consists perhaps in recalling that a storm is followed by
a pathetic death. We don't remember the plot as set forth in

handbooks. . . . Memory automatically strips any intense experience down to its poetic essentials, a few vivid juxtapositions."[1] It is hard to suppose that Mr. Kenner really believes that the connection between the scenes of a Shakespearean tragedy is of the same kind as the connection between Pound's "ideograms"; hard to believe that a critic who constantly postures as an Aristotelian and has presumably read the *Poetics* can bring himself to say it. But he does say it; and even a very different writer, perhaps the most serious and responsible critic of modern poetry that we have, R. P. Blackmur, after having almost squarely faced the consequences of the rag-bag quality of the *Cantos*, shies off at the end and reduces the gravity of his conclusions by a sneer at the common reader. He concludes his essay "Masks of Ezra Pound" with these words: "'A catalogue, his jewels of conversation.' The *Cantos* are an anthology of such jewels and read as most people read anthologies, as indeed all but a few read any sort of poetry, for the felicity of line and phrase, for strangeness, or for an echoed aptness of sentiment, the reader can afford to forget the promise and ambition of which the poem cheated him. He will have been equally cheated in all but the smallest part of his reading."[2] But this is quite untrue. The cases are not parallel. The reader of an anthology reads whole poems. He may flit uncritically and unhistorically among them; but each exists in its own right; each communicates to him as a whole. This is not the experience of a reader of the *Cantos*. There are magnificent lines and passages indeed; but they are rarely whole poems; they are almost all fragmentary, or blurred at the edges, or contaminated, either with rubbish or with alien matter. I do not see that the anthology sipper is cheated at all as he goes from a Shakespeare sonnet to the "Coy Mistress" to "Mariana" in the *Oxford Book of English Verse*; but if he is cheated it is in a wholly different way from the exasperated reader of the *Cantos* finding what satisfaction he can in splendid or beautiful fragments, neither complete in themselves nor having any intelligible connection with a larger whole. Only the wilful blindness of

---

[1] Hugh Kenner, *The Poetry of Ezra Pound*, p. 91.
[2] R. P. Blackmur, *Language as Gesture* (New York, 1935), p. 54.

addiction could lead this admirable critic to append a false conclusion to the judgment he has made.

A similar trope is employed by Mr. Hugh Kenner again. The *Cantos* have been found disconnected, incoherent and obscure. Very well, then: "Probably very few graduate students enjoy a confident, other than habitual awareness of the presence of connection between the two stanzas of the familiar 'Lucy' poem, 'A slumber did my spirit seal.'"[1] It is symptomatic of Mr. Kenner's culture that the only persons he can think of as likely readers of Wordsworth are graduate students, and that the handiest way he can find to get out of a tight spot is to belabour his pupils. But even if his suggestion were true, and even if the condition of Mr. Kenner's graduate students were of any importance in the general context of European letters, how would all this make the *Cantos* any better? This technique of non-explanation is continued in his third appendix, "The Cantos; further notes"; notes which merely paraphrase confusion—a set of muddled jottings which are supposed to represent the "themes" of the poem, and do nothing whatever to show that the themes combine into an intelligible order.

Time after time we find that the major critical questions that modern literature ought to arouse are left virtually unattempted. The honourable exception is in the work of Mr. Yvor Winters, who has subjected Imagist poetic theory, and its poetic practice, and the relation between the two, to a searching and stern examination. I could not hope to emulate the rigour with which he has performed his task; it is only to be regretted that the devastating accuracy of his analysis has been partly obscured by some extremely eccentric judgments of individual poets; and what seems to me an untenable view of the moral relations of poetry. But in the ability to stand back and see twentieth-century poetry in a historical perspective, Mr. Winters stands alone. Others, with all their sensibility, industry and acumen, have been docile followers of a rather elderly Zeitgeist. We are left with a crowd of claqueurs, bemused epigoni, Hudson Reviewers, wedding guests each helplessly fascinated by his own Ancient Mariner: or morose bystanders who retain de-

[1] Hugh Kenner, *The Poetry of Ezra Pound*, p. 194.

tachment at the price of insensibility. It is a paradox that to-day, when criticism is more active, more strenuous and better equipped than it has ever been, it has never managed to see the most typical work of its own time in the light of a mature literary experience.

Some reasons for this state of affairs have been suggested—reasons connected with the special kind of enjoyment that modern poetry gives. But there is I think another one; the real roots of the novelty in modern literary practice have been very little examined. We shall find the roots of English Imagist poetry in the French Symbolist area, the area that is bounded by Mallarmé and Rimbaud. And this is well enough known. Mr. Eliot has acknowledged his discipleship to Laforgue and Corbière; both Eliot and Pound in the early days made great play with Rémy de Gourmont; and there is a valuable study by René Taupin of Imagist-Symbolist relations.[1] But these known linkages seem to have made little impression on the general critical consciousness. Mr. Eliot's encomium on the Metaphysical poets obscured the fact that his poetical methods have very little in common with theirs; and the extreme Anglican decorum of much of his critical writing has not inclined us to look towards Paris of the eighties for the origins of the new poetry. And Pound's odd and dazzling collection of antiquities—his exhortations to read Provençal, to read Guido Cavalcanti, to read Golding's translations of Ovid, to read Confucius—have brought about more bewilderment than illumination. Where there is a recognition of the powerful Symbolist spell it is apt to fall into the opposite excess of assuming that the Mallarmé-Rimbaud complex is the type of normal poetic situation. A recent study which I have encountered assumes quite openly that Mallarmé's *Coup de Dés* and *Finnegan's Wake* are the two great monuments of modern Western culture. For a less extreme example we could turn to Miss Elizabeth Sewell who proposes to inquire into the structure of poetry in general (*The Structure of Poetry* is the title of her book) precisely by examining the work of Mallarmé and

---

[1] René Taupin, *L'Influence du Symbolisme Francais sur la Poésie Américane, 1910–1920* (Paris, 1929).

Rimbaud. She finds that Mallarmé pushes poetry as far as it can go towards the abstract and ordered structure of mathematics, Rimbaud towards the disordered concreteness of dream. And these, she suggests, are the two poles between which poetry exists, Number and Nightmare. Number and Nightmare—a splendid fragment of oracular incantation; but it seems odd to use these two extravagant indices to point out the normal structure of poetry. It is as if to say, to one who would inform himself on the nature of man: "Some people are mathematical logicians, others are delirious. You had better examine these two cases, for normal human experience lies between them."

The disordered concreteness of dream which Miss Sewell calls Nightmare is illustrated by her mainly from Rimbaud's *Bateau Ivre* and *Illuminations*; we could illustrate it too from *The Waste Land*, the *Cantos*, from large parts of *Ulysses* and from *Finnegan's Wake*. It is essentially the Imagist method, some of whose consequences we have discussed. To turn now for a brief glance at the opposite extreme, Number, Mallarmé's method, the effort to turn poetry into a self-contained structure divorced as far as possible from concrete referential content. I am acutely aware that anything one says about Mallarmé may be wrong. Attempts to wrestle with Mallarmé's poetry, and some reading of what much better qualified critics, both French and English, have said about it, reveal such a diversity of possible judgments that one cannot feel very much confidence in saying anything. It is quite certain, however, that aspiration towards an impossible "purity", a liberation of poetry from all reference to the actual world, is a constant movement in Mallarmé. His critical writing everywhere reveals this. The question that remains is how can poetry move in this direction; how did Mallarmé think it could be approached? I say approached, for obviously this purity cannot be achieved. Words have meanings, references to things that are not words, and these references are inescapable. Pure poetry is always a mirage. Miss Sewell's answer is a simple one, and it is manifestly wrong. She supposes that Mallarmé attempts to make his poetry a pure structure of sounds, or since poetry is now generally read from the printed page, of sounds and appearances—what she calls the sound-look aspect of words. She sees in Mallarmé's poetry an intricate pattern of sounds and syllables, partly constituted by the exacting rhyme-schemes of his sonnets, partly by a system of internal rhyme, assonance and alliteration. Certainly this system is there and can be examined. Equally certainly it is grossly inadequate as an explanation of how the poems are constituted. This is revealed by the miserable poverty of the analyses that her method enables her to give. All she can find to say of a sonnet like "Le vierge, le vivace et le bel aujourd'hui" is:

> The essential of this poem is the i pattern. The rhymes make this clear at once, the octet rhyming on ui and ivre, the sestet on ie and igne. No line is without its i sound. . . Added to it is the v pattern. This starts by being intimately associated with the i. . . .[1]

And so on. This is not nonsense; it is a part of the structure of the poem: but if, as she suggests, it *is* the structure of the poem such poetry could not have the slightest interest for any rational being.

And of course this is not Mallarmé's procedure. His intelligence is far too subtle ever to have supposed that such an infantile simplification could have been more than an auxiliary to his purpose. If I may attempt a suggestion where so many better-informed writers have made suggestions already, it is that Mallarmé endeavours to make poetry a paradigm for an experience, without the actual content. He tries to give, with the minutest delicacy, the structure of an experience without the actual experience; a structure that might be filled out, if we insist on filling it out, with many actual experiences. But the poem does not commit itself to any of them, or concern itself with them except in a minimal unavoidable way. Mallarmé's work has been described as a kind of poetical algebra. I have often wondered whether people who use this phrase know what they mean by it. But it will be clear, I imagine, what I might mean by it. Algebra performs structural operations

---

[1] Elizabeth Sewell, *The Structure of Poetry* (London, 1951), p. 144.

without concerning itself with the actual value of the symbols it employs: Mallarmé's poetry tries to do something of this kind. Or we can use the analogy (it has more than once been consecrated to poetic purposes) of a jar, whose shape is beautiful, satisfactory, complete—and can be filled indifferently with ashes, brandy, weak tea, water or nothing at all.

Mallarmé's sonnet "M'introduire dans ton histoire" has given rise to a number of explanations, and its last line "le seul vesperal de mes chars" became at one time a proverbial phrase for the sonorous unintelligible gibberish of which his poetry was supposed by its enemies to be made up. The poem has been variously seen as an ingeniously veiled obscenity; as a less indecorous piece, but still on an erotic theme; as the account of an imaginary triumph after a real amorous failure; of a real triumph after coldness and disappointment. The scene from which it takes its departure has been variously figured as the intimate meeting-place of two lovers, a carriage going for a drive in the evening, and a firework display. This will be enough to illustrate the dubieties that are possible in reading the poem, and the impossibility of assigning to it a definite referential content. What then remains? A structure; partly indeed a structure of sounds and syllables such as that suggested by Miss Sewell; but also a structure of meaning—timidity, the sense of sanctities violated, the chill of repulsion and failure, followed by a grandiose triumph. How does Mallarmé contrive to keep his poem in this state of abstraction, without unduly arousing—and certainly without satisfying—the reader's ordinary desire for a concrete content? Partly (though more in some other sonnets than in this one) by an elaborate deformation of syntax which absolutely prevents the reading of the poem as anything approaching narrative or description; partly by using metaphor and image in such a way that the tenor of the metaphor (what it might convey in a prose paraphrase) is left uncertain or undiscoverable. One example must suffice, a metaphorical phrase to which it is almost impossible to assign a literal meaning because it couples together incomparable classes of objects. "Tonnerre et rubis aux moyeux"; thunder and rubies at the axle-trees. We cannot locate *thunder* and *rubies* together in any imagined physical space. When Mr. Eliot adapts this phrase—

> Garlic and sapphires in the mud
> Clot the bedded axle-tree

—he is less bold. Garlic and sapphires are both material objects, they can be found in the same mud in which a wheel is supposed to be buried. True, the metaphor still has to be interpreted, but we are not dazzled at the start by a coruscating obliquity on its surface. Thunder and rubies together are a sort of no-road sign, forbidding access to a referential meaning. And this no doubt is only one of many devices by which Mallarmé, while preserving a structural relation between different parts of the poem, prevents us from giving it a defined content.

Mallarmé remains the extreme example of this kind of poetic effect; but it has though less consistently become a familiar feature of modern poetry in English. Even *A Cooking Egg* affords a slight illustration—we know Pipit's position in the poem, her relative status, even if we do not know who or what she is. We could find the same sort of thing in parts of Auden's work; but for clearer and more abundant examples we should look in the poetry of Wallace Stevens. The parallel between him and Mallarmé has often been remarked. Of course the deliberate exploitation of such effects is a very specialised, very recent, and very untypical development in poetry. They are far remote from the main poetic stream. Epic and dramatic poetry could not proceed in this way; and most lyric does not. Nightmare and Number may, as Elizabeth Sewell suggests, be the two poles of poetic experience, but the exploration of each of them simply draws us away from the great temperature area in between where nearly all poetry has its being. And this brings us back, after a long excursion, to our original subject, poetry and tradition. In spite of much talk of tradition, the characteristic, idiosyncratic features of twentieth-century poetry have taken it away (in a phrase which I quote from Mr. M. H. Abrams) from "the central tradition of poetics, which looked upon poetry not as a verbal structure nor (in C. Day Lewis's phrase) as an image composed of images, but as a verbal representation, artistically ordered, of thinking, feeling and acting human beings".[1]

Crystal-gazing as a critical method had better be reduced to a minimum; but it is hard to believe that poetry in the future can make any further progress in the Imagist-Symbolist direction. If it were to remain in that mode it would either lead a fading invalidish life and then die altogether, or become an esoteric plaything. Either could happen. Then, if I were one of the morose depreciators of modern poetry that I fear I have often made myself sound like, I should proceed to say that this whole experiment has been a dead end, and that poetry must retrace its steps. But this is not what I want to say. If we are to use metaphors, mine would not be a cul-de-sac but a détour, a diversion from the main road. Traffic along the main road has been proceeding all the time, and we do not sufficiently remember this. In talking of modern poetry we ought to recall more often than we do that Hardy was writing till 1926, and that among the poets of our century are Robert Frost, Robert Graves, John Crowe Ransom, Edwin Muir and John Betjeman. But the détour has been considerable, and most of the heavy traffic has chosen to travel on it. It is probably time it rejoined the main highway. But, to abandon the metaphor, which is becoming inconvenient, it is no use imagining that things will ever be the same again. This is like the social illusion of going back to pre-war days, with which we used to delude ourselves for a short time after 1918, and have abandoned for ever, ever since. All we can say is that some of the most brilliant poetic innovations of the most original poetic talents of our day are probably inimitable and unrepeatable. They cannot be developed any farther, and they have been of a kind from which it is very difficult to learn. Yet they cannot be forgotten or ignored. This I believe is the difficult situation that poetry finds itself in to-day.

[1] M. H. Abrams, Review of Frank Kermode's *Romantic Image* in *Victorian Studies*, Sept. 1950, p. 77.

A LITERARY REVOLUTION

A few years ago, when the *Rock-Drill* section of Pound's *Cantos* appeared, a reviewer justly remarked that the most part of it is simply not poetry in English. After some further commentary on this cento of Greek, Latin, French and Italian tags, Chinese ideograms and Egyptian hieroglyphs, all pressed into an English setting, he concluded by saying, "This is the poetry of the future." A Johnsonian phrase seems called for: surely while his breath was forming this proposition into words his understanding must have suspected it to be ridiculous. Perhaps it was intended only as a pious hyperbole. Prophecy is not a useful subject for debate; we can only usefully inquire by what motive it was prompted. Evidently there is some loss of faith in poetry written in English (or presumably in any one language), some sort of belief that the future of poetry is bound up with a composite polyglot discourse. What Wyndham Lewis called the Demon of Progress in the arts is still at work. Here as often he operates by making lunatic extrapolations from events that have actually occurred. There is not the slightest evidence that the integrity of individual linguistic traditions is weakening, or that poetry could live and transmit itself through a jumble of half-comprehended multilingual fragments. But this is an inference, if it is anything so respectable, from a real historical development—from the fact that the English literary community has undergone a great expansion in this century.

I want to return to this topic in a moment, but first I would dwell briefly on a few social-economic platitudes and their implications for literature. Literature is among other things a commodity; and if one has deciphered the Coca-Cola signs in Arabic script along the shores of the Suez Canal, read advertisements for Nestlé's milk in Malay newspapers, bought Gillette razor-blades in Hanoi, Lucky Strikes in Innsbruck, or Courvoisier brandy in Chicago, one cannot doubt that commodities to-day have an international range. Once we get above the level of the merest domestic subsistence, we live in a culture that is no longer regional, no longer national, but composite and eclectic, and therefore becoming steadily more uniform.

IMAGE AND EXPERIENCE

This cosmopolitan civilisation based on science, technology and social democracy, can be regarded with complacency or with misgiving. We can point to the enrichment and variety of experience that it makes possible in any one particular spot; we can point too to the fact that one spot begins to look very much like another. Of course we want to have our cake and eat it. The great international capital where everything can be had and anything may happen is one of the achievements of our civilisation; but we cannot wish it to become the universal model. We want our own region and the regions that we visit to retain their individual qualities. Provincialism is deeply rooted in our nature. We have all known those peasants of London, Paris or New York who can hardly conceive of life outside the bounds of their brick and concrete *pays*. It would be a melancholy state if peace were only to be secured by making everywhere exactly like everywhere else. But of course uniformity does not imply agreement. Two dogs of the same breed are just as likely to fight over a bone as two different ones; and to be oneself makes it no more likely that one will want to quarrel with one's neighbour.

The international exchanges, cultural missions and conferences in which our world abounds have probably done nothing to bring about a unity of culture; and if they did they would do nothing to bring about international agreement. There is really no political argument for internationalising culture and arts. Some of the arts are by their nature more capable of international diffusion—music and painting, most happily. We have an international style of architecture at present—much less happily, for a variety of reasons. But literature, tied to language as it is, is absolutely prevented from developing in the same way; and technology and communications hardly affect the situation. This huge mongrelised commercial civilisation, living on the same products, made in the same factories, sold out of similar shops, is powerless before the fact of language. By the mercy of heaven, French literature remains French, Italian literature remains Italian, and English literature remains English. And contacts between them seem to be of the same nature as they have always been—fertilising, refreshing, but no

58

more massive and tending no more to standardisation than they were in the sixteenth century or the eighteenth. This is the great bulwark against the dreary entropy of taste that is rapidly afflicting cookery, building and interior decoration.

It is the language barrier, the blessed and almost total failure of such projects as Esperanto and Basic English, that guarantees continued diversity. Within a single linguistic area it is harder to see what is actually going on, and far harder to know what state of affairs is to be desired. In this respect the English linguistic area is unique. More than any other, English is a world language. A greater number of people speak Chinese; but they are nearly all in China, and belong to a common culture. Users of English are scattered all over the globe, and belong to enormously differing social and cultural systems. This has been the case for long enough. The English linguistic community has been growing steadily for over two hundred years. And yet I spoke of the English *literary* community undergoing a great and rapid change this century; and I think this is true. Until recently many parts of the English-speaking world were hardly parts of a literary community at all, whether as producers or consumers. They are now active in both directions. And America, which was always a literary community from the time of the first settlers, has had an enormous expansion of its literary public and its literary consciousness in the last fifty years. The result of these developments is that English writing is a commodity of international diffusion as writing in no other language can be. And this has had a profound though not easily definable effect on the literature of our century.

The greatest realignment of forces has been in Anglo-American literary relations. They have become completely transformed in the last fifty years; and this has had both a broad general effect on the sense of values, and a quite specific effect on the modern literary revolution that we have been discussing. If we are to discover the nature of our recent poetic upheaval we must pay some attention to these circumstances. I am persuaded that there is a massive cultural phenomenon here that has not yet been properly examined—still not properly examined, in spite of the establishment of American literature as an academic discipline, and the conscientious exhortations in the London *Times Literary Supplement* to recognise its existence. It is not a question of recognising its existence, but of realising its effect on the whole English-speaking literary community. Up to some time in the middle of the nineteenth century, American literature was not so much subordinated to English as a part of it. It drew its standards and its style from English sources, and it had a quite straightforward appeal to an English audience. On late-Victorian English bookshelves Emerson stood beside Carlyle, and Longfellow beside Tennyson. I suppose no one can date exactly the beginning of a separate American literary personality. The programme is outlined in Emerson's "American Scholar" lecture of 1837, and his other lecture "The Poet" of seven years later; and the programme preceded the performance. However much of the American spirit and material may have appeared in earlier writing, what a European would recognise as a distinct American style in poetry appears only with Whitman, and in prose only with Mark Twain. But the distinct American style does make its appearance, and from that time on the question of the relationship between American and English literature has been active. A robust British Victorian view of the matter is expressed by Matthew Arnold.

> I see advertised *The Primer of American Literature.* Imagine the face of Philip or Alexander at hearing of a primer of Macedonian Literature! . . . we are all contributors to one great literature—English Literature.[1]

This is not quite the proprietorial pronouncement that it sounds; Arnold is merely asserting the primacy of language in the cultural tradition, and its power to override local differences. And this is not self-evidently absurd. But both Emerson and Whitman saw the matter otherwise. And surely by now there is no longer anything to argue about—as a mere question of fact. There is an American literature, distinct in its material, its characteristic interest and to a large extent in its style from English literature. At present its power in the world is a good deal greater.

[1] Quoted in M. Cunliffe, *The Literature of the United States* (London, 1954), p. 9.

A LITERARY REVOLUTION

But once we let go of the mere fact and begin to consider its implications there is a great deal that still needs inquiry and understanding. In all the discussion of American literature and its status it has never I think been remarked, on either side of the Atlantic, that we have here a cultural situation unique in the history of the world. We have two civilisations, widely different in social habits, political assumptions, and relation to the international community, producing two different literatures, but in the same language, and having behind them a common literary heritage. I do not believe that there is any stage in the history of our civilisation when a situation quite like this has prevailed. There is no real parallel in the Hellenistic or Imperial Roman world. We have seen provincial and colonial styles appearing in a metropolitan literature. But this is something quite different. American writers are not in the position of Apuleius or Seneca or St. Augustine. They are writing in English, with a background of English literature—but out of an established, unified and quite un-English civilisation. The only similar relation is that between the Spanish literature of Spain and that of the Spanish-speaking countries in the New World. This is less striking, for the civilisation of Latin America is not a unified one like that of the United States; and the relation is in any case only another instance of the same distinctively new state of affairs.

So far as Emerson and Whitman were only proclaiming their right to a distinctively American subject-matter they were not saying anything particularly controversial. A new country offers new material. And shorn of the patriotic rhetoric, some of their claims amount to no more than this. When Emerson says that the American writer should see in "the barbarism and materialism" of his own day "another carnival of the same gods whose picture he so much admires in Homer" he is saying what may be doubted, but he means little more than that America has the right to make an epic of its own matter if it can. "America is a poem in our eyes; its ample geography dazzles the imagination, and it will not wait long for meters."[1] But when the meters, if not precisely Homeric ones, actually arrive

[1] "The Poet", 1844.

61

with Whitman, hardly more than ten years later, they make a larger claim for themselves. Whitman writes in the preface to *Leaves of Grass*, "The Americans of all nations at any time upon the earth have probably the fullest poetical nature. The United States themselves are essentially the greatest poem."[1] There is implicit in these words not only the announcement of a new subject-matter, but a new scale of literary values. It is repeated in *Democratic Vistas*: "America demands a poetry that is bold, modern and all-surrounding and cosmical, as she is herself. . . . Erect, inflated and fully self-esteeming be the chant; and then America will listen with pleased ears."[2] And then we turn back and realise that the new scale of values had already been announced by Emerson himself. Acknowledging that the ideal poet has not yet appeared in America, Emerson also fails to find him in five centuries of English poetry. "These are wits rather than poets, though there have been poets among them. But when we adhere to the ideal of the poet, we have our difficulties even with Milton and Homer.[3] Milton is too literary, and Homer too literal and historical." There is to be an improved scale of values for America, then, by which Milton and Homer will be insufficient.

And that is the real problem raised by the emergence of a second literature in the English language. Linguistically it cannot help inheriting five centuries of English literary tradition—a tradition always vitally connected with that of Europe as a whole. And yet so far as it is a new literature springing from a new world it is socially and experientially unrelated to much of the English tradition. I think there can be no doubt that a distinctly American set of literary values has emerged in recent years; and that its co-presence with European ones is still capable of causing bewilderment. An Englishman in America cannot help being aware that a number of shrines in the literary pantheon command very different degrees of devotion in the two countries. If the status of Henry James is internationally agreed, that of Hawthorne, Melville and Thoreau is not. They do not assume much importance in the English

---

[1] Preface to *Leaves of Grass*, 1855.   [2] *Democratic Vistas*, 1871.
[3] "The Poet".

literary imagination; and Henry Adams none at all. American literature is a much more national affair than English has ever been or felt itself to be. Writers are esteemed for their American quality, for their share in establishing a peculiarly American consciousness; and a good deal of what goes on in the study of American literature seems to the outsider to belong to social rather than to literary history. On the other hand the Englishman becomes intermittently conscious that there are areas of the English literature of the past that look quite different to Americans, who stand outside the English social hierarchy, have no nostalgia for fogs and gaslight, and are not accustomed to babble of green fields.

The difficulties that this state of affairs may lead to can be illustrated from a recent critical study by Mr. Richard Chase. His important book *The American Novel and its Tradition* sets out to define a specially American kind of novel. Mr. Chase, following Hawthorne, describes it as the "romance-novel", and to this category he finds that the greatest American fiction belongs. It diverges from the English tradition and cannot be accounted for by English literary standards; it diverges even from the traditions of classical tragedy and Christianity, which Mr. Chase sees to lie behind the work of the English novelists. His aim then is to isolate a distinct literary kind, with its own quality. Yet his definition is couched in terms that suggest mainly deficiency. The romance-novel as he describes it sounds like something that does not quite manage to become a novel of the ordinary sort. The word romance, he says, in this context, "must signify, besides the more obvious qualities of the picturesque and the heroic, an assumed freedom from the ordinary novelistic requirements of verisimilitude, development and continuity; a tendency towards melodrama and idyll . . . a willingness to abandon moral questions, or to ignore the spectacle of man in society, or to consider these things only indirectly and abstractly".[1] And again, "Like other romance-novels, *Moby Dick* is thus somewhat disqualified for engaging the moral imagination in the sort of close involvement with real life which makes the context for moral ideas in

[1] Richard Chase, *The American Novel and its Tradition* (New York, 1957), p. ix.

such novels as those of Balzac, George Eliot or James himself."
Now, melodrama is an inferior form, idyll a slight one; a
willingness to abandon moral questions and a failure to engage
the moral imagination with real life sound like serious dis-
qualifications; and the compensatory merits of the romance-
novel sound more like special pleading than a real balancing
factor.

Yet as the book goes on the reader is mildly surprised to find
that these apparent deficiencies have only to be seen as part of a
distinctively American tradition to be immediately transformed
into virtues. It is not necessary to say that something bad does
not become good by becoming American; or that this is not what
Mr. Chase intends to convey. If the romance-novel is an independent form, as I have no doubt it is (there are English and
French examples of it as well as American ones—*Wuthering
Heights* and *Le Grand Meaulnes* occur immediately to mind),
it has its own standards and its own kind of integrity. One does
not define *The Tempest* by its unlikeness to *Antigone*. This is
just one example of the sort of difficulties that the dubious relation between English and American literary values can lead us
into.

My own conviction is that the difference in standards should
be simply accepted. This sounds like a pusillanimous agreement
to differ; and since I do not mean that, I should say welcomed,
rather than accepted. There should always be debate, as there
always has been in the European literary tradition; but real
debate, which recognises that the two parties start from different
points. This is only to recognise the obvious. Surely by now it
is inevitable that out of the vast number of literary possibilities
England should continue to interest itself in some that mean
little to America, and that America should have selected or
created others which are outside the English literary sphere.

Yet there was a period, and a very recent one, when it seemed
that a common Anglo-American literary community with a
common set of values was likely to develop. It was a period
when the ascendant values were formalist ones—those which
most easily transcend local and national difference. It is the
period with which we are particularly concerned, that of our

recent poetical revolution. There was a decade or so when all the newest and most promising poetry being written in English was written by Americans; but they had to come to England to do it. It is remarkable, one might note in parenthesis, that Robert Frost had to find an English publisher before his peculiarly American genius could make itself known. But of course I am thinking of the revolutionary work of Pound and Eliot. Pound in his early days preserved a passionate interest in the destinies of American poetry. He kept up continuous contacts with Harriet Monro and her Chicago periodical *Poetry*; and with William Carlos Williams. He was always on the look-out for new American talent. Yet he lived in London, was much inclined for some years to talk of London as the cultural capital, and most of his early work appeared in English periodicals and editions. Mr. Eliot's destiny from 1915 onwards was far more exclusively linked to the English scene. No doubt the example of Henry James counted for much. He was revered by both Pound and Eliot, and he is the one great example of a writer whose status is equally assured on both sides of the Atlantic and who drew equal nourishment from the old and the new. But the brilliant and shimmering edifice he constructed is a sort of rainbow bridge, connecting the two worlds, kept up by miracle, and affording no foundation for later building. The post-Jacobean period of Anglo-American literary alliance seems to be an even less substantial structure.

The two American poets who were radically changing the direction of poetry in English were, it is true, expatriates, but they were expatriate Americans; and that means that their relation to the European poetic tradition was radically different from that of any English poet of their own time, or of any other time. The situation I am trying to describe is initially a matter of simple geography, but the cultural effects are more complicated. When an American goes abroad he is apt to say he is going to Europe. An Englishman says he is going to Paris or Austria or Florence. He can't go to Europe since he is in it already. From the Western side of the Atlantic Europe is apt to appear as a large geographical and cultural block, set over against America. From England, peripheral though its

European position may be, Europe can never appear in this light. Indeed the Englishman has a rather feeble sense of Europe; he is inclined to think merely of particular places, whose acquaintance he makes gradually and sporadically. This is the crude origin of the difference I wish to point to, but it has manifold consequences in the literary field. Some of them are massive and obvious—the greater openness of America to a variety of European influences, for instance; some of them are subtle, extending to delicate details of poetic technique and expression.

There is a whole chapter of cultural history here, and this is not the place even to outline it. Let me instead look for a generalisation and a few pertinent examples. If we shift our ground from physical to mental travel we find an exact analogy. When the mental traveller from England makes his explorations into other European cultures he remains an Englishman who has connected his own literature and civilisation with some of its ancestors and collaterals. The American who moves away from his native grass-roots tends to become at one bound a cosmopolitan. His education encourages him to be so. Consider the number of college courses called Masterpieces, or Great Books, or World Literature, or something of that kind— in which the undergraduate is given in a single year a guided tour around the great monuments of European culture from the *Iliad* to *Finnegan's Wake*. When Pound first came to Europe he was a graduate student in Romance languages. It is not easy for an Englishman to be a graduate student in Romance languages, for the educational system does not encourage the blunderbuss study of a large group of tongues. In surveying Pound's early career one hardly knows whether to be more astonished at the inaccuracy of his knowledge or the wideness of its range. His first book of verse, *A Lume Spento*, contains some startling illiteracies. The student of Romance languages had not even a schoolboy's competence in Latin. Yet in a few years he was to write a book called *The Spirit of Romance*, which is a series of glimpses of Romance literature from the *Pervigilium Veneris*, through medieval Latin, Provençal, early Italian and Spanish to old French. It has not any particular scholarly value and does not pretend to it, but it is even now an extremely attractive, lively, first-hand account of the divers works that it describes.

Pound is after all very clear about what he wants. He cares for poetry, and he wants only such knowledge as a practising poet can directly use. His attitude is one of glad discipleship to a variety of foreign literatures. He is followed in this by Eliot, much more discreetly. The rather self-consciously cosmopolitan air that we find in Mr. Eliot's early poems and in *The Waste Land* is to be found too in *Harmonium*, the first volume of Wallace Stevens. It is noticeable that the distinguished critic of this generation, Mr. Edmund Wilson, regards this internationalism as the character of the literary scene even to-day. In a recent interview published in the London *Sunday Times* he remarked, "The whole world is getting to be more alike in certain ways. We're all having to deal with more or less the same kind of society, so that national literatures and all that are becoming less important."[1] It is in some such faith that the polyglot mosaic of the later *Cantos*, and possibly *Finnegan's Wake*, appear to have been composed.

Our literary revolution, then, is a cosmopolitan affair. Biographically speaking it is a revolution of expatriates and exiles; and this is so before and quite apart from the enforced exile brought about by revolution and war. It is an age of arbitrary migrations and displacements. Henry James, in this as in other ways, is the father of much in modern Anglo-American letters. Eliot follows him in turning his back on the American scene and ultimately adopting English nationality. Pound's active years were spent in London, Paris and Rapallo, and he was never again in his own country until he re-entered it in tragic and problematical circumstances after the last war. Joyce deliberately elects a career of "silence, exile and cunning", has no other theme but Dublin, yet writes of it in memory, from Trieste, Zurich and Paris. Lawrence after writing one great novel straight out of his native experience spends the rest of his life in restless wandering over the world, in search of somewhere to settle. And in a younger generation Auden reverses the usual course of literary migration and leaves England to

[1] *The Sunday Times*, Feb. 1, 1959.

settle in America. Yeats is almost alone among the great writers of the early part of this century in writing out of the heart of his own country.

This cosmopolitanism may be simply accepted and embraced, as an essential part of the contemporary scene. Edmund Wilson seems to take it in this way, and there are many who have been willing to extend and generalise the idea. Geographical eclecticism has gone hand in hand with historical eclecticism, and both have been extended to other arts than literature. André Malraux founds his art-criticism on the idea of the "imaginary museum". The modern painter, thanks to the technical advance that has made improved methods of reproduction possible, and thanks too to history and anthropology, has at his disposal the whole body of painting of all times and all countries, so that his relation to the past is radically different from that of any of his predecessors. There has been no comparable technical revolution affecting literature, and the great un-international fact of language forbids it; but the enormous diffusion of historical and anthropological knowledge has had something of the same effect—as the Great Books courses bear witness. And Mr. Donald Davie, with some qualifications, has suggested that the modern poet too lives in an imaginary museum, and that his writing is inevitably affected by it. He must proceed by pastiche and allusion, and must acknowledge by nods and becks and lifted eyebrows his awareness "that there are modes of experience or ways of saying things which the poet is aware of though his poem on its own account is not".[1] Mr. Davie makes this a recommendation; it seems to me a concise recipe for some of the most meretricious effects in modern poetry; but his way of thinking is obviously relevant to the poetry of the last fifty years.

We can consider this denationalisation of the literary scene in another way. We can consider the audience. The audience for literature in English has no longer any homogeneity, except that provided by its tendency to read literature written in English. Its members may live in Edinburgh or Hampstead or Brooklyn or Seattle or Sydney, or quite possibly Jamaica or

[1] *The Listener*, July 12, 1957.

Bombay. No community of experience can possibly be assumed between them. We can see this most clearly by thinking of the destiny of the novel, since the direct mimesis of experience is more in the foreground there than in any other form. The typical situation through the eighteenth and nineteenth centuries was the assumption of a shared experience between writer and reader. The reader of Fielding or Dickens was assumed, and on the whole rightly assumed, to be as much in possession of the social data and the literary conventions on which the novel was founded as the writer himself. The English reader of Faulkner is commonly quite uninformed about the world Faulkner portrays, or rather about what sort of relation the novels have to historical reality. He reads him as he reads Dostoievski. He presumes that behind Faulkner's imaginative vision lies a world and a society, but it is one that is wholly mysterious to him, apart from the novels themselves. I persuade myself that I see a similar situation in Lionel Trilling's study of Forster; Professor Trilling sees his subject as a moralist in a dateless, unlocalised sense, or relates him to broad general currents of ideas; while an English reader must I think always start his appreciation of Mr. Forster (it will not conclude there) with a vivid sense of his contact with a particular social life, and his provenance from a specialised cultural milieu. It is no use approving or deploring this state of things; it is simply there. For writers like Faulkner and Forster, each of whom has been able to write out of a specific culture, it will merely mean a diversity of readings. For the writer who is aware of his large denationalised potential audience, the situation is different. It offers temptations—the temptation to exploit by snob-appeal a false assumption of common experience; or to exploit by a kind of bullying exoticism the absence of community. It can happen with Hemingway. We are asked to agree that we are all friendly with head waiters and very good at bull-fighting. Yes, we reply, with a false complicity, we are like that too: or alternatively, in abject submission, No, we are not like that at all; we lead very quiet lives; do tell us Mr. Hemingway, you are so clever and so brave. There is a kind of impurity here, both in the reaction of the audience and in the fact that it has

been played for; an impurity not caused but probably much en-
couraged by the huge international swamp of readers to which
such a writer appeals.

So that I cannot regard the detribalisation of literature with
much complacency. I doubt whether the Anglo-American
literary community is a real community, or that any particular
effort should be kept up to make it so. I believe that a writer
to-day should be suspicious of any attempt to appeal to the vast
faceless international audience. It may be that he has no community left. It is a melancholy thing that one of the most moving
of all sonnets, "Heureux qui comme Ulysse", can so often now
be no more than the motive to a historical regret. There is no
pays to return to. But I think we should try to make one, and
that the writer should, so far as it is in his power, write from
and for those whom he knows, whose habits and experiences he
shares. It will be the best chance he has of bringing something
living to those whose experiences he does not share.

And this brings me back to the poetic revolution of the child-
hood of the century, to its singularly rootless character. Many
of the great works of modern literature seem to exist in a
vacuum, to spring from no particular society and to address no
particular audience. *The Waste Land* is founded on a vegetation
myth that is universal rather than particular. It draws its religious symbolism from Buddhism and the Upanishads as well as
from Christianity. Since this poem aims at a kind of compre-
hensiveness and universality the feeling of non-attachment to
any particular cultural context is wholly appropriate. *Finnegan's Wake*, in spite of its obsessive attachment to Howth
Castle and environs, aims to represent nothing less than the
total dream of man, so it too must be based on a universal re-
surrection myth, and deserting any one language descend into
the mind's workshop where language itself is formed. These
are highly idiosyncratic encyclopedic successes; as the *Cantos*
is an idiosyncratic encyclopedic failure. In any case their being
depends on their encyclopedic quality. The smaller forms need
a more precise focus. Eliot's early quasi-satirical poems and the
satirical pieces in Pound's *Ripostes* and *Lustra* both suffer from
the lack of it. Burbank with his Baedeker, Bleistein with his

cegar, Mr. Hecatomb Styrax and the Milwins hardly seem more aimless, clueless and unattached than the lyric speakers who reflect on their condition. Satire needs a firm social base. The violently energetic, cruelly trenchant pamphleteering of Wyndham Lewis, locally so powerful that one begins to think of a comparison with Swift, never makes its full effect as a whole because it has no consistent standpoint, no basis in society or intellectual tradition. There is a similar spirit in criticism. Its main symptoms are a continual talk about the European tradition, and a continual unwillingness to accept the canon of European letters as it is. There was an itch to be continually tinkering with reputations, usually in a destructive fashion—to hound out Virgil or Petrarch, to dislodge Milton, to make it impossible for any right-thinking person to read Shelley, or whatever it might be. All such attempts to erase sanctified names from the public monuments are symptoms of insecurity. I try to say this neutrally. Probably things could not have been other than they were; I am only concerned to remark on what they were.

The general cultural cosmopolitanism that I have been trying to observe, strongly reinforced in our case by the presence of two powerful American writers who felt themselves to be intellectual citizens of the world, can be seen—indeed I cannot help seeing it—as in some sense opposed to the English literary tradition. It is hard to find the right shade of definition in talking of this. Of course the English poetic tradition has been from the start a matter of continual influence from Latin culture—mostly from France but nearly as much from Italy. Often a native growth has been opposed by a highly authoritative influence from abroad, and the two have had to be reconciled in a new synthesis. One thinks of the problem Dryden and the neo-classic critics had in reconciling the presence of Shakespeare with the formal ideals of drama derived from France. But then Shakespeare himself would be unthinkable without the great body of Romance literature from which he drew much of his material. And so it has always gone on. This continual and extremely civilised dialogue has been the very substance of the English literary tradition. Of all men Pound appeared to be the most vociferously aware of it. ("All English poetry is a history of successful steals from the French," he said.[1]) Yet he is curiously unaware of its real nature. In his early days Pound was an indefatigable propagandist for Provençal poetry and its value as a technical example to the English verse of his time. But he hardly seems to recognise that English poetry had begun to absorb the Provencal lessons in the thirteenth century, that whatever was relevant in them had long since passed into English poetics. That is perhaps why his own verse on Provençal themes has so much the air of Rossetti and the nineties; he is not really learning anything that he did not learn from existing English lyric verse. What comes out is the style of his own day, or the day before; though of course he is writing it with his own immense personal distinction. The programme for the aspirant English poet or student of poetry outlined in *How to Read* neglects all the process of gradual growth and assimilation that has made up poetry in English, neglects all the slow, thorough absorption that is necessary for a real education, and would substitute a huge, barbaric, indigestible meal of gobbets. Pound's energy and enthusiasm, his impatient fury to extend the range of twentieth-century poetic vision, are extremely sympathetic qualities.

> English and American culture of the generation preceding mine, and the completely contemptible and damnable activity of the literary bureaucracy in power . . . has been occupied with the inane assertion of the non-existence of the giraffe, and not of the giraffe alone, but of whole tribes of animals, the puma, the panther, the well-known Indian buffalo.[2]

Yes, indeed; but the implied analogy of a poetic tradition with a menagerie is not a happy one. It is surely a good thing to know something of the variety of the animal creation; but if you live in Norfolk there is not much sense in breeding pumas and panthers; except as isolated curiosities it is necessary to stick to what suits your soil and climate. The lunatic jumble of asyntactical English, tags of Latin, Greek, Italian, German and French, interspersed with Chinese ideograms which have neither auditory nor conceptual significance for the Western reader—this kind of thing in the later cantos is an extreme pro-

[1] *Literary Essays of Ezra Pound*, pp. 15–41. [2] Ibid., p. 78.

jection of the eclecticism Pound exhibits at the start. And if one is for better or worse a writer in the English language a continual crotchety hostility to the English poetic tradition is a poor ground for experiment. I trust it is not an offended provincialism that speaks. I have never been in a position to hold the whole of European literature from Homer in the mind; but I have cared for the Latin and Italian poetry that I know as much as any, and I have been as devoted to French poetry as to English: it is for this very reason that the barbarous tasteless hewing up of gobbets, the gross jumbling of incompatible fragments seems so offensive. It is surely astonishing that Pound and Eliot, the two poets of our day who have shown themselves most sensitive to rhythm, and have done the most to quicken a sense of linguistic decorum, should have practised so much insertion of unacclimatised and undigested fragments into their work. It is a curious experience to hear Mr. Eliot's own reading of *The Waste Land,* and, every time we arrive at one of the quotations in a foreign language—"Frisch weht der Wind der Heimat zu", or "O ces voix d'enfants chantant dans la coupole"—even though the concession is made of pronouncing them all pretty uniformly after the school of Stratford-atte-Bowe, to note the hideously awkward gear-change, the intrusion of an alien rhythm and an alien vowel-system, into verse otherwise distinguished by the fineness of its auditory imagination. It is a curious thing that Joyce, perhaps the most technically accomplished master of every variety of English prose that we have ever seen, should conclude his career with the polyglot jargon of *Finnegan's Wake.* It is almost heartbreaking when the gibberish is compared with the breathtaking beauty and power of some of the intervening passages that are still written in an accessible language.

This is meant as criticism of the past, not as present polemic, for this phase of experiment has gone by. But it is perhaps a symptom of some more general condition in the revolutionary literature of this century. Every great spiritual change demands in the end a change of idiom, rhythm and poetic method to compare with it. But the technical developments can occur without being the response to any deep movement of the spirit. The changes begun by Wordsworth and Coleridge were the technical counterparts to a great revolution in philosophy and general outlook—the change from a philosophy of mechanism to one of organism. That is why the Romantic movement is such a massive and inescapable fact, even to those who dislike its ideas and some of their literary manifestations. I do not believe that the poetic revolution of the twentieth century is a fact of the same order. It was not a spiritual revolution. The Romantic movement left a legacy of feelings and ideas to the whole nineteenth century. I can see no sign that such an inheritance has come down from the great literary figures of the twenties. They had nothing to leave. Their revolution was one of technique and sensibility, not a movement of the spirit in any profound sense. Coleridge talks of Wordsworth's union of deep feeling with profound thought. Mr. Eliot's characteristic doctrine is that the poet does not think, and need not personally feel—though happily his own thoughtful and deeply felt poetry belies his principles. Joyce seems to have had no development, no attachment, no beliefs outside his art; all is contained within an intricate technical code. Pound's early poetry suffers from the lack of an adequate subject-matter; it too often seems to be technical experiment in a void: there are a few climactic moments when matter and accomplishment come together; then all is dissipated in a waste of sterile eccentricity. It is notable that the two great writers of this period who are least interested in novelty of technique, Yeats and Lawrence, are the two whose work reveals a continual spiritual quest.

To return for a moment to Mr. Eliot's notion that the poet does not think. "It is the general notion of 'thinking' that I would challenge. . . . Did Shakespeare think at all? He was occupied in turning human actions into poetry." The whole passage deserves careful consideration. One must take it to mean that it is not the business of the poet as such to be a "thinker". He may take over his "thought" bodily from his age, or from other writers; and in any case his poetic quality will be independent of the philosophical value of his thinking. This is the kind of argument that is formally hard to refute, yet seems to be leading in the wrong direction. It marks a tendency in modern discussion of poetry—the tendency to under-play the role of poetic thought. What gives Romantic poetry as a whole its strong deep and steady movement is not only that it was part of a more inclusive movement in thought, politics and society; it is also that the most living questions of the age were actually worked out in poetry. Poetry was the medium in which the poets did their thinking. This is strikingly true of Wordsworth, Keats and Shelley, less true of Coleridge, but true again of Byron so far as he thought at all. In reading *The Prelude*, Keats's *Odes* and the two *Hyperions*, or *Prometheus Unbound*, one is conscious of thought that profoundly affects the poet and his fellows, actually being worked out in the process or writing the poetry. One who has read these works, even if he had read nothing else, has felt much of the force and pressure of the age. A reader of the characteristic modern works—shall we say *The Waste Land, Hugh Selwyn Mauberley* and *Ulysses?* —will have experienced something far more peripheral, some-thing that cannot take him, as the works of the Romantic poets can, close to the very centre of the time. It will be said of Mr. Eliot that his poetry, especially after *The Waste Land*, is the record of a developing spiritual experience, and that its thought is both central and deeply felt. And this is true. But it is true in a very special sense. Faithful to his own critical insight, Mr. Eliot does not "think" in his poetry. He is following a tradi-tional and well-tried road, not exploring a new region. The poetic ordonnance is his own, handled with a beautiful sensitive-ness and invention; but the underlying structure of the thought is something discovered not devised; and it has been dis-covered and expounded many times before. The numerous quotations from the liturgy and the spiritual classics bear witness to this. There is thought and there is poetry; but they are not part of the same process. The poetry is not in the thought and the thought in the poetry in the *Four Quartets* as it is in the *Odes* of Keats.

It is the absence of any deep current of thought, any massive and widely shared direction of the spirit that throws so much of the emphasis of modern literary activity on technique and formal experiment. Pound's idea of the study of literature as the study of technical invention is the most extraordinary case in point. The shrewdness and wit of the technical comment in his pamphlet *How to Read*, the tinny assertiveness of everything else, show up the paradox in its sharpest form. But in many other places a rift can be observed between means employed and total end proposed—technical experiment pursued for its own sake and no longer controlled by any central purpose. The best illustration is *Ulysses*, manifestly a work of genius but almost unique among works of comparable scale in ice-bound self-containedness, the absence of any view of life, of any ethic or metaphysic, asserted or implied. What is there instead? An immense system of correspondences, elaborate literary and symbolic parallels. This is the system that is exposed in Stuart Gilbert's study (we can take it as authoritative since it is derived from Joyce himself), where each of the eighteen episodes of *Ulysses* is paralleled to an episode of the *Odyssey*, and has besides its particular hour, organ of the body, art, colour, symbol and technique. It can safely be said that no one would have been aware of these correspondences as elements in the pattern, except in the vaguest and most fragmentary way, unless he had been informed of them from the outside. Yet this sterile elaboration is a real part of the structure. Or we can take the Oxen of the Sun episode—that is the scene in the lying-in hospital—where the process of embryonic development is paralleled in a series of pastiches of every notable prose style in English from the Anglo-Saxon chronicle to Walter Pater. Brilliant writing, one can imagine no one else who could have done it—but in the end a device, an ingenious piece of machinery and nothing more. And of course I am selecting only obvious examples; the student of Joyce could illustrate the use of wanton intricate ingenuities *ad infinitum*.

After the Romantic movement had done its work the relation of man to nature, the relation of man to man, were all changed, all different from what they had been before. The change was brought about by forces that to a large degree worked through literature, and in any case were expressed in it. The great forces at work in the early twentieth century do not realise themselves in literature to anything like the same extent. If the young man of 1840 was different from the young man of 1800 the main reasons were Wordsworth and Byron. If the young man of 1940 was different from the young man of 1900 the main reasons were Marx and Freud. We noticed earlier that Romantic modes of feeling and expression were a model for three succeeding generations; and that our twentieth-century revolution already seems to have exhausted a large part of its influence. There are technical reasons for this, that we have tried to suggest; some of the typical experiments of the twenties are specialised, inimitable, perhaps in the end self-annihilating. But we can now discern a much larger and more general reason for the restricted influence of the new poetry. It was not the vehicle of a great spiritual force; it did not have behind it the flow and impetus of a great movement of society and ideas. It may be that literature will never have this power again; it is perhaps through the sciences, or the pseudo-sciences of psychology and sociology that these forces will express themselves; and that literature will be the vehicle not of ideas or the great streams of feeling, but merely of the sensibilities. We have so little notion of what our society is going to look like in fifty years' time that it is useless to speculate.

To take a shorter view, we might ask ourselves what developments have outlived the revolutionary decade, and what changes in the poetic landscape have been effected. There are a number of signs in England of an attempt to return to some pre-lapsarian innocence. In poetry and in talk about poetry, in the novel and in talk about the novel, a half-defiant parochialism is set up against the cosmopolitanism of the preceding age; and in this I may be thought to share, though it is not my intention. Two influential novelists of the present generation who are not at all parochial but very much men of the world, Mr. Angus Wilson and Sir Charles Snow, have expressed or implied or suggested a large lack of interest in the experimental fiction of the twenties and thirties; their suasions are towards the large-scale socially-oriented novel, the presentation of the world as it actually works, without any fiddle-faddle about form and verbal nicety. This too may begin to sound like some of the things I have been saying; but it is only a parody of them, and I wish to detach myself from it as delicately as I can. Personally I find the ethics and social attitude of Henry James antipathetic; the achievements of Joyce are probably quite unrepeatable; the sensibility of Virginia Woolf seems dangerously specialised and limited. Yet I believe that the novel will only continue as a serious form of art by learning whatever it can from these writers, and applying it, inevitably, to different social and human material. The social-descriptive tradition of the novel, the emphasis on mimesis rather than on the creation of something that is satisfying in itself by its form and texture, has had a long and honourable run in English. The novel has often got on pretty comfortably without much self-consciousness in formal matters; but I doubt if it can do so again. It may be in just this field that the new pseudo-sciences begin to encroach on literary preserves. The striking success of such books as *The Lonely Crowd* and *The Organisation Man*, abominably written as they mostly are, and lacking any conceivable appeal to the emotions and the sensibilities, seems to suggest that the appetite for this kind of examination of society may be satisfied outside the field of art altogether. If we are to have great slabs of social realism they may as well be simply real. For over sixty years (much longer if we think of France) there has been a growing sense of prose fiction as something that must combine adequacy to experience with its own kind of formal perfection; something that can be still prose but can work with some of the subtlety and directness of poetry. The rise of this sense coincides with the decline of the long poem. No one writes epics now, and if they did no one would read them. The novel has taken their place. And it feels the need of the refinement of structure and texture that poetry has acquired in its longer and more arduous career. If the novel were to continue on the lines of *Finnegan's Wake* and *The Waves* it would soon cease to exist: if it were to refuse to learn what can be learnt from them it might as well cease.

The remark about the novel and the long poem brings me to a larger but related matter. The boundaries between prose and verse are no longer so clear as they were. The important division seems to come in another place. This is partly a technical affair. The practice of free verse, which is in essence an attempt to isolate a personal organic, meditative rhythm, without reference to any of the accepted metrical patterns, comes to coincide with the careful and self-conscious organisation of prose. They have worked together to make the distinction often merely typographical. Apart from their appearance on the page, parts of *Finnegan's Wake* are much like what we used to call verse, parts of the *Four Quartets* much like what we used to call prose. But there is a more than technical reason. The immense expansion and prestige of the natural sciences, the extension of scientific method to more or less humane studies, has meant that the real dividing line in our discourse comes now not between prose and verse, but between any writing organised for an aesthetic purpose and all other kinds of writing whatsoever. This fact has been widely recognised in the criticism of the last forty years, and the dichotomy between "scientific" and "emotive" writing, with a variety of terminology, has been widely em-employed. It was recognised already by Mallarmé in 1895 when he wrote that the form called verse is simply literature itself; it begins as soon as there is any conscious attempt at style. This remains true although *vers libre* is little practised in English to-day. In what is called formal verse at the moment there is in fact a considerable approximation to the rhythms of prose, and prose of any but the humblest pretensions will not easily forget, or be forgiven if it does, the refined orchestration of the great formalists.

I have left to the last the most considerable and certain of the legacies of the earlier modern poetry—the establishment of a modern poetic diction. It is largely the work of Mr. Eliot, whose constant concern it has been. He has adapted the oft-quoted phrase of Mallarmé, and said of himself and his friends that it was their concern "to purify the language of the tribe". In another place he has said that the creation of a proper modern poetic idiom was the task of poetry in the early part of the century;[1] and the passages on language in the *Four Quartets* show how enduringly he has been engaged with this matter. This is

---

[1] *Selected Essays* (London, 1932), p. 115.

the greatest exception to what has been said up to now about the intractability of Imagist poetry as a model. Here Eliot's writing, both in practice and in theory, has been a decisive influence—not by generating direct imitation, but by the much better way of guiding and informing taste and providing some impeccable but not easily imitable examples. And the lesson has been learnt; the new sense of decorum about poetic language that it has inculcated has become almost too acute. It makes difficulties with an obviously great poet like Hardy whose control of diction is obviously uncertain. Perhaps we are becoming too squeamish; but if so it is an evidence of how far the chastening of our poetic idiom has gone. Recent writing tends to speak as though this had always been a conscious preoccupation of poets, but it is hardly so. The Elizabethans seem to have been only intermittently conscious of the question of poetic diction, and the Romantics after Wordsworth hardly conscious of it at all. Nineteenth-century poetic idiom seems to have grown up almost without conscious criticism; and the praetorian cohorts of Romantic verse were a fairly disorderly band by the time they came to be demobilised in the earlier part of this century. It was at that time that the idea of a poetic language based on living speech was revived. Ford Madox Ford was a great propagandist for it, and Pound, whose diction up to the time he met Ford was of the purest Wardour-Street school, seems to have taken up the doctrine from him; and it became of course a part of Imagist doctrine. But to talk of a poetic language based on living speech is in itself little more than a pious aspiration. Actually to create such a language, and to make it not only contemporary and alive, but also rich and flexible enough for all the purposes that poetry requires—that is a very different matter. Mr. Eliot achieved it at a very early stage in his career. Some of the irony of *Prufrock* has faded, and the stanza poems of 1921 seem by now rather insecure; yet in all of them the precision of the language in general, the judiciously evocative phrases, never allowed to get out of hand, the sparing and controlled richness, are all as valid examples still as at the time of their first appearance. But he has described these ideals of language himself:

A LITERARY REVOLUTION

> The common word exact without vulgarity,
> The formal word precise but not pedantic,
> The whole consort dancing together.

And this, or something like it on a lower level of accomplishment, is a piece of craftsmanship that younger poets have been able to learn. There is neither a metric, nor a rhetoric, nor a subject-matter to-day that has become traditional and generally available, but there is a diction.

So the poetry of the present and the immediate future has not been too richly endowed by its predecessors, but neither has it been left destitute. There are no indubitable prophets among its fathers, so it has inherited no body of extra-literary doctrine; and this is perhaps not a misfortune; the too-easy availability of Wordsworthian natural religion was not a certain blessing to the nineteenth century. As I have tried to show, poetry has been left a good deal of machinery that it cannot use; but it has also been left a set of admirable tools, still sharp, still usable, still unimpaired by having been turned to meaner purposes.

At this point I should like to call up the shade of Hardy, the last greater writer both in prose and verse to stand wholly outside the modern movement. His life just overlaps the early years of modern literature with which we have been concerned, but of course his formation belongs entirely to an earlier age. By looking at his work we can get some idea of what English writing has gained and what it has lost in our century. It is hard to imagine a novelist of his stature to-day who would not be free of his more obvious defects. Bad writing we have always with us, but the peculiar kind of bad writing that is often found in Hardy—the stiffness, the polysyllabic humour, the pseudo-scientific jargon, the dialogue that is neither natural nor stylised, but merely artificial—these would hardly be tolerated in the present age. Nor would the abuse of coincidence, the feeling that the novel had been written to a thesis instead of according to its own internal development. Since Hardy's time we have come to demand that language should be a more responsive instrument, and that fiction should work through it, not merely employ it as a necessary but

81

unconsidered means. And yet in the end none of this seems to matter very much; no one feels that Hardy's stature is ultimately affected by what we can only label his deficiencies. The images of acting, feeling and suffering human beings are too deeply felt and too powerfully communicated for our consciousness of a clumsy method to be more than a critical afterthought. His knowledge of his own world is both intimate and profound. It is a local rustic world, but by knowing and feeling it to the core Hardy has made it also into the image of the great world. Without the aid of fertility rituals or the collective unconscious he has shown how the provincial can become the universal.

His poetry triumphs over obstacles in the same way. Here the obstacles are even more marked. By the current criterion of a chastened and accomplished diction many of them are put out of court at once. The reader is tripped up on ponderous pieces of scientific vocabulary; archaisms abound, not used purposively, but simply as convenient chunks of ready-made poetics; syntax is distorted to fit a metre and words are dragged in to make a rhyme. None of the accomplished younger poets of the mid-century, disciplined and made conscious of their craft by the Imagist regimen, would be guilty of such gaucheries. Yet again the triumph occurs—partly for the same reasons as in the novels, reasons that have more to do with humanity and vision than technique. But there is another reason too, the ever-present lyricism, a very varied, meditative yet musical rhythm, something extremely personal, apparently unstudied, through which we nevertheless hear the centuries-old voice of English lyric poetry. It is notable and touching to see Pound paying his tribute to one whose attitude to poetry was at the opposite pole to his own. Pound wrote of Hardy in a letter of 1922, "He woke one to the extent of his own absorption in *subject* as contrasted with aesthete's preoccupation with *treatment.*"[1] And again in 1934: "The old man's road (vide Tom Hardy) CONTENT, the INSIDES, the subject matter."[2]

This points us in another direction from formal refinement and purifying the language of the tribe. Yet there seems no reason why the two directions should be permanently opposed.

[1] *Letters of Ezra Pound*, p. 178.   [2] Ibid., p. 248.

A LITERARY REVOLUTION

The early poetic exercises of the modern movement were a discipline, an askesis, conducted almost without regard to the purpose for which the training was undertaken. But weight-reducing and body-building are tedious performances unless the stripped and strengthened body is going to be used for something. And of course it has been; but no thanks to the prevalent poetic theory. Doctrines that would make meaning merely a sop to the intellect, distil poetry to a pure invisible essence, purge it of the taint of personality, all have their value, but in the end become confining and sterilising. In the famous essay in which the impersonal theory of poetry is announced Mr. Eliot wrote, speaking of the relation of the poet to his work:

> I shall therefore invite you to consider, as a suggestive analogy, the action that takes place when a bit of finely filiated platinum is introduced into a chamber containing oxygen and sulphur dioxide.[1]

We are puzzled by this; but before the suspense becomes intolerable we are given the answer: sulphurous acid is produced, and the platinum remains unchanged. The analogy we are invited to consider is that of the catalyst—a substance in whose presence alone a chemical reaction takes place, but which itself does not participate in the reaction and remains unaffected by it. So should the poet behave; the argument concludes "The mind of the poet is the shred of platinum."

The language of criticism is frequently metaphorical. We need not deplore this, and we can learn much from attending to the metaphors. For certain purposes and at a certain historical point it was doubtless very apt and very salutary to liken the poet to a finely filiated bit of platinum. At the present conjunction of the stars it might also be well to remember the quite unmetaphorical saying of an earlier writer—that the poet is a man speaking to men.

[1] *The Sacred Wood*, p. 54.

II

FREE VERSE

For some reason the concept of free verse has never wholly naturalised itself in English. Many people still prefer to call it *vers libre* and the unassimilated French term suggests that the thing itself is not regarded as a normal part of English poetic practice. Yet at any time in the last fifty years a fair proportion of current poetry has been written in free verse of one kind or another. Much of it no doubt was ephemeral; but it includes poems by T. S. Eliot, by Ezra Pound, by D. H. Lawrence, and by Edith Sitwell that have become a part of English poetry, and have given to the verse of their age much of its peculiar character. It would seem then that we have in free verse materials for a yet unwritten chapter of English poetical history. Only a chapter, and probably not a very long one; for we find comparatively little written in free verse before this century, and we find little now. Most of the younger poets seem for some time to have written in fairly strict form, and the older ones in stricter forms than they used to. Sir Herbert Read records the beginning of this development as early as 1932,[1] with the plaintive and, I think, untrue suggestion that it is a return to academic timidity. In France the picture is quite different. There we find not only that *vers libre* was well established before 1900, but that it still is. The establishment of the *vers libre* is one of the major French poetical revolutions. It engaged the attention of some of the most acute literary intelligences of the eighties and nineties—even of those who did not themselves practise it, like Mallarmé. Rémy de Gourmont went so far as to say that the revolution in poetic form, of which the *vers libre* was the most

---

[1] H. Read, *Form in Modern Poetry* (1932), Preface.

obvious feature, was the one enduring legacy of the Symbolist movement. And to-day it can be said, as it has by a recent critic, Mr. Geoffrey Brereton: "After being the instrument of a small minority, free verse of various kinds has become the more usual medium, while the regular forms tend to be the exception."[1]

A natural consequence of this development is that the idea of *vers libre* in French does not at this time of day arouse any particular reaction; it is simply an accepted technical term like the Alexandrine or the sonnet or any other. Whereas in English, from the time of its first appearance, the idea of free verse has always been met with a certain dubiety and reserve. Among the old-fashioned poetry-reading public of my own youth it was rather naïvely regarded as a kind of cheating—an evasion of the real difficulty of writing verse. Among a quite sophisticated and up-to-date public to-day I suspect that it has a tang of slightly antiquated novelty, like free love. Some of those who have indubitably written it are chary of confessing it. "No verse is free for the man who wants to do a good job", Mr. Eliot has remarked, with one of those delicate equivocations in which his critical works abound. And the protagonist of modern metrical experiment, Mr. Ezra Pound himself, suffered a strong revulsion against it towards the middle of his career. Yet if those who to-day feel obscure doubts on this subject are presented with some of the poems actually written in free verse—*Ash Wednesday*, Lawrence's *Snake*, Mr. Pound's Chinese translations—they at once admit that these are good poems with which they have long been familiar. There is, I think, a subject for inquiry here. Since so much that is both valuable and original has been written in free verse, we should be able to admit it less grudgingly into our critical vocabulary; and I offer these remarks as some slight assistance to that end.

One quite appropriate reason for caution in approaching the term is that we are not at all clear about what, in English, it means. Since this is an inquiry into its nature, we are not at this stage in any position to define it, or even to describe it at all closely. Let us instead begin with a loose catalogue of those

---

[1] G. Brereton, *An Introduction to the French Poets* (1956), p. 237.

obvious properties by which we distinguish free verse from traditional verse, regular verse, metrical verse, or whatever one likes to call it. The obvious distinguishing marks are these. First and most obvious, the lines will be of irregular length, and these variations in length will not occur in any definite pattern. While the staple may be something like the length of the standard English heroic line—ten syllables—there will be many short lines, and very likely some a great deal longer than any recognised in traditional versification. Secondly, many of these lines are not assignable to any recognised metrical scheme; we cannot label them iambics, trochaics, anapaests, or anything else. In extreme cases no line of any recognised verse form appears at all; and there are who cherish the suspicion that what they are presented with is simply prose printed in short lengths. This suspicion is regarded as shrewd and damaging by those who dislike free verse, and as callow and Philistine by those who approve of it. And leaving value judgments out of it, it may turn out to have something in it after all. Thirdly, rhyme may be altogether absent; or if it appears, it does so sporadically, in no regular pattern, and many lines are left blank.

This will do for a rough general description; but as soon as we begin to examine actual examples in any detail it becomes clear that a great variety of different effects are obtained by these means. And as I begin to compare examples I come to suspect that more than one principle is at work and that free verse is not a uniform phenomenon at all.

We shall not find much verse of the kind that I describe before this century. There are some examples, but they are mostly very special cases—attempts to find an equivalent for a foreign form, or means of obtaining an admittedly unusual effect. There are the choruses of *Samson Agonistes*; these are supposed imitations of the Greek tragic chorus, and have besides been considerably influenced by Italian models—notably the choruses of Tasso's *Aminta*. There is Arnold's *Strayed Reveller*; and the versification of that poem is accounted for by the fact that its hero is a reveller, and that he has strayed. And there is the isolated example of Whitman. By and large it is

only within the last fifty years that free verse is used by any
number of poets as their normal mode of expression. And it is
with this modern free verse that I am mainly concerned.

At this point we may turn for assistance to France, where
free verse, as we have seen, is more strongly established, and
where literary inquiry is often pursued with more zeal and more
pertinacity than in England. We do indeed discover that there
has been more theorising about free verse in France, and that
it has resulted in distinctions of greater clarity. Even so the
clarity is hardly blinding; origin, purpose, and technical principles are all matters of controversy. We discover at once that
the French distinguish between *vers libre* and *vers libéré*—verse
which is born free and verse, so to say, which has been liberated
from some pre-existing chains. We have not this distinction in
English—partly I suppose because the neat verbal antithesis
between *libre* and *libéré* is not available in the English language,
but more because the idea of emancipation from an exact
metrical code assumes far greater importance in French literary
history. The conventions of French classical versification were
both more powerful and more elaborate than anything that
was known in English, and much of the greatest French verse
was written within them. Above all they had a longer run.
Enfin Malherbe vint; but *enfin* though it may have been, Malherbe had arrived about 1600, forty years before Mr. Denham
and Mr. Waller began to effect their memorable refinement of
our numbers; and the process they began was not complete
until the time of Pope, a century or more after Malherbe. And
at the other end of the story, the Romantic emancipation,
Coleridge was writing his *Christabel*, in a metre, as he said,
"founded on a new principle", in 1799, thirty years before the
early lyric verse of Hugo burst upon the French literary scene.
And as for the power of prosodic convention, it will perhaps be
sufficient to remark that an enjambment has never caused a
riot in the English theatre. So that in French poetic history the
liberation from a set of defined rules—the exact placings of
the caesura, the alternation of masculine and feminine rhymes,
the demand for *rime riche* and all the rest of it—is a much more
serious matter than it is in English; and the French have there-

fore the concept of *vers libéré*, a verse which takes its starting-point from traditional versification, but handles it with great licence and much neglect of the less essential of the old conventions. Further, they distinguish this from *vers libre*, which has on the face of it no connection with traditional versification at all. Since in English most of our greatest poetry has been written in verse which either enjoyed a pre-lapsarian liberty or was liberated without much fuss, we take the commoner kinds of *vers libéré* for granted, and do not even give them a name. We then confound together the extremer kind of *vers libéré* with anything else that looks formally eccentric and call them all "free verse". Nevertheless I think the French distinction is a valuable one for us, and I shall return to it later.

To look for a moment at what the French critics have said about the origin and purpose of their own *vers libre*, since we may be able to get some hints from it. The question of origins has always been hotly contested. It is of course far earlier than in English; it belongs with the symbolist experiments of the later nineteenth century; and a large number of starting-points have been suggested. The *vague et soluble* versification of Verlaine—*vers libéré* which could be liberated still further into *vers libre*; the experiments and propaganda of Gustave Kahn in the eighteen-eighties; the *Livre de Jade* of Judith Gautier; Rimbaud's *Illuminations*; poetic prose generally; the *Petits Poèmes en Prose* of Baudelaire in particular; or the work which in part inspired them, Aloysius Bertrand's *Gaspard de la Nuit*; the verse of Whitman; or the form to which it seems most nearly allied—the *verset* or Biblical verse. These matters have been learnedly discussed by Professor Mansell Jones in his *Background to Modern French Poetry*: but even in his exposition this cloud of witnesses generates a certain obscurity. What does emerge with tolerable clarity is that, whatever common ground there may be between the *vers libéré* and the *vers libre*, the extremer kinds of *vers libre* owe most to poetic prose. They are adaptations of prose rhythms rather than of anything in traditional versification. This, I think, has never been seriously said about English free verse, and the suggestion may be worth investigating

FREE VERSE

As for the directing purpose behind the new versification, it belongs of course with the general liberation of the sensibility characteristic of the Symbolist movement; but it has been expressed in a variety of forms. Gustave Kahn, for example, said that he was seeking in his free verse "une musique plus complexe", while his contemporary Laforgue was seeking an immediate psychological spontaneity, a way of rendering the sensation as directly as possible.[1] Mallarmé in *Crise de Vers* suggested that the use of the Alexandrine should be reserved, "ainsi que celui du drapeau", like the country's flag, for solemn and formal occasions; while for lesser and more personal affairs, free verse in all its variety would be more suitable.[2] Still earlier Verlaine, who disliked the actual *vers libre*, had consciously sought in his own *vers libéré* a slighter and more hesitant rhythm than that of official French verse. And these views have their analogues in English. The early essays of Yeats, though they are not contemporaneous with any very distinct experiments in free verse, are full of Verlainian echoes about the need for a faint, fluid, and tenuous kind of verse rhythm.[3] Indeed the desire expressed by Kahn for a new musical articulation of verse is constantly repeated in English at the close of the last century and the beginning of this one. T. E. Hulme, in an essay on modern poetry of about 1908,[4] actually cites Kahn and traces the origin of free verse to his work; but in his own commentary he gives the purpose of the new versification a more psychological twist, and finds it in the desire for greater individual expressiveness and spontaneity. Later in the same piece he goes near to echoing Mallarmé in distinguishing between the old and the new versification. He equates traditional

---

[1] G. Kahn, *Premiers poèmes, avec une préface sur les vers libres* (1897), p. 17.

[2] S. Mallarmé, *Œuvres complètes* (Pléiade, Paris, 1945), p. 362.

[3] W. B. Yeats, *Essays* (1924), p. 201: "With this change of substance . . . would come a change of style, and we would cast out of poetry those energetic rhythms, as of a man running, which are the inventions of the will, with its eyes always on something to be done or undone; and we would seek out those wavering, meditative, organic rhythms which are the embodiment of the imagination." Ibid, p. 492: "Unlike the rhetoricians, who get a confident voice from remembering the crowd they have won or may win, we sing among our uncertainty; and, smitten even in the presence of the most high beauty by the knowledge of our solitude, our rhythm shudders."

[4] T. E. Hulme, *Further Speculations* (Minnesota, 1955), pp. 67 et seq.

verse with the passion for permanence, eternity, and absolute beauty; and free verse with what he describes as the modern search for the fluid, and for the maximum of individual and personal expression. Fixed forms are suited to the themes of the older poetry—heroic action, for example; modern poetry, according to Hulme, is small-scale and intimate. "To put this modern conception of the poetic spirit, this tentative and half-shy manner of looking at things, into regular metre, is like putting a child into armour." And this, I think, is a sloppier, less accurate attempt at saying what Mallarmé was saying in *Crise de Vers*. Rather later, Ezra Pound, without any nonsense about being tentative and half-shy, echoes both Laforgue and Mallarmé.[1] Later still, D. H. Lawrence gives his *raison d'être* for free verse, and he too, though with a very different accent, finds it in immediate psychological spontaneity.[2]

II

But it is thirsty work digging out these channels without allowing any of the Castalian water to flow through them; so with the few historical and theoretical hints we have managed to fish up, let us turn to actual examples. Only one more critical remark to introduce them: Mr. Eliot has said that there

[1] *Literary Essays of Ezra Pound*, ed. T. S. Eliot (1954), p. 9: "Rhythm. I believe in an 'absolute' rhythm, a rhythm, that is, in poetry which corresponds exactly to the emotion, or shade of emotion to be expressed. A man's rhythm must be interpretative, it will be, therefore, in the end, his own, uncounterfeiting, uncounterfeitable. . . . Form. That most symmetrical forms have certain uses. That a vast number of subjects cannot be precisely, and therefore not properly rendered in symmetrical form."

[2] D. H. Lawrence, *Phoenix* (1936), pp. 220–4: "This is the unrestful, ungraspable poetry of the sheer present, poetry whose very permanency lies in its wind-like transit. . . . Much has been written about free verse. But all that can be said, first and last, is that free verse is, or should be, direct utterance from the instant whole man. . . . There is some confusion, some discord. But the confusion and the discord only belong to the reality, as noise belongs to the plunge of water. . . . All we can say is that free verse does *not* have the same nature as restricted verse. It is not of the nature of reminiscence. It is not the past which we treasure in its perfection between our hands. Neither is it the crystal of the perfect future into which we gaze. . . In free verse we look for the insurgent naked throb of the instant moment. To break the lovely form of metrical verse, to dish up the fragments as a new substance, called *vers libre*, this is what most of the free versifiers accomplish. They do not know that free verse has it own *nature*, that it is neither star nor pearl, but instantaneous like plasm."

are only two ways of coming at free verse—by starting with a
conventional pattern and continually receding from it, and by
starting without any pattern at all and continually approaching
some conventional one. Let us look at a piece of his own verse
and see how it fits these prescriptions. I shall take the first
twenty lines of *Prufrock*, an excellent example of their kind.

> Let us go then, you and I,
> When the evening is spread out against the sky
> Like a patient etherised upon a table;
> Let us go, through certain half-deserted streets,
> The muttering retreats
> Of restless nights in one-night cheap hotels
> And sawdust restaurants with oyster-shells:
> Streets that follow like a tedious argument
> Of insidious intent
> To lead you to an overwhelming question. . . .
> Oh, do not ask, What is it?
> Let us go and make our visit.
>
> In the room the women come and go
> Talking of Michelangelo.
>
> The yellow fog that rubs its back upon the window-panes
> The yellow smoke that rubs its muzzle on the window-panes
> Licked its tongue into the corner of the evening,
> Lingered upon the pools that stand in drains,
> Let fall upon its back the soot that falls from chimneys,
> Slipped by the terrace, made a sudden leap,
> And seeing that it was a soft October night,
> Curled once about the house and fell asleep.

This passage is pretty evidently "free verse" in the loose
English sense. The lines vary in length from six syllables to
fourteen; they do not on first reading seem all to belong to a
common rhythmical movement; and some are hard to fit into
any metrical pattern at all:

> Like a patient etherised upon a table;
> Of insidious intent.

The rhymes are irregularly disposed, sometimes in couplets,
sometimes alternately; and many lines are blank.
On the other hand, no one could doubt for a moment that

what he was reading was verse; in fact a number of the lines taken individually are perfectly regular verse.

> Of restless nights in one-night cheap hotels
> And sawdust restaurants with oyster-shells:
>
> Lingered upon the pools that stand in drains,
>
> Slipped by the terrace, made a sudden leap,
>
> Curled once about the house and fell asleep.

These are, of course, perfectly normal iambic decasyllables. Now the iambic rhythm in English has great dominating power. Whether this is a historical accident or an intrinsic quality of the language I do not know; at all events the iambic decasyllable has been the staple line of English verse since Chaucer. And the effect of this is that where it is found in a passage of mixed and varied lines like this it tends to impose the suggestion of itself on all the rest. And the experience of reading this passage, I suggest, is very much that of reading blank verse, rather irregularly rhymed. This sounds a contradiction, but I mean that the general run is like that of blank verse, not like that of the couplet or any stanzaic form, even though rhymes actually occur. There are of course a number of short lines; but we are never much surprised by short lines in blank verse, partly because we are so accustomed to the broken lines at the ends of speeches in dramatic verse, and partly because the short lines in Virgil have given them a sort of classical precedent.

The long lines present rather more of a problem.

> The yellow fog that rubs its back upon the window-panes

is difficult to fit into a metrical scheme. But it turns out on investigation that this and the lines that follow it do actually *contain* blank verse, though they do not so appear on the page. Re-read as:

> The yellow fog that rubs its back upon
> The window-panes, the yellow smoke that rubs
> Its muzzle on the window-panes, licked
> Its tongue into the corner of the evening,

and it becomes perfectly recognisable blank verse, though it is not printed as such. The line arrangement as it stands is, so to speak, a kind of punctuation, that suggests a movement different from that of blank verse, though the blank verse movement is contained within it. It is in fact very like some of the mis-lineated passages in badly printed versions of Jacobean tragedy. And we then recall that Mr. Eliot has himself told us that he founded his versification partly on that of Webster and Tourneur; and we realise how similar this passage is to their handling of blank verse; and that besides their authentic metrical qualities Mr. Eliot has even perhaps seized upon an accidental incompetence of the seventeenth-century printing-house and turned it into a positive prosodic effect.

So it has become quite clear what kind of verse we are faced with here. It is free verse of the first type—that which starts from a conventional form and continually recedes from it. The result is to produce a rhythm that is perfectly easily accommodated to our previous notions of verse rhythm, yet is also strikingly original. When I first read these verses about thirty years ago it was their novelty that most impressed itself upon me; now it is their traditional quality, the fact that they can be read as a perfectly natural development of Jacobean blank verse handled, it is true, very freely, but with the same kind of freedom as that employed by the dramatists we know Mr. Eliot to have studied. It is in fact *vers libéré* rather than *vers libre*.

If we consider the motives to free versification already mentioned, which of them seems to fit this passage of *Prufrock* best? A new music? Perhaps a little, though this verse does not strike one as aiming very distinctly at musical or auditory effects. The free expression of the poet's individual sensibility? Mr. Eliot has repeatedly disclaimed any such intention. The direct transcription of a particular moment of experience? This passage is rather a summation of many moments, and seems in essence meditative and reminiscent rather than an attempt at direct transcription. I do not think any of the suggestions we have heard up to now provides the real reason for the existence of this kind of *vers libéré*. The real one, I should suggest, is simpler and less egotistical than the complete expression of the poet's sensibility; more vigorous and less *faux-naïf* than the half-shy snatching at a fleeting moment. Mr. Eliot has himself remarked that the peculiar task of the poetry of the early part of this century was the development of a proper modern poetic idiom,[1] related to the living speech of the day, not merely related, as so much contemporary poetic language was, to a rather tired selection of recent literature. Now it is extremely difficult to develop a new poetic idiom without at the same time developing a new poetic form, simply because the existing forms are accidentally but inevitably associated with certain kinds of poetic diction and vocabulary. Ezra Pound's contemporaneous desire to break the tyranny of the iambic has the same root. And the kind of free verse we have been discussing seems to arise not from any passion for freedom or informality as such, but simply as the necessary accompaniment of a renewal of the diction of poetry which was taking place and had to take place about that time.[2]

"Donne I suppose was such another" who found that a solution, stretching and dislocation of the old measures was necessary to accommodate his new vocabulary. Periodically this need will recur. But we should not think of it as the normal or inevitable poetic situation. Critics who have a fixation on the nineteen-twenties, as Sir Herbert Read seems to have in his *Form in Modern Poetry*, are apt to demand that this state of affairs shall be perennial. The poets know better. Mr. Eliot has continued the passage cited just now by saying that when the modern idiom has been established a period of musical elaboration can follow.[1] And that is what we might now expect, a period of formal and exact versification like that of the *Four Quartets*—but a formal versification which will have learnt much by the practice of a period of free verse.

To turn now to a second example, this time from D. H. Lawrence. Many of Lawrence's poems seem to me admirable

[1] T. S. Eliot, *The Music of Poetry* (W. P. Ker Memorial Lecture, Glasgow, 1942), p. 27.

[2] We might say of Mr. Eliot's early versification what Kahn said of the versification of Rimbaud and Verlaine: "De très habiles dissonances sur la métrique ancienne donnaient l'apparence qu'un instrument nouveau chantait, mais apparence illusoire; c'était, avec bien du charme et de la ductilité en plus, avec un sens très critique, l'ancienne rhythmique." *Premiers poèmes*, p. 15.

chiefly for other things than their form; some of them are simply failures on formal grounds. I will take a passage from what is surely both a good poem and an interesting piece of versification.

A snake came to my water-trough
On a hot, hot day, and I in pyjamas for the heat,
To drink there.

In the deep, strange-scented shade of the great dark carob-tree
I came down the steps with my pitcher
And must wait, must stand and wait, for there he was at the trough
   before me.

He reached down from a fissure in the earth-wall in the gloom
And trailed his yellow-brown slackness soft-bellied down, over the
   edge of the stone trough
And rested his throat upon the stone bottom,
And where the water had dripped from the tap, in a small clearness,
He sipped with his straight mouth,
Softly drank through his straight gums, into his slack long body,
Silently.

Someone was before me at my water-trough,
And I, like a second comer, waiting.

He lifted his head from his drinking, as cattle do,
And looked at me vaguely, as drinking cattle do,
And flickered his two-forked tongue from his lips, and mused a
   moment,
And stooped and drank a little more,
Being earth-brown, earth-golden from the burning bowels of the
   earth
On the day of Sicilian July, with Etna smoking.

The opening sentence, which is also a self-contained stanza of three lines, is a sufficient advertisement that we have here a rhythm that starts from no conventional verse form. In the following group of lines we are more aware of rhythm as a positive aesthetic tool, directing and taking charge of the feeling. And since I would rather be childishly explicit than merely vague, I will point to the places—"deep, strange-scented shade", "great dark carob-tree"—where the collocation of long heavy syllables deepens and darkens the shadow; where the delayed, self-retarding movement of "must wait, must stand and wait" contrasts with the sudden swiftness of "for there he was at the trough before me". But this rhythm which is being used so vigorously is not a verse rhythm; it cannot be assimilated, however loosely, to any conventional verse pattern.

And I should say the same, though I will not pause to illustrate in detail, for the next section, "He reached down from a fissure . . ."—where part of the effect is gained by rhythmical repetition and repetition of words—slack, stone, straight—and partly by a slack trailing rhythm which represents the slack trailing movement of the snake. But again no approach to conventional verse.

Then, observe what occurs. There is a short, rather flat two-line passage almost like a note of punctuation; and then:

> He lifted his head from his drinking, as cattle do,
> And looked at me vaguely, as drinking cattle do,
> And flickered his two-forked tongue from his lips, and mused a
>   moment,
> And stooped and drank a little more,
> Being earth-brown, earth-golden from the burning bowels of the
>   earth
> On the day of Sicilian July, with Etna smoking.

What we have here is something quite different; it is in fact a passage of freely handled blank verse—quite normal blank verse with a very free use of anapaestic substitution. This is perfectly straightforward in the first two lines; in the third and fourth slightly obscured by the line division; but alter the typography and break the line after "mused", and again we have two perfectly straightforward blank-verse lines. The fifth line is considerably modified and expanded, and fits only uneasily as it stands into the basic pattern; but we return decisively to the norm in the last line—

> On the day of Sicilian July, with Etna smoking.

What has happened here is the converse of what happens in the passage from *Prufrock*. There the prevailing movement was the rhythm of blank verse, and it became considerably stretched, modified, and deformed. Here the prevailing movement is no discernible verse rhythm at all; it is, if you like, a prose rhythm, conditioned almost entirely by the experience itself—the movements of the snake in the hot, still, Sicilian day; and used extremely purposefully as a major part of the aesthetic effect. And then, as so often in strongly rhythmical English prose, the attractive force of the iambic decasyllable is so great that the rhythm slips into it, and becomes a kind of blank verse, very subtly handled and not at all out of harmony with the rest. As the poem goes on, this recognisable verse rhythm is again broken, and we return to the prose rhythm, often straightforwardly conversational prose rhythm, but pointed and emphasised by repetition and parallelism. And ever and anon there are returns, sometimes tentative, sometimes decisive, to the blank-verse line. And though I do not for a moment suspect Lawrence of thinking explicitly in these terms, these intermittent approaches to a normal verse rhythm, from a basis of rhythm differently conceived, are an important part of the effect of this beautiful poem.

And now for the third example, this time from a very conscious technician, Ezra Pound. It will actually consist of two examples, and I am displaying great moderation in confining it to two, for Pound has been the most tireless experimenter of our time both in various kinds of free verse and in many traditional measures. Here is the first sample:

> Dark eyed,
> O woman of my dreams,
> Ivory sandalled,
> There is none like thee among the dancers,
> None with swift feet.
>
> I have not found thee in the tents,
> In the broken darkness.
> I have not found thee at the well-head
> Among the women with pitchers.
>
> Thine arms are as a young sapling under the bark;
> Thy face as a river with lights.

I can find no trace in this of any conventional verse rhythm;

the most obvious formal features are repetition and parallelism. These at once suggest Bibilical prose, or rather English prose translations of Biblical verse; one is reminded of the Song of Solomon, and this is appropriate enough, for the poem from which the passage is taken is called *Dance Figure, For the Marriage in Cana of Galilee*. In addition, there is a very heavily marked stress. Pound has commented on this himself: "There is vers libre with accent heavily marked as a drum beat (as par exemple my 'Dance Figure')."[1] I do not quite know how this is done; but evidently the three opening lines, each with two heavy stresses, establish at the beginning the expectation of a strong accentual rhythm, though not a symmetrical one. This is *vers libre*, not *vers libéré*; but we still find the strongly marked pattern mainly in terms of stressed and unstressed syllables, and this disposal of accents is used to make a melody of its own. Here I think we can rightly invoke Kahn's reason for the existence of *vers libre*—the desire for a new music. I mean that in this poem the accents are not disposed in a largely fortuitous way, as in ordinary prose, not primarily to reinforce descriptive effects, as in Lawrence's *Snake*, not to refer, however tenuously, to some pre-established expectation of conventional verse rhythm—but to achieve an independent and novel musical organisation.

And now for a much more difficult example. It is from *Homage to Sextus Propertius*. In this poem Pound speaks through the mask or *persona* of Propertius, including many more or less distorted renderings of Propertius's own verse; and this passage deals with one of the recurrent topics of the series—the limitation of his own (Propertius-Pound's) muse, the refusal of the great public themes and the confining of his poetry to such subjects as will please his mistress, not a very intellectual or public-spirited girl.

> When, when, and whenever death closes our eyelids,
>
> Moving naked over Acheron
> Upon the one raft, victor and conquered together,
> Marius and Jugurtha together,
>   one tangle of shadows.

[1] *Literary Essays*, p. 12.

FREE VERSE

Caesar plots against India,
Tigris and Euphrates shall, from now on, flow at his bidding,
Tibet shall be full of Roman policemen,
The Parthians shall get used to our statuary
                        and acquire a Roman religion;
One raft on the veiled flood of Acheron,
    Marius and Jugurtha together.

Nor at my funeral either will there be any long trail,
    bearing ancestral lares and images;
No trumpets filled with my emptiness,
Nor shall it be on an Atalic bed;
    The perfumed cloths shall be absent.
A small plebeian procession.
    Enough, enough and in plenty
There will be three books at my obsequies
Which I take, my not unworthy gift, to Persephone.

Now here, as it seems to me, we have admirable verse, but very little that is familiar to hang on to; no clearly marked accentual rhythm, no echoes from the Authorised Version. Pound's comment about *Dance Figure* which I quoted just now goes on like this: "On the other hand I think I have gone as far as can profitably be gone in the other direction (and perhaps too far). I mean I do not think one can use to any advantage rhythms much more tenuous and imperceptible than some I have used. I think progress lies rather in an attempt to approximate classical quantitative metres (NOT to copy them) than in a carelessness regarding such things."[1] Since the date of this comment (1917) is the same as the date of the *Homage to Propertius* we may reasonably suppose that it has some relevance to the verse we are examining. The rhythms of *Propertius* certainly incline to tenuity; and since it is a poem on a classical theme it is there if anywhere that we might expect to find the approximation to classical quantitative measures of which Pound speaks. Even so, the remark quoted lets in a fitful gleam rather than a flood of light. Clearly this is not a direct imitation of any classical metre, nor is any regular quantitative pattern to be found in it. Nor do I find any regular quantitative measures anywhere else in Pound. English is such a strongly

[1] *Literary Essays*, p. 12.

accented language that any attempt at quantitative measures in it usually fails, simply because the accentual pattern overwhelms any other. And when people talk about classical measures in English what they usually mean is imitating in an accentual pattern the quantitative patterns of ancient verse. I beg leave therefore to take this about classical quantitative measures with a pinch of salt, and to describe in my own terms what I believe to be going on in this verse. First, a steady consistent avoidance of the iambic-anapaestic rhythm that forces itself upon us in most English verse. Where there is any suggestion of regular accentual verse pattern it is a trochaic-dactylic one, rare and difficult to sustain in English; so rare in fact that unless it is very plainly and heavily marked, which here it is certainly not, it is not readily recognised at all. Secondly, a deliberate use of quantitative effects to modify accentual rhythm. Third, the use of a number of devices— rhythmic parallelism, verbal repetition and parallelism, sometimes open and sometimes concealed—as a means of formal organisation.

To illustrate. The four lines beginning "Caesar plots against India" so successfully avoid the suggestion of any common verse rhythm that they can be read simply as prose, and almost invite it. On further examination accentual rhythms of an orthodox kind do make their appearance, tentatively; but never the obvious iambic-anapaestic, always trochaic-dactylic.

$$\overset{/}{\text{Cae}}\overset{x}{\text{sar}}\ \overset{/}{\text{plots}}\ \overset{x}{\text{a}}\overset{x}{\text{gainst}}\ \overset{/}{\text{In}}\overset{xx}{\text{dia,}}$$

Caesar plots against India,

$$\overset{x}{\text{Ti}}\overset{/}{\text{bet}}\ \overset{x}{\text{shall}}\ \overset{x}{\text{be}}\overset{/}{\text{full}}\ \overset{x}{\text{of}}\ \overset{/}{\text{Ro}}\overset{x}{\text{man}}\ \overset{/}{\text{po}}\overset{x}{\text{lice}}\overset{}{\text{men.}}$$

Tibet shall be full of Roman policemen.

The line

Moving naked over Acheron

suggests at first no possible verse rhythm; but it avoids doing so largely because the syllable "-ing", though unaccented, is quantitatively long (long by position in the Latin sense; the final "-ng" and the initial "n" of "naked" make it so); and that forbids us to trip over it as we do an ordinary unaccented syllable. If we insist on doing so, this becomes a rather tripping trochaic line: and Pound is so far justified in talking about quantity that he does actually use a quantitative effect to modify or obscure an accentual rhythm. As for rhythmic parallelism, it is clearly illustrated in the first line

When, when, and whenever

death closes our eyelids

And the lines which I said just now almost demand to be read as prose turn out to contain rhythmic parallelisms of the same kind.

Tigris and Euphrates shall, from now on, flow at his bidding,
Tibet shall be full of Roman policemen.

It is only the presence of the river Euphrates that has washed away an obvious rhythmic echo between the two lines:

Tigris shall, from now on, flow at his bidding,
Tibet shall be full of Roman policemen.

A variety of formal devices, then, in these apparently informal lines, though not reducible to any one scheme.

One could go much farther into the matter; but I have done enough, I hope, to show that this is neither traditional versification slightly disguised, nor prose chopped up into short lengths. But there is no one obvious guiding principle in such a technique, and no convenient label serves to describe it—nothing short of a complete analysis. The technical devices used are not in themselves new; trochaic rhythms, considerations of quantity, verbal and rhythmical parallelisms can all play their part in traditional verse. But in traditional verse they are normally subsidiary to a prevailing measured accentual rhythm, decasyllabic, octosyllabic, or what not; and in English nearly always iambic. Here the prevailing measured accentual rhythm disappears; no single technical principle is put in its place, and the burden of formal organisation is carried by a number of normally subsidiary elements, which, because they have never been a matter of formal rule, are used in the most varied, individual, and unpredictable way.

For this reason I doubt whether such a verse could ever become standard, the normal practice of a school, generally available to the majority, like the couplet in the eighteenth century. The adventurer on this sea is left without a chart, and unless his instinctive auditory sensibility is exceptionally acute, without a rudder either. The conditions for success are too difficult, and failure, if there is failure, is too complete. And this is why Pound himself, about two years after the time we are speaking of, had a temporary revulsion of feeling, and decided that "the general dilution of vers libre, Amygism, Lee Masterism, general floppiness had gone too far, and that some countercurrent must be set going. . . . Remedy prescribed, Emaux et Camées (or the Bay State Hymn Book). Rhyme and regular strophes."[1]

III

We have discovered, then, three types of versification, all in English called free verse. The first is simply traditional verse expanded and distorted in various ways. The second is a kind of verse which starts apparently without formal principle, except a free rhythm dictated by the nature of the experience itself, yet constantly approaches, and sometimes slips into, traditional iambic versification. The third very carefully avoids the cadence of normal iambic verse, and employs a variety of means— quantitative effects, verbal and rhythmic parallels, and I am sure others connected with speed and quality of sound—which brings about a planned and intricate formal organisation, that is nevertheless almost indescribable. Is it really appropriate to give them a common name? Are they founded on a common principle? I do not think so. For *Prufrock* (and this applies too to *Gerontion, The Waste Land,* and all Mr. Eliot's earlier versification) we do not need a new principle at all. We are simply confronted with an extension of the liberties that have been normal in English verse over a great deal of its history. This is not quite true of the mixed, loose versification of Lawrence, though when this becomes conspicuously recognisable as verse it is of a quite traditional kind. And I do not think that Pound's free verse can be reasonably reduced to traditional versification at all. Since all he has to work with is the English language,

[1] Note in the *Criterion*, July 1923.

no doubt all the formal devices he employs can be found somewhere before, but he employs them in such different proportions
and combinations that the result is in effect a new thing.

Some of these devices, such as parallelism and repetition,
verse has always had in common with prose. So that if they are
found where immediately recognisable verse rhythm is absent
it is easy and natural to say that this kind of free verse is derived
from prose. This has in fact been said about French *vers libre*;
but whether it is true or not of French, I doubt whether as a
matter of historic fact it is true of much English free verse,
except perhaps that of Whitman. There is no demonstrable
transition between English poetic prose, usually composed in
pretty lengthy tracts, and the relatively short forms of free
verse. And we have nothing significant in English to compare
to the *Petits Poèmes en Prose* of Baudelaire or Mallarmé. There
is, however, one important respect in which free verse begins
to approximate to prose. It is this. In prose the small stylistic
divisions are necessarily syntactic divisions. If a phrase in
prose has a rhythmic unity it is because it is a sentence or a
syntactical part of a sentence. There is nothing else to give it
unity. There is no other determinant at work to impose a
rhythmical configuration; a rhythmical figure is always what
Gerard Manley Hopkins called a "figure of grammar". Now
it is hardly otherwise with free verse. What makes a free verse
line a line at all? It has no outwardly determined length, as an
Alexandrine or an octosyllable has. It is only a line because it
is a rhythmical unit, and it is only a rhythmical unit because it is
a unit of sense, a unit of syntax.

In traditional verse of course this is not so. The line has a
length and shape independent of sense or syntax—the length
or shape that we describe when we call it an Alexandrine or an
octosyllable.

> I have met them at close of day
> Coming with vivid faces
> From counter or desk among grey
> Eighteenth-century houses.

The line "From counter or desk among grey" is not a syntactical unit; it breaks at an adjective, another adjective and the

qualified noun being in the next line. And it is a line because that length and shape have been determined by all the other lines. Now in free verse you cannot get this effect, since the lines do not establish any determined pattern. So, even in such an uncomplicated example as *Prufrock*, almost every line is a sentence, or a grammatical subdivision of a sentence, or a self-contained descriptive phrase, or something of the sort.

This is platitudinous enough, but its most important consequence is perhaps a little less so. That is that in conventionally metrical verse there are always two rhythms at work, one provided by the ideal metrical norm, whatever it is, the other by the syntactic structure; while in free verse there is only one, that provided by the syntactic structure. It is a commonplace that the most powerful effects of traditional verse are achieved by playing off the syntactical movement against the metrical movement—making then coincide very closely as in the Augustan couplet, or making them diverge very widely as in Miltonic blank verse. All this powerful range of effects is closed to free verse, since there is no ideal metrical norm to appeal to. And that is why, I think, we nearly always feel in free verse a certain tenuity and slightness of rhythm, feel it the more the farther we recede from accepted metrical form. Freedom, in fact, is most significant against a background of known and established order. And this slightness of rhythm in free verse is why we find such very different literary characters as Mallarmé, T. E. Hulme, and D. H. Lawrence all saying or suggesting that metrical verse remains the medium for the great permanent and public themes, free verse becoming the medium for the slighter and more fugitive ones.

This division of labour may well be disputed; but what cannot, I think, be disputed is that the whole free-verse movement, with its reliance on one rhythm, as in prose, rather than on the contrasted play of two rhythms, as in metrical verse, has tended to bring about a blurring of the distinction between prose and verse. Many examples of this could be given, and some such uncertainties are of quite early date. Novalis's *Hymns to the Night*, for example, were written as verse in manuscript, but first printed as prose. One of Rimbaud's *Illuminations*, a piece called *Marine*, is printed as verse in editions of Rimbaud's works, but on its first appearance in the magazine *La Vogue* in 1886 was arranged as prose.[1] More modern editors have performed similar operations. Yeats boldly opened his *Oxford Book of Modern Verse* by printing the famous Monna Lisa passage from Pater's *Renaissance* as free verse; and an extremely scholarly and useful American anthology, Brynnin and Fryer's *Modern Poetry*, includes, with normal prose typography, extracts from Joyce's *Finnegan's Wake* and Djuna Barnes's *Nightwood*, which if they are to be given a formal label can only be described as novels.

I have already mentioned the vulgar suspicion that much free verse is really prose, distinguished from other prose merely by courtesy and typography. Perhaps I have now been serious about free verse for long enough to allow me to confess that I sometimes share this suspicion. I will take as an example a light and quite charming piece by Ezra Pound.

> The very small children in patched clothing,
> Being smitten with an unusual wisdom,
> Stopped in their play as she passed them
> And cried up from their cobbles:
>   *Guarda! Ahi, guarda! ch' e be'a!*
>
> But three years after this
> I heard the young Dante, whose last name I do not know—
> For there are, in Sirmione, twenty-eight young Dantes
>   and thirty-four Catulli;
> And there had been a great catch of sardines,
> And his elders
> Were packing them in the great wooden boxes
> For the market in Brescia, and he
> Leapt about, snatching at the bright fish
> And getting in both of their ways;
> And in vain they commanded him to *sta fermo!*
> And when they would not let him arrange
> The fish in the boxes
> He stroked those which were already arranged,
> Murmuring for his own satisfaction
> The identical phrase:
>   *Ch' e be'a.*
> And at this I was mildly abashed.

[1] P. Mansell Jones, *Background to Modern French Poetry* (1951), p. 121. I have obtained much help, especially bibliographical, from this book.

IMAGE AND EXPERIENCE

I don't want to break this butterfly on a wheel, but there does not really seem to be any reason at all why this should be regarded as verse; except that it is small and self-contained, and there is no particular precedent in English for printing small pieces of this kind in prose, and it is therefore easier to promote them to the status of verse.

All this suggests that in recent literature the distinction between prose and verse has assumed far less importance than it used to have. Verse abandons the obvious distinguishing feature of regular metric, and relies on many techniques that it has in common with prose. Prose has been willing to let slip many of its descriptive and narrative functions in favour of a lyricism or dexterity of verbal architecture that once belonged especially to verse. We have got used to this perhaps without noticing it. We have in fact been approaching the point of view suggested in Mallarmé's critical writing—that the fundamental distinction is not the one between prose and verse, but between language used in a purely utilitarian way on the one hand, and language organised for an aesthetic purpose on the other. Mallarmé calls the first "l'état brut de la parole", the second "l'état essentiel".[1] In the first, the brutish or utilitarian state, the word is simply a piece of money, a counter having a defined value, to be exchanged between one mind and another; in the second, the essential or aesthetic state, the word with its fixed exchange value disappears in the verse, the poetic phrase, re-creates a new whole, "de plusieurs vocables refait un mot totale". Or, to desert Mallarmé's delicate and sidelong mode of expression—the referential value of the words becomes less important because they are now parts of an aesthetic unity with its own different kind of value. Manifestly this can happen just as well in prose as in verse; in fact it begins to happen as soon as there is any intention beyond the mere exchange of referential counters. Verse begins, in fact, as soon as there is any attempt at aesthetic organisation—and this Mallarmé hails as one of the great discoveries of Symbolism.

—Une majestueuse idée inconsciente, à savoir que la forme

[1] *Œuvres complètes* (Pléiade), p. 368.

appelée vers est simplement elle-même la littérature; que vers
il y a sitôt que s'accentué la diction, rhythme dès que style.[1]

Seen from this point of view, then, the phenomenon of free
verse is simply an instance of the general fusion between verse
and imaginative prose that has been characteristic of our
century. But if one were to infer from this that a sort of demo-
cratisation of verse had gone on, that it had approached nearer,
in abandoning the strict form, to the average purposes of life,
one would be very wrong. The drawing together of verse and
prose of which I speak has not been an overture to the world,
it has rather been a closing of the ranks against it. To speak of
this cleavage between the world of science and organisation and
affairs and the world of imaginative literature would be to
embark on another subject. But even here I can hardly keep
out the host of witnesses, all with their various axes to grind,
who are eager to testify to it. Villiers' Axel saying, "As for
living, our servants will do that for us"; Yeats complaining
that it was impossible to write poetry in London because
people will talk to you about the sort of thing that is in the
newspapers; Virginia Woolf objecting to the materialism of
Bennett's novels; the now disbanded logical positivists with
their principle of verification; the kind of critics who talk about
dissociation of sensibility; and the other kind who talk about
scientific and emotive language. Whatever they think they are
doing, they are all testifying to the same process, the process by
which, in the post-symbolist phase through which we have lived,
literature has sought to weave a circle round itself, to separate
itself from the outer world, and the outer world has been
very willing that it should do so. When literature is surrounded
on all sides by a chasm as profound as this, it is not surprising
that a mere internal division such as that between prose and
verse should have receded into unimportance.

[1] *Œuvres complètes* (Pléiade), p. 361.

III

PSYCHOANALYSIS AND LITERARY INTERPRETATION

I

THE position of Freud in relation to the arts to-day is something like that of Plato in the Renaissance. The thinker who above all others loomed behind the contemporary artistic imagination notoriously took a low view of the artist and his functions. The platonising critics of the Renaissance knew too well that Plato had turned the poets out of the Republic, and in any general consideration of poetry had first, tacitly or overtly, to get this objection out of the way. So the familiar arguments were marshalled; the poets were the first guides and teachers of mankind; they provide notable examples of moral virtue; far from imitating phenomenal things that are only shadows they see behind them to the Ideas themselves—and all the rest of it. To-day, when there can hardly be a writer or critic of importance who has not been deeply influenced by Freudian thought, those who concern themselves with the nature of poetry have first to make a pious act of dissociation from their master's view of what poetry was. For Freud's conception of art was strongly influenced by his clinical interests, and his clinical interests were at the service of a strictly positivist philosophy of life. In his view the neurotic and the infantile personality are under the domination of the pleasure principle; the business of the mature man is to come to terms with reality. In this stern quest the arts have no help to offer. The productions of the artist are like the fantasies of the neurotic or the child—compensations for satisfactions that reality denies. Art is fantasy, it is day-dreaming; Freud states it formally in *Der Dichter und das Phantasieren*, and it is implied by what he says about the

PSYCHOANALYSIS

arts in innumerable other places. We have often been reminded of this lately; since the recent centenary there has been so much discussion of the bearing of Freud's doctrine on so many departments of human activity that it could hardly have been otherwise. What has been said above about Freud's valuation of art is virtually a repetition of a paragraph from an admirable article on "Freud and the Arts" in *The Times Literary Supplement* for May 4, 1956. This article continues:

> The simple view of art as "substitute activity"—as a form of activity more closely related to play than to work—has been widely accepted by stolid physicians and others whose criterion of mental health is simply adjustment.

Dissatisfied with this view, like all who have been concerned seriously with the arts, the writer then proceeds to criticise it. The answer (it has now become conventional) is that the differences between art and fantasy are more striking than the resemblances; the neurotic, the day-dreamer, is possessed by his fantasy, while the poet is in command of his. The point was made earlier by Lionel Trilling, who is duly cited here. Charles Lamb is also quoted, answering the Freudian argument in the terms of an earlier age. "The poet dreams being awake. He is not possessed by his subject but has dominion over it." By this simple *ignoratio elenchi* Freud is supposed to be put in his place. But the neurotic or the day-dreamer is partly in control of his fantasy; he can within limits alter its form and its terms. Even night-dreams can be modified by the conscious behaviour of waking life. It is doubtful whether the artist's control over his fantasy is in principle different from this. In a crudely literal sense the poet is of course in command of his fantasy; he is free to put down on his page what words he will, he can turn his theme in any direction that he likes. But without having recourse to any extreme theory of inspiration, or to any extreme example, such as the *Sonnets to Orpheus*, the poets have always known and their readers have always recognised that there are points at which the theme resists alteration or direction. Some of the great unfinished poems (*Christabel* or *Hyperion*) are so because of a cessation of the fantasy, or because of a mistaken effort of the will to force it into a new direction. In fact the poet's dominion is more over his craft than over his conception or his material; it reveals itself in the linguistic embodiment, in the work of expression and revision, in all that makes a poem, because it is a verbal construct, something different from an unwritten dream. It is true that a poem is not simply the record of eavesdropping on the unconscious. No one except the surrealists ever thought it was. But the element of the dictated, the unmodifiable, the given (given perhaps by the individual unconscious, but perhaps by the unrecognised pressure of a culture or a genre) is always present. And of this the poet is not in command. So it is doubtful if the stock answer of the affronted man of letters is as compelling as it looks at first.

If we wish to rescue the arts from the relatively humble station to which Freudian theory would confine them we can take another road. Unless we are too afraid of the obvious we should begin by saying that art is distinguished from non-artistic fantasy by the absolute requirement that it should be embodied in material or linguistic form; and that this at once introduces a whole range of considerations outside the sphere of fantasy itself. And then we can distinguish between different levels of fantasy. The psycho-pathologist may not, but the student of the arts must. There is neurotic fantasy, and the idle day-dreaming of normal persons, and, we must admit, a good deal of bad art, which are all, as Freud would say, an evasion of the demands of reality, a refusal, permanent or temporary, harmful or more or less innocent, to come to terms with the world. And there is fantasy which can look very like this to the careless, the uninterested or the uninstructed, which deserts an obvious and easily perceptible reality in the effort to compass a more comprehensive reality. This is the kind to which significant art belongs, and it has always been one of the tasks of criticism to discriminate between this and its inferior simulacrum. In practice the distinction is perfectly familiar. Arnold's and Mr. Eliot's dismissal of Shelley's poetry was a relegation of it to the first inferior class—immature wish-fulfilment and day-dream. The business of his defenders is to show that the lack of commerce with familiar and tangible reality in Shelley's poetry is in fact a means of comprehending a wider vision of authentic human experience. The same distinction is often found in biographical dealings with artists. When a poet's progress is described as a "savage pilgrimage" it is tacitly claimed that the asperities and inadequacies of his life are purposive and are directed to a goal worth attaining. The comment "What a set, what a world!" implies that the particular artistic circle under discussion was inadequate to the demands of existing social reality without having any tendency to fulfil demands of a wider scope. The latter judgment is always the easier to make. Rimbaud was certainly a *voyou*; whether he was a *voyant* is a matter for debate.

To this sort of debate Freud has contributed little or nothing. He was cautious in his claims for the illumination that psychoanalysis could cast upon the arts. He insisted that it could do nothing towards explaining the nature of the artistic faculty or the means by which the artist works, artistic technique; and he never professes to make qualitative distinction, to distinguish between good art and bad. Perhaps this needs a little elucidation. No one can doubt Freud's wide literary culture. He always acknowledged his debt to the imaginative writers; it was not he, but the artists and poets, he said, who discovered the unconscious. He had the profound respect for the arts that the scientific intellectual educated in a German context generally has—and the tendency to regard them as profoundly mysterious. Even when he had assimilated the poetic activity to day-dream, not different in fundamental nature from the dream of sleep, he does not think that this affords any insight into the process by which some of these fantasies are transmuted into art. All art is fantasy, but not all fantasy is art. The task of judging what is art, and of judging, by intrinsic criteria, between the things that come within art's scope, is not one for psychoanalysis. So when Lionel Trilling says that Ernest Jones and similar psychological interpreters cannot explain the meaning of *Hamlet* "because they have no adequate conception of what a literary meaning is", he is probably saying little more than the founder of psychoanalysis would have approved.

Provided that we are allowed to make qualitative distinctions between fantasies that it was not Freud's business to make, we have not much call to be affronted at his placing of the arts. We could agree that art is fantasy, if it were not that the word fantasy carries at least a mildly pejorative connotation. The more elevated term is imagination; but the two are not unrelated. Yeats said that fantasy was "uninformed imagination", making the same distinction between different levels of fantasy that we have just suggested. Art is fantasy, we have always known it; art can thus be called play, we have always known that it was something different from the business of the world. To deny this in the name of the seriousness of art results in a solemn, scrupulous, joyless falsification of the whole nature of the artistic activity—the belief, for example, that all literature would be *Middlemarch* if it could. We have always known too that it is in his fantasy and his play, as much as in his practical activity, that man reveals the depths of his nature. Like other fantasies art does not occupy the whole of life; it has its intermittences. In the intermittences we return to the world; and it is the peculiar property of the kind of fantasy that is art that at its best it allows us to return to the world with a renewed and enriched vision of the world's possibilities. Freud himself, with his typical sardonic positivism, saw the road back from the dream-world of art to the world of actuality in that by publishing his fantasies the artist wins money, fame and the love of women, from the lack of which the fantasies had originally sprung! We need not waste much time over this defence of poetry; but the non-Freudian claim that art allows us to return to the world with an enriched view of its possibilities needs some expansion. It is sometimes made in a rather different form. Professor Trilling says that art *leads us back* to reality, while the dream does not. This no doubt springs from a laudable desire to provide a moral and social justification for the arts: but I do not see in what sense art in general *leads* us back to reality. (There are of course specific works which attempt to do just that, provide deliberate bridges between the realm of aesthetic contemplation and that of actual experience.) But the world of art and the world of reality are separate worlds; there is a discontinuity; we cannot be led from one to the other except by a bridge which is not itself of the nature of art. When we cease to contemplate a work of art and return to our affairs we relax one kind of attention and resume a different one. But we return to the world of reality after the experience of art with a livelier and more extensive vision. We return from day-dream with a narrowed one.

But in what sense does the experience of art extend the vision of what reality can hold? If this is to be more than a pious formula it needs to be stated in plain terms. In the first place the extension and enrichment may be present in a straightforward historical sense. The artists have in fact sometimes (not as often as has been said, but sometimes) profoundly modified both the personal and the general sensibility, been the pioneers of new modes of feeling and behaviour. Such modifications are not the product of art alone; they may be produced by other historical and social developments, and the relation between these factors and the arts is a complicated and reciprocal one. In a second and more fundamental sense art allows us back into a world that has been enriched merely by its own existence—enriched by the addition of newly perceived relations between forms, rhythms and colours which become part of our lives—and are art's creation alone. This is quite distinct from the simple effects on feeling and behaviour; and non-artistic fantasy does not supply it. It is not the possession of the aesthetically cultivated alone, and we need not go to some idealised William Morris community in a medieval never-never land to see it at work. Jazz, popular songs, sentimental or sensational films, espresso-bar décor, are often denounced as commercially inspired fantasy substitutes for real living. They are also on their level works of art. They fulfil the essential precondition of embodiment in verbal, melodic or material form; and quite apart from the doubtless cheap satisfaction of doubtless immature or indefensible wishes, they provide, generally in a rather poor way, the satisfactions of verbal pattern, melody, rhythm and visual design; and it is doubtful whether life in the contemporary subtopian scrub would be tolerable without them. They are real, and they are of the same kind as the enjoyment of better art by more instructed people.

There are two ways, then, in which we can come back from

art to actuality the richer for our experience. Neither of them seems to be a matter for the psychoanalyst. The first, the social and historical enrichment, is the affair of the cultural historian, and a cultural historian with a different perspective from that given by psychoanalysis. (Freud's excursions into cultural history are the most dubious parts of his work.) And to speak of the second, the purely aesthetic enrichment, is not for the psychoanalyst either, it is for the aesthetic critic—precisely what Freud was willing to admit the psychoanalyst is not. The psychoanalyst cannot tell us what distinguishes art from other kinds of fantasy; and he cannot therefore discuss its particular kind of connection with actual living. The light that psychoanalysis can bring is something preliminary and external to art itself. What psychoanalysis has done is to bring a new, far deeper and more systematic understanding of the way human fantasy in general works, of its genesis, its mechanism and its materials. These deeper-dug and better-laid foundations will inevitably affect what the cultural historian and the aesthetic critic can build. The new insights will show themselves in two ways—first in an increased understanding of the way an artistic production may be related to its creator's experience; and second (this really applies to literature alone) in a new way of interpreting the conflicts of character and motive within the work itself. Freud has given us notable examples of both; of the first in the study of Leonardo; of the second in a number of comments on Ibsen and Shakespeare. In one respect he has abandoned a field that he could well have explored. When he said that his science could do nothing to show the means by which the artist works, I hope to show that, as far as the poets are concerned, he was claiming too little; it is precisely in this field that his illuminations have been most direct.

II

It is certainly necessary at this point to change Freud's emphasis; he is of course perfectly aware of the aesthetic enrichment that art can bring. He writes of it in these terms:

The writer softens the egotistical character of the day-dream by changes and disguises, and he bribes us by the offer of a purely formal, that is, aesthetic pleasure in the presentation of his phantasies. The increment of pleasure offered us in order to release yet greater pleasure arising from deeper sources in the mind is called an "incitement premium" or technically "fore-pleasure". I am of the opinion that all the pleasure we gain from the works of imaginative writers is of the same type as this "fore-pleasure", and that the true enjoyment of literature proceeds from the relief of tension in our minds.

Thus Freud would assimilate the aesthetic activity to the erotic play which is enjoyed as a mere preliminary and incitement to the serious business of the sexual life. But surely he is mistaken. It is this "fore-pleasure" alone that distinguishes art from other kinds of fantasy formation. It is this that makes art; and no theory that introduces it as a kind of mask to conceal a deeper source of satisfaction can be adequate for one who is studying art as such; though it may have something to say to one who, like Freud, is mainly interested in the place of art in the general economy of psychological life. Nowhere, so far as I know, does Freud make any suggestions about the nature of this "purely formal, that is, aesthetic pleasure". He seems to have regarded it as a mystery. There is of course the possibility of attempting to explain even the formal satisfaction of art in psychoanalytical terms. We enjoy enclosed forms because we were so comfortable in the womb, we enjoy upright and free-standing forms—for the reason that, in Freudian theory, we always enjoy upright and free-standing forms; and so forth. But to anyone with any deep and varied experience of the arts these explanations must seem so fragmentary and tendentious as to be of very little value. Readers of Cassirer and Suzanne Langer are familiar with the idea that it springs from a more radical and generalised symbolic activity than the kind discussed by Freud, a symbolic activity that is fundamental to man quite apart from his vital and sexual needs. We are surely more likely to be convinced by something like Mrs. Langer's contention that the art of music symbolises our sense of the organisation of experience in time; that the art of painting symbolises our sense of the organisation of space in the world around us; and that they provide the only symbolic language in which such apprehensions can be expressed. Freud's "fore-pleasure" turns out to be the gateway to a whole range of symbolic experience that lies outside the limits of his specialised point of view.

But Freud was talking about literature. And the formal satisfactions of literature have always been a more difficult matter to discuss than those of music or painting. We are told by musicians that music has no necessary relation to the emotions and experiences of actual life; we can conceive of painting that has no reference to our experience of actual objects. (Though I would add that for many "non-representational" paintings this claim seems to me to be falsely made.) But we cannot even conceive of literature that makes no reference to persons, objects, events and experiences such as those we know in the actual world. A brush-stroke need not refer to anything besides itself. A word necessarily must. I do not know that "pure music" or "pure painting" is necessarily an illusion. But I know that "pure poetry" is. The formal element in literature has never been as easily separable as it is in these other arts; and in many discussions of it the contenders are not at all sure what they are talking about. In this matter Freud is simply willing to confess his ignorance. Other related considerations, such as "aesthetic distance", the autonomy of the work of art, never seem to have occurred to him. His overt discussions of works of literature are confined to those aspects of them that imitate or represent or symbolise the experiences of actual life. And this limitation of range he has in common with many professed literary critics. It is a limitation, but it need not prevent him from having something valuable to say. If Freud "has no adequate conception of what a literary meaning is", this is a disability he shares with many of those who have written about literature; and it is one which serves to remind us that in spite of the formalists, in spite of those who would liken the ultimate satisfactions of literature to those of "significant form" (whatever that means) in painting, in spite of those who would tell us that all art aspires to the condition of music, the particular art of literature is always concerned with human persons, human experiences, human emotions, analogous to those that we experience in daily life; and a large part of any adequate discussion of literature must be conducted in these terms.

III

But of course the insights of psychoanalysis can be profitably used on a literary work only if we know what we are trying to do with them. Many of those who have been willing to employ them have not. They have been incapable, for example, of distinguishing between the analysis of a work of art and an analysis of the character of its creator. Many of those who have attacked psychoanalytical interpretation have been incapable of distinguishing between the different ways in which a scientific or philosophical theory may impinge on a work of art —on the one hand as a conscious factor in its formation, like scholasticism in Dante; on the other, as a heuristic procedure applied to works that are wholly innocent of any such theory. We have been told, for example, that psychoanalytic interpretations of *Hamlet* must be nonsense because Shakespeare did not know about psychoanalysis.

Perhaps the commonest critical practice has been to use the literary work as a means of analysing the nature and personality of the individual artist. Needless to say, this is not literary interpretation. It is using literature as material for study of quite another kind. Personally I often find such inquiries fascinating, though one must confess that their results are clouded by uncertainty. The concentration of contemporary criticism on the work itself as an autonomous object makes this kind of study unfashionable in the more austere literary circles. To read back from the poem to its creator is regarded as irrelevant or illegitimate or both. Certainly at its worst it can lead to a merely dubious kind of biography. However, the mischief does not come here, for as literary students we are not primarily concerned with biography. One of the dogmas we all accept to-day, I think rightly, is the separation between the literary personality of a writer and his historic and social personality. The psychologist does not seem to accept this. For him the work of art is a set of symptoms, and like any other set of symptoms it leads us straight back to the actual self. When Freud had finished his delightful study of Wilhelm Jensen's *Gradiva* he wrote to the author asking for confirmation of the analysis, biographical confirmation from Jensen's own "impressions and memories". Jensen refused to collaborate. This may have been simply the distaste of an elderly man who felt his privacy was being invaded; but it is likely also to be a testimony to the artist's sense of the dichotomy between biographical experience and the completed work of art.

However, a critical purism must not blind us to the fact that there *are* cases where this dichotomy is less than absolute. There is a kind of imaginative writing (the Germans call it *Erlebnisdichtung*) where the author takes as his material the unfolding panorama of his own experience. I do not mean that he writes factual autobiography, but that his real theme is the development of his own experience and his own attitude. Two long poems cover the whole of Byron's writing life; and they must I think be read in this way. Anyone who reads Lawrence's novels chronologically finds it hard to avoid seeing in them a long continuous *Bildungsroman*. Here it would be absurd, besides being virtually impossible, to avoid some biographical reference; and the more refined the biographical reference can be the better. If we believe that psychoanalysis, for all its dubieties and limitations, has increased our understanding of the workings of human nature, we must also believe that it can give us the means to a fuller understanding of works of this kind.

There are however some difficulties of method. Freud's method of dream interpretation depends on using the free associations of the subject. He always insists that we cannot interpret an isolated dream without these associations. If we do so we are revealing ourselves not the subject. Now we have not normally got the writer's free associations to the significant elements in his work; so in theory we are deprived of essential data and cannot proceed. And Freud actually utters cautions to this effect. It is true that he did not always observe his own rules, for he does give us many interpretations of literature without extraneous help from the authors—who were either dead like Shakespeare or unco-operative like Jensen. And I believe in this respect that Freud's practice was sounder than his theory. In spite of great literary insight, Freud was after all not a critic, and I should be ready to maintain that we have in effect got the writer's free associations, though only by the application of rather more literary expertise than psychologists normally possess. By examination of imagery and repeated symbolism (what Leo Spitzer has called "image-clusters") we can find out what emotional associations a writer has with certain elements in his work, and could quite reasonably proceed with the analytic process, fairly confidently and without danger of projecting our own attitudes. Doubtless this has not often been done successfully, and doubtless it will not be, for it needs the alliance of two specialised kinds of skill that are not often found together. I do not know how much pain is caused to psychologists by the amateur excursions of literary critics into their territory; but I do know what one feels about the retaliatory expeditions into criticism made by some psychologists.

A different and more interesting problem is the interpretation not of the writer's mind, but of the work itself. We do not ask (we shall not if we are wise) what connection the mental states revealed in *Hamlet* have with Shakespeare's mental states, or whether they have any at all. We ask instead—but what do we ask? What can we reasonably expect psychoanalysis to tell us? We can in the first place ask what psychological patterns are revealed in the work in a very crude and obvious sense—we can, that is to say, take the characters in a play or a novel as though they were real people, and interpret them psychologically, as far as the evidence permits. This simply provides us with another set of tools for character analysis. And character analysis has always had a place in criticism. It was, for example, the mainstay of Shakespearean criticism from Johnson to Bradley. When Ernest Jones examines *Hamlet* in this way he is not doing anything revolutionary, he is simply using a new set of concepts to play the old and well-established game of finding out why Hamlet behaved so oddly. Goethe says, "A beautiful, pure and most moral nature, without the strength of nerve that forms a

hero . . . " and all the rest of it; Ernest Jones says a neurotic with
an excessively strong attachment to his mother. You may
prefer one explanation to the other, but they are not different
in kind. I will not go into the question of how far such inquiries
are relevant to the understanding of the play. Personally I take
the view that Shakespeare's plays are not expanded metaphors
or patterns of imagery, but are about characters in action; and
that to talk about the characters is therefore relevant. What we
must ask however is how much new light psychoanalysis can
bring to this sort of enterprise. This depends on the nature of
the work. I cannot think that it would make much difference to
Pride and Prejudice. But *Hamlet*, which I must admit is the
most favourable example one could take, has since the beginning
of the nineteenth century been regarded as an enigma, and the
enigma has generally been seen to centre in the character of the
hero himself. Sophisticated Shakespeare criticism may wish
to discount many of the nineteenth-century heart-searchings on
this theme; but there they are; and there have been contemporary ones. Mr. Eliot in a famous essay found *Hamlet* an
artistic failure because it did not provide any "objective correlative" for Hamlet's behaviour, it is in excess of the apparent
circumstances. Ernest Jones's study does not indeed provide an
answer to Mr. Eliot's objection on Mr. Eliot's own terms. The
apparent circumstances remain what they were. But it does
provide an explanation of Hamlet's conduct deducible from the
apparent circumstances, entirely consonant with them, and
without going outside the limits of the text. And since the
explanation lies in the realm of universal unconscious experience it also explains the universal appeal of the play, even when
its motivation was not clearly understood. And if we are to
object, as it seems Mr. Eliot would, that concealed, unapparent
causes of this kind are not artistically valid we should have to
condemn so many solutions of continuity, breaks of motivation,
in so many imaginative works that I think we should find ourselves in an impossible position. I believe, then, that here
psychoanalysis has brought us a clear gain—just such a gain
as any increase in psychological understanding might be
expected to bring. Dr. Jones's further speculations about

Shakespeare's circumstance and state of mind when he was writing *Hamlet* are not open to the same commendation. For those I resign him to critical justice.

It must be added that this line of approach is likely to be particularly unhelpful with modern psychologically inspired literature. Since the psychoanalytical insights have been put in on purpose no great revelation is to be expected from fishing them out. Freudianism cannot tell us much about the conflict in *Sons and Lovers* that is not perfectly explicit in the text because Lawrence was aware of Freudian doctrine before he finished the book.

But in such cases (and no doubt in others, in older literature too) another kind of approach may prove useful. Freud wrote in *Der Dichter und das Phantasieren*, "The psychological novel in general probably owes its peculiarities to the tendency of modern writers to split up their ego by self-observation into many component-egos, and in this way to personify the conflicting trends in their own mental life in many heroes." From this point of view, then, the work of fiction as a whole represents the totality of psychic life, and the conflicts in it are internal psychic conflicts. (We need not follow Freud in supposing that they must represent the writer's personal psychic life and psychic conflicts.) Instead of regarding the characters as substantial human beings to be understood as best we may, we now regard each as the representation of some internal psychic factor. Lawrence's gamekeepers and stallions are symbols of the id, Clifford Chatterley represents the maimed or neurotic ego. And though this should not, I believe, excuse either us or the author from realising the characters as people, it can be an extremely significant way of seeing a total pattern. Clearly there can be no objectivity or certainty about such interpretations. Freud's picture of the structure of the mind belongs to the "mythological" part of his doctrine, and we are under no obligation to use the Freudian rather than the Jungian or any other picture. Both, I should claim, are rich and illuminating myths. They have the same sort of status as "the conflict between reason and the passions" or "the search for self-realisation", which are traditionally accepted as among the forms of psychic experience, and traditionally used to explain the works of the imagination. They have the advantage that they are perhaps more fundamental, certainly less moralistic than more traditional and "unscientific" formulations; but we use them in the same way. They are simply among the categories naturally available to the modern mind—a way of relating our literary experiences to our other kinds of experience.

IV

But none of these illuminations is after all central to our literary experience. They are only techniques for doing what has been done by one means or another for centuries. Lionel Trilling has pointed out in his essay "Freud and Literature" that the great importance of Freud for letters is more fundamental, and lies in a different area altogether. It is that Freud has "naturalised poetry"; has shown that the working of the unconscious is itself mythopoeic, poetic; that the mind can work without logic yet not without directing purpose. Within the limits of his essay he does not elaborate this. What follows is an attempt to do so.

That the mind can work mythopoeically—without logic yet not without directing purpose—the importance of this notion to modern poetic theory hardly needs to be emphasised. The poetics of the twentieth century has been almost obsessed by the thought that the language of poetry is not discursive language, that a poem does not utter propositions, that it must not mean but be. The formulations are many and the ramifications almost innumerable. The directing force behind all of them is the desire to find a place for poetic utterance in a world increasingly dominated by the ideals of scientific positivism. The intention is understandable enough, but one may still be disquieted by some of the results. Objectless beliefs, pseudo-statements, words which refer us to nothing beyond themselves, poems sundered by an absolute and impassable gulf from other forms of experience—they all look suspiciously like manœuvres to get out of a difficulty. And manœuvres undertaken with this object alone commonly lead straight into new difficulties. The difficulties about what is left of poetry after it has been thus drastically purged are not our concern at the moment. I am concerned with another difficulty—what is left for the critic to say about matters which he has been at pains to render almost ineffable. This has often been met by making the language of criticism itself as impenetrable to ordinary modes of apprehension as the language of poetry is alleged to be. To much of what has been said about poetical discourse in the present century it is impossible to attach any meaning at all. One can observe the principle on which the counters are being manipulated, but they have virtually no reference to actual experience of poetry. And indeed the object of such pronouncements is not to lead us back to the concrete experience of poetry but to produce a state of stupefaction in which we will consent to the notion that poetic utterance is different in kind from ordinary discursive communication, without inquiring how it actually works.

And Freud has shown us another way. He has given us minutely documented illustrations of a mode of expression which is non-discursive, non-logical—yet does not exist in some mysterious aesthetic limbo, but is native and central to the human mind. It is generally accepted that Freud's greatest work is *The Interpretation of Dreams*, and Freud himself thought so. It is there, especially in the chapters on the dream-work and on dream-symbolism, that we find Freud quite unintentionally throwing the most penetrating light on the mode of functioning of the poetic imagination. It is probably not too much to say that in Freud's researches on symbolism and on the dream mechanism—"distortion", "projection", "condensation" and "displacement", to use his own terms—we have the most vivid of all illustrations from extra-literary sources of the way poetic expression works. Had Freud not familiarised us with such mechanisms it is doubtful whether some of the most characteristic developments of contemporary criticism would have taken place. The Empsonian concept of ambiguity, which has been so fruitful in consequences for later poetical exegesis, appears at first to owe everything to semantics, to the work of Ogden and Richards; but as he applies it, it becomes something

123

much more like a Freudian dream-interpretation, and, I should suspect, is more fundamentally indebted to this source. Wilson Knight expresses himself in traditional moral and metaphysical terms, but his discovery of symbolic patterns in drama, underlying and partly differing from the overt pattern of character and incident, could hardly have been made without the habits of thought to which psychoanalysis has accustomed us.

It is neither necessary nor possible here to indicate more than a few of the many applications of this part of Freudian research to literature. Freud's term "condensation", for example, indicates the process by which a figure in a dream may stand simply for himself, an actual historical or social person; for some emotional attribute exhibited by that person or associated with him; for some other person with similar or associated attributes; for a whole class of persons. Similarly with an object, action or word—two or more objects, a whole cluster of pertaining or associated attributes may be compressed into one. Freud is talking of dreams; but in literature we now accept as commonplace this kind of compression and multivalence, the shifting boundaries of the symbol, as a pre-Freudian generation could not have done. This viewpoint does not reveal anything of great interest in a modern work like *Finnegan's Wake* for *Finnegan's Wake* both represents a dream and deliberately employs the Freudian mechanisms. The possibility of this kind of interpretation has so patently been put into the work that not much gain is to be expected from isolating it. It is in older works, that have been long familiar, whose symbolic vocabulary seems to have become stereotyped for us, shall we say *The Ancient Mariner* or *The Faery Queen*, that we need to be warned against over-simplified interpretations, one-to-one equivalences, allegorical equations. It is here than an acquaintance with the natural history of symbolism as Freud has revealed it can be a saving revelation of possible depths and complexities of meaning. And this, one may add, can be quite independent of a "Freudian" (in the *Reader's Digest* sense, that is, sexual) interpretation of the symbols or of the work as a whole. It may be said that this is only a twentieth-century version of medieval typology, the four-fold interpretation of Scripture and so forth. To this the answer is that it is not. It is something new. The conditions of medieval interpretation were stereotyped; they were laid down beforehand and were extrinsic to the work. What we have now is the possibility of rich and varied levels of meaning, to be deduced and controlled only by the poetic context itself.

Of course no method of interpretation is proof against being run to death, or immune to being employed by fools.

Freud has himself made some of the applications of this part of his theory. He has for instance discussed the phenomenon of dissociation, familiar in dreams, by which one character is split and presented as two. In the essay on "Character Types in Analytic Work" he suggests that Macbeth and Lady Macbeth are essentially two sides of a single personality, involved in the same situation. Macbeth's fears on the night of the murder do not develop further in him but in the lady. He has the hallucination of the dagger, but it is she who succumbs to mental disorder. He hears the cry "Sleep no more . . . Macbeth shall sleep no more"—but it is she who suffers from sleeplessness and betrays herself in sleep-walking. And this suggests an answer to questions that frequently arise where a character cannot be successfully understood in naturalistic terms. Other instances of the same dissociative process readily occur; Don Quixote and Sancho Panza, always together, always opposed; two complementary factors of a total personality; the I-as-actor and the I-as-spectator, a dichotomy so often found in dreams, and found in the novel in such cases as that of Chad Newsome and Strether in *The Ambassadors*, who both go through the same process—one by actively participating in it, the other by watching it.

Freud gives the name "displacement" to the process by which the centre of an original stimulus-situation appears in the completed dream in some quite subordinate position—displaced and so concealed. A good illustration of this process revealed in literary terms is given in Dr. Tillyard's study of *Lycidas*. Explanations in terms of convention, the pastoral elegy and so forth have never seemed enough to account for the power of this poem whose outward occasion seems to have been

mere formal obituary tribute. Dr. Tillyard suggests of course
that the ostensible theme is not the real one; the core of the
poem is not to be found in the death of King, but in Milton's
apprehensions about an early death that he feared on his own
behalf, fears for the frustration of his own high ambitions. And
I persuade myself that I can detect a similar process at work in
Gray's *Elegy*, which does not derive its power either from its
good manners, as Dr. Richards has suggested, or from the pro-
fundity of its concern with the fate of the rude forefathers of the
hamlet, but from Gray's own consciousness of unused powers.
And here I should be specific about what the nature of the
Freudian illumination is. Not, certainly, possibility of a reductive explanation of these poems, bringing them down to the
level of merely personal conflicts. What Freud can do for us
here is something quite different. It is to show that what might
appear to be a rather perverse literary device, a meaningless
obliquity, is in fact deeply rooted in our psychological habit.
The elaboration of a raw personal situation into a form in which
it can be more readily accepted is not a matter of evasiveness
or decorum, but a profound psychological necessity.

To read Freud on the working of the unconscious in dreams
almost inevitably recalls Coleridge on the imagination. "It
dissolves, diffuses, dissipates, in order to recreate." And as
the most significant part of the Coleridgean doctrine, to my
mind, is the connection between the primary and the secondary
imagination, between the power used in all human perception
and the specific power of the poet, so the most significant consequence the literary student can draw from these Freudian
studies is that much of poetical procedure is closely analogous
to, is, as it were, a special case of the procedure of the unconscious itself. The poet is working as the mind of man works
at its deeper levels. We are back with Lionel Trilling—Freud
has naturalised poetry. But we are also back with contemporary poetic theory. We have not indeed been shown a
language that is non-referential, for there is no such language,
except in the realm of inarticulate exclamation, endearment
and abuse. But we have been shown a language that is referential in a way more complex and many-sided than that used in

ordinary discourse; and one in which the symbols have a special status. I do not for a moment believe with Eliseo Vivas that we give a special kind of non-transitive attention to the symbols of poetry; but it is true that the symbol in poetry (a character, a metaphor, a presented object) is the only means available for presenting a complex cluster of feelings and impressions; it is unique, it exists in its own right. Although of course it refers to another kind of reality existing on another plane, it does so in ways so intricate, so impossible to trace exhaustively, that we are compelled to regard the symbol as in a sense final, as an object of contemplation in itself. And I suspect that this is what most of the contemporary pother about the unique nature of poetic communication is really about.

It may be said however, and often is, that this is just what we do *not* learn from a study of Freud; that his method is purely reductive, that he pays very little attention to the dream-symbols in themselves, that he uses them, in an extremely cavalier fashion, simply as a means of getting back to an original psychic experience that underlies them. This is for instance one of the many criticisms that Jung levels against Freud. From the point of view of the arts it sounds a damaging one. The reductive mode of procedure is precisely the wrong one for the study of the arts; we should not want to rush off behind the presented surface in pursuit of another reality supposed to lie behind it; or if we do, it must be only a temporary excursion to help us to contemplate the presented surface more adequately. Now here we must make a distinction. It is true that Freud's method is radically reductive, that he is only interested in the manifest content of a dream or fantasy in so far as it reveals a latent content. This is his clinical method, and Freud's procedures are always dictated by his clinical interests. But the illumination his *Traumdeutung* can bring, the insight it gives into the natural history of symbols and their modes of association, is something quite independent of clinical interests; and the literary student is free to acknowledge his debt while rejecting *in toto*, if he likes, infantile sexuality and the Oedipus complex; rejecting too, if he likes, Freud's not very interesting positivist philosophy. It is not too much to say that if all

IMAGE AND EXPERIENCE

Freud's conclusions as a strictly medical psychologist were to be disproved (and doubtless some of them have been) he would still remain a pioneer explorer of the workings of the imagination.

v

Freud sums up his observations on dream symbolism in the *Introductory Lectures* by saying:

> We get the impression that we have to do with an ancient but obsolete mode of expression, of which different fragments have survived in different fields, one here only, another there only, a third in various spheres in slightly different forms.

It is an older and less differentiated use of language than the discursive—a usage in which an object and its associated qualities and the emotions that it and they arouse are presented together, and the word or the image means neither the one nor the other but all together. To this ancient mode much of poetic expression belongs; it is both more precise than the language of science or of everyday discourse, because it uses the unique, particular, unparaphrasable image; and more comprehensive (therefore in another sense less precise), because the unique image may have bound together in it many layers of meaning; or perhaps we should say ever-widening circles of meaning, like the waves that spread out from a stone thrown into a pond.

This view of poetic language comes very close to that expressed by Owen Barfield in his book *Poetic Diction* (1927, revised 1951), an isolated and in some ways eccentric work, still perhaps not as well known as it deserves. To put it briefly, and to simplify an argument that is in fact pretty fully worked out, Barfield condemns the idea that language was originally concrete, and then used metaphorically to produce abstract terminology—that *spiritus* was originally just *breath*, and then by metaphor became *the principle of life*. He opposes to this the notion of a single primitive meaning in which abstract and concrete were united, undifferentiated; *breath* and the *principle of life* were one. In this phase of language *sun, light,* and *sight* might all be represented by one word. Poetic language, he suggests, restores this primitive wholeness; instead of the modern dissociated concrete and abstract it presents both in one; to complete the Coleridgean phrase I began to quote earlier "it struggles to unify".

Now Barfield is entirely innocent of Freudian ideas, and to judge by his general attitude he would be most unwilling to seek allies in that quarter. We meet, therefore, two quite different approaches to poetic language arriving at virtually the same standpoint. And this is striking. The ghost of Vico too seems to be hovering in the background, and if we were to call him to witness no doubt he would add his suasions in the same direction. What distinguishes Freud from the others is that he is able to adduce a mass of positive evidence about the way in which symbolism actually works. And Freud's contribution to the interpretation of poetry will be found to lie in these detailed and laborious researches on symbolism, far more than in the elucidation of the family saga or the mythology of the ego and the id.

VI

Up to now we have left out of account the question that for some minds ought to have been raised at the beginning— whether psychoanalysis has any bearing on literary interpretation at all. The line of argument used to show that it cannot have is sufficiently familiar: psychoanalysis and the study of literature are two incommensurable disciplines; their methods and their presuppositions are entirely apart; the work of art is autonomous, its ontological status makes it untouchable by psychological methods, it is one entire and perfect chrysolite, not to be penetrated to the slightest degree by tools of this order. No doubt it would be possible to answer this sort of contention on its own terms; but it is hardly necessary. For there comes after all a time when common-sense breaks in, a time when our experience of the way the world works begins to seep through the almost watertight structure of contemporary criticism. Freud is one of the great revolutionary thinkers of our age, and the one whose thought touches lived and experienced life most closely. However much his specific doctrines may be subject to modification he remains the writer who has altered the moral and emotional landscape of the West more fundamentally than anyone since Rousseau. Since he has had such a profound effect on the way we look at our whole nature it would be a strange thing if he had had no effect on the way we look at literature. So strange a thing that we may be forgiven if we refuse to accept its possibility, and prefer instead to investigate the changes in our literary outlook that his work has actually brought about.

Part Two

IV

TWO EXILES: BYRON AND LAWRENCE

JUST as every age seems to have some great intellectual figure who sums up in his own person its most characteristic and accepted tendencies, so, I should like to suggest, every age has its own rebel, some single figure in whom the submerged faculties and the unexpressed longings of a whole social order become open and articulate. For the eighteenth century I suppose we should fix on Rousseau, for the early nineteenth, Byron. Both are European figures; each of them, by that curious modern amalgam of literary achievement and personality that was unknown to older cultures, altered the landscape of the heart in the Europe of his day—and, for good or ill, altered it ineffaceably. If we are to look for a similar hero in whom to incarnate the revolt of the twentieth century, we should be hard put to it to find one—at any rate to find one who was effective over so wide a range. The fragmentation of Western culture in our own day almost obliges us to abandon the concept of European influence, at least in the aesthetic and imaginative sphere. We are moving into a world dominated by the one great international force of science, and by literatures more parochial and less international perhaps than they have mostly been before. If one were asked to name the most profoundly revolutionary influence on the imaginative writing of this century, one would be compelled to cite the name of a scientist—Freud. And if one were asked to name a single poet or novelist through whom this influence had been transmitted to the imagination of Europe, it could not be done; there would probably be half a dozen different answers—each valid for a different area of the European scene. So let us turn to what is nearest to hand—to the English scene. And here I think we can find a claimant to the vacant title—we can find a single writer who incarnates the rebellion, the discontent and the aspiration of the half of our century that is now completed; surely it is D. H. Lawrence. And though he is not a European figure in the same sense as Byron and Rousseau, I should be willing to place him in the same series, and to measure him by the same scale.

Since it may be thought that he is a lesser man both by his achievement and the range of his influence, perhaps we should begin by explaining why. In the first place, he absorbs into himself and his work two of the great currents of feeling that have most influenced the imaginative life of our century— one, the impulse to map and explore the interior world that has been so greatly strengthened by modern psychology; the other, the deep disquiet about the consequences of industrial civilisation that grows stronger as that civilisation rises to greater material triumphs. And secondly, as for the range of his influence, I think it is quite as great as that of either Rousseau or Byron, though it is exercised in a different field. The old Europe—Childe Harold's Europe—blew to pieces in 1914; and this may be the prelude to a new synthesis, or simply the outward evidence of dissolution and decay. But it may also be something else. The 1914 war was the first time that the new world powerfully and decisively stepped in to redress the balance of the old. It marks the first appearance of America on the European scene, not as a vision, an ideal or a refuge— it had been that for a hundred and fifty years—but as a present and potent reality. And it is from this date too that I should mark the emergence of an Anglo-American cultural world which both overlaps and extends beyond the European one. Its relation with the European one is a complicated subject; and all I want to say is that it is to this world that Lawrence belongs; that it is a large and varied world, besides being an extremely powerful one: and that a writer who makes a deep impression on it can justly claim to be as wide-ranging, as little of a parochial figure as any of his European predecessors.

Rousseau is outside my field. In a sense he stands behind both Byron and Lawrence. It is these two, Byron the rebel of the nineteenth century, and Lawrence of the twentieth, that are our immediate theme. And immediately I want to shift my terminology. I have described them as two rebels—superficially and as a means of working into the subject. But a rebel suggests the leader of a party; or at least one who belongs to a party— someone who works with a splinter group within a society to overturn or alter the whole. And this description does not fit either Byron or Lawrence at all. Neither had much talent for belonging to parties, and their typical reaction to a society that had rejected them, or that they had rejected, is not to go under-ground within society itself, but simply to get to hell out of it. Byron as Childe Harold sheds the dust of England off his feet without a sigh,

> to cross the brine
> And traverse Paynim shores, and cross Earth's central line:

Lawrence as Lovat Somers, looks back from the boat "when they had left Folkestone behind and only England was there, England looking like a grey, dreary-grey coffin sinking in the sea behind". Exiles, then, rather than rebels; each self-exiled from the organised community of his birth, each using his out-side vantage-point to launch his guided missiles into the com-fortable herd he had left behind.

There is no need to labour the difference of their social stations—Byron the aristocrat, Lawrence the miner's son; but we might add that each developed in such a way as to reduce these differences rather than to increase them. Byron's is a con-sciously aristocratic revolt, born of strong individual self-assertion and a good deal of personal petulance and caprice. But his wandering, unsettled way of life, as well as his politics, brought him constantly into touch with the people, and into situa-tions which he had to deal with simply as man to man, or as man to woman. Byron is not above playing the English milord when he feels like it; but the overwhelming impression from the letters is that that pose was a superficial one, that his many and varied encounters all ultimately took place on the ground of naked human worth, the authentic contact of one human being with another that the class-bound English traveller so often goes abroad in search of, and is so often constitutionally unable to find. Lawrence starts from an entirely opposite point, as a defender of the warmth and vital knowledge of his own class against the exhausted values of bourgeois civilisation. Yet he actually passed much of his life moving on equal terms with representatives of the upper bourgeoisie that he attacked, and like Byron ultimately exists on a plane where the acute class-consciousness that he had felt ceases to matter. What starts as difference ends as likeness. Each begins with an extreme aware-ness of being embedded in his particular class situation, and each ends with the assertion of values which would destroy that kind of distinction between human beings altogether.

But if we think of the manner in which these values were asserted we are brought to a much more important difference. Byron is as little as possible of a theorist. He has no programme, and the ordinary literary student who tries to find out what Bryon stands for is often at a loss. All that is revealed on the surface is a mass of romantic fantasy, historic and geographical description, brilliant reporting mixed with more or less facti-tious self-dramatisation, irony with sentiment—and apparently no guiding principle whatever. With Lawrence the case is different. Besides the intense imaginative activity embodied in the novels and tales we have an almost equally large body of expository work, a self-conscious philosophy of life, fairly consistent and well-organised. So that the rough popular portraits of the two men are widely divergent—Byron the spoilt aristocrat accidentally endowed with a genius for exploiting his personality; Lawrence the untrained prophet of an antino-mian creed. But in fact both were engaged on the same quest, the quest for self-realisation. The differences in method are partly indeed the result of differences in temperament and cir-cumstance, but far more, as I hope to show, the result of a difference in historical phase, a whole new orientation of the European consciousness between Byron's day and our own.

Another odd contrast is that whatever Byron is actually doing, whatever the actual tendency of his work, what he professes is often quite contradictory to it. While his whole course of life is a vindication of instinct and unchartered freedom, he con-

stantly appeals to the standards of reason and good sense, even
of conventional morals. "We must make an effort. A month's
effort must make us rational," he writes to Lady Caroline
Lamb, with whom he was having, although somewhat un-
willingly, a wildly irrational love-affair.

> Yet must I think less wildly; I have thought
> Too long and darkly, till my brain became
> In its own eddy boiling and overwrought,
> A whirling gulf of fantasy and flame:
> And thus untaught in youth my heart to tame
> My springs of life were poisoned,

as he wrote in *Childe Harold*. And he is extremely firm in his
determination to keep his illegitimate daughter away from the
influence of her disreputable mother and turn her into a good
Christian. Such sublime unconsciousness of his own actual
tendencies is inconceivable in Lawrence. We cannot imagine
Lawrence determining to think less wildly or reproving his
heart for being untamed. "My great religion is a belief in the
blood, the flesh, as being wiser than the intellect"—that is what
Lawrence professes. And here, as often, we have a curious
sense of topsy-turvy—of Byron the libertine appealing to
reason and Christian morals, and Lawrence, that monogamous
and thoroughly married man, appearing as the apostle of instinct
and the passions.

The paradox is there, and it is sometimes diverting; but it
begins to disappear if instead of setting Lawrence against
Byron we set the two of them against a wider background of
European thought. I have said that they were both engaged on
the same quest. We can see this more clearly as soon as we try
to place them in the moral tradition of Europe. I am aware of
course that there is more than one moral tradition in Europe—
shall we say, perhaps, four major ones—Platonic, Christian,
secular humanist and utilitarian? But they all turn out to have
one thing in common: whatever ends they propose for man (and
they propose different ones), they all propose as a means the
domination of the passions by reason. The exact procedure for
dealing with the passions may vary—subdue them by abstinence,
tame them by allowing them a reasonable indulgence—but all

these great moral traditions are at one in holding that man's ful-
filment must be found by making reason, whether it is the
Platonic *nous* or Benthamite calculation, the sovereign guide.
All the accepted teachers and leaders of Western man could use
—and many of them do—the illustration that Plato uses in the
Phaedrus for the nature of man—the image of a charioteer
guiding a good and a bad horse, the destiny of the whole
equipage depending on his being securely in charge. In Plato
only the chariots of the gods move easily and are obedient to the
rein; all others move with difficulty for they are dragged out of
their course by the bad horses. The best of men are those who
restrain their horses most successfully. The worst are at the
mercy of the horse of vicious temper. "Hence ensues the ex-
tremest turmoil and sweating; and herein, by the awkwardness
of the drivers many souls are maimed . . . and all such after
painful labour go away without being blessed by admission to
the spectacle of truth."

Such is Plato's myth—a myth which the moralists of Europe
would mostly be willing enough to adopt. Let us now look at
the treatment of wild horses in the myths of Byron and Lawrence. In Byron's *Mazeppa* the hero is an old Cossack telling a
story of his youth. He had an illicit love-affair with the wife of
the Polish lord whom he served; and in punishment he is bound
on the back of an untamed horse which is then set free to gallop
where it will. A nightmare ride follows in which Mazeppa is
entirely helpless to guide the horse in any way. The beast
rushes off eastward towards its home on the steppes, and at last
when both man and horse are almost at the end of their strength
the neighing of other horses, and the helpless Mazeppa finds
himself in the midst of a whole herd of wild coursers.

> With flowing tail and flying mane,
> Wide nostrils never stretched by pain,
> Mouths bloodless to the bit or rein,
> And feet that iron never shod.
>
> They saw me strangely bound along
> His back with many a bloody thong,
> They stop, they start, they snuff the air,
> Gallop a moment here and there

—and then Mazeppa's horse drops dead, and he himself loses consciousness. When he awakes it is to find a beautiful Cossack maiden bending over him. She brings her mother and father, they carry him to the nearest hut, succour him; and eventually Mazeppa recovers and becomes the Cossack king. What was meant as a punishment has brought him to a throne. I need hardly labour to explain the symbolism; Mazeppa has sinned through passion; he is given a punishment that fits the crime—delivered over to a force more wild and tameless than himself; his own will and power of control is completely suspended. His wild horse carries him to the land of the wild horses—the realm that is to say where the untamed passions are at home. This looks like the end of his earthly career, but he survives the ordeal and emerges renewed and powerful, a king among his own people.

This is Byron: but I think we may agree that this is in spirit a very Laurentian fable. And Mazeppa's encounter with the wild horses almost inevitably recalls that strange passage at the end of *The Rainbow* where Ursula endures a similar ordeal— though to be sure it is only in a quiet English Midland landscape, and we are never quite certain whether it is vision or actuality. Ursula, it will be remembered, has abandoned her love-affair with the young officer Skrebensky; she is almost in despair about her destiny and about the world she lives in. She is walking across the fields in the rain, when suddenly she becomes aware of a group of horses trampling in the mist near by. She is half afraid, half attracted; but in any case the horses have cut off her advance.

> But the horses had burst before her. In a sort of lightning of knowledge their movement travelled through her, the quiver and strain and thrust of their powerful flanks, as they burst before her and drew on, beyond. . . .
> . . . She was aware of the great flash of hooves, a bluish iridescent flash surrounding a hollow of darkness. Large, large seemed the bluish incandescent flash of the hoof-iron, large as a halo of lightning round the knotted darkness of the flanks. Like circles of lightning came the flash of hooves from out of the powerful flanks.
> . . . Cruelly they swerved and crashed by on her left hand.

She saw the fierce flanks crinkled and as yet inadequate, the great hooves flashing bright as yet only brandished about her, and one by one the horses crashed by, intent, working themselves up. . . .

. . . They had gone by, brandishing themselves thunderously about her, enclosing her. . . . They stirred, they moved uneasily, they settled their uneasy flanks into one group, one purpose. They were up against her.

In an agony of fear she scrambles into the branches of an oak tree, and jumps from them to safety on the other side of the hedge. Like Mazeppa, she lapses into unconsciousness. She is ill and feverish—but as she emerges from this state it is to witness a new creation. She looks out at the same people, the same dreary landscape, but now she sees in them the germ of a new life. And she has the vision of the rainbow with which the book ends, the vision of "the earth's new architecture, the old, brittle corruption of houses and factories swept away, the world built up a living fabric of truth, fitting to the over-arching heaven". I have neglected the part that this episode plays in the book's economy as a whole (it is, as a matter of fact, an inadequately prepared conclusion, imperfectly integrated with the rest). The only point I wish to make is that it is again by submission to the contact of the wild horses, the agents, as it seems, of passion and ferocity; by the temporary obliteration of personal integrity and awareness, that Ursula's mystic reintegrating vision is achieved. In Lawrence as in Byron the wild horses are not creatures to be dominated and subdued—their wildness is itself the instrument of redemption.

This is just an illustration of what I mean by putting Byron and Lawrence together in opposition to the moral tradition of Europe. Of course the point could be developed far more fully; but it is hardly necessary. Other resemblances between these two writers will now perhaps seem less accidental, more the necessary consequences of their essential activity. A writer whose sympathy is with the wild horses rather than with the charioteer who restrains them is not likely to be a formalist. His poetical procedure will be more like a gallop than a ceremonial procession. So it is with both Byron and Lawrence. Hence the difficulty of illustrating their true quality in a small space—and the paucity of telling quotations in this lecture.

140

BYRON AND LAWRENCE

Byron's verse is often undistinguished in detail; it suffers badly from the present critical practice (or is it already on the way out?) of minutely examining short extracts. The sweep of a whole canto of *Childe Harold* or *Don Juan* is needed before we can see what he is at. Neither the emotional élan nor the irony reveal themselves in smaller doses; and when they do reveal themselves they turn out to be curiously independent of formal structure. *Childe Harold* has no more of it than a guide-book, and *Don Juan* is a splendid hotch-potch, and unfinished at that. Lawrence too needs the range of a long novel to work out his ideas. He is formally superior to Byron in that having worked them out, he can often re-present them in a more compact and orderly fashion as a short story or a *novella*; but for the initial working he always needs to splash about on the large untidy canvas. And as with Byron, the critic can always find local patches of villainously bad writing, which in the end do less than we should expect to damage the whole.

We encounter in both cases a kind of writer who can only achieve form by re-living an actual experience. Two long poems span the whole of Byron's literary career; and through *Don Juan* and *Childe Harold* we can trace pretty accurately the development of his nature. Seven long novels extend over Lawrence's life; and if they are read chronologically, as they commonly are not, they give an equally close picture of their author's own growth. *The White Peacock* is in large measure a disguised and romanticised autobiography, just as the first two cantos of *Childe Harold* are; by the third canto Byron has cast off the archaic Gothic-romance persona of the Childe, who had never been an effective creation, or much more than a masquerade costume. He writes the rest of the poem frankly in his own person; in fact, under the pressure of a real distress, he has learnt to speak the truth direct. In the same way Lawrence in *Sons and Lovers*, compelled by an urgent personal necessity, casts off the sentimentalised middle-class setting of *The White Peacock* and tells the story of himself and his family as it really was. In both cases, later on, direct autobiography gives way to a more objective creative activity. Yet in both cases the developing personality of the author subsists—both as a continuous thread on which the work is strung, and intermittently as an actual actor, sometimes well to the front of the stage. Don Juan's travels do not follow those of the historic Byron as Childe Harold's did, but they do constantly reproduce scenes from Byron's experience: and the desultory conversational manner, the ironic or reflective asides, keep Byron constantly in the foreground of our consciousness, not only as the artificer and manipulator of the story, but as the living, growing, ever-changing substance out of which it is all spun. Lawrence's middle and later novels do not as a rule contain his own experience as directly as *Sons and Lovers* had done— it is not present in *Women in Love* or *The Plumed Serpent* in the same way as in the earlier book—but to the attentive reader the living reality only just below the surface is the constantly developing fabric of Lawrence's own insight. And, there are several lapses into the earlier manner; the middle part of *Aaron's Rod* and a great deal of *Kangaroo* are simply authentic bits of Laurentian travel-diary fathered on to a fictitious personality.

Now to all defenders of the objectivity and impersonality of art, the pursuit of formal perfection, these methods are most reprehensible; and those who continue to be impressed by Byron and Lawrence must I think propose for consideration some other criterion of excellence altogether. These two writers are only intermittently creating separate works of art, with an independent, self-subsistent life of their own. The continuous activity on which each of them is engaged is the writing of his own *Bildungsroman*—the story of his own continual search for self-realisation. Parts of this are done as direct autobiography; parts crystallise out as fables in which warring or separable elements of the personality are personified as fictional characters; parts may even be inspired by an objective interest in the outer world. But the underlying reality beneath all these different kinds of literary conception is always the changing and developing self; and this is the fundamental distinction between writers of the kind we are discussing and those who are primarily reporters, story-tellers or linguistic craftsmen.

BYRON AND LAWRENCE

I think it is probable that exile is a necessary condition for the full development of such a literary programme—physical spatial exile, or at least some anomalous relation to one's own native society. If the life-work is to be the long objectification of the process of self-development it is above all necessary that the personality shall not set and harden too early, that life shall remain fluid and unbounded. Both Byron and Lawrence are rich in metaphors that enshrine this necessity.

> It is the way our sympathy flows and recoils that really determines our lives. And here lies the vast importance of the novel, properly handled. It can inform and lead into new places the flow of our sympathy away in recoil from things gone dead.

So Lawrence writes, ostensibly about the novel in general, in reality about his own work. And he goes on in another place to contrast it with religion, science and philosophy, which are all "busy nailing things down, to get a stable equilibrium". Not so with the novel:

> If you try to nail anything down, in the novel, either it kills the novel, or the novel gets up and walks away with the nail.

It is useless to look for similar statements of principle in Byron. Byron does not go in for statements of principle. We must look instead for the principles that are actually exalted in his verse. If we had to choose one, surely that most frequently celebrated is unconditioned freedom—sometimes hailed by name, sometimes recognised in symbol, most often perhaps in the symbol of the sea.

> Once more upon the waters! Yet once more!
> And the waves bound beneath me as a steed
> That knows his rider. Welcome to the roar!
> Swift be their guidance, wheresoe'er it lead!
> Though the strained mast should quiver as a reed,
> And the rent canvas fluttering strew the gale,
> Still must I on.

That is Childe Harold, and the Corsair similarly rejoices in:

> Ours the wild life in tumult still to range
> From toil to rest, and joy in every change.

143

There is no need to elaborate the parallel to these sentiments in the actual lives of both Byron and Lawrence, of which the refusal to be nailed down, the willingness to go on to the next experience seems to be the one guiding principle.

For a man who makes his career as a normal member of the society that gave him birth, to preserve this degree of fluidity is almost impossible. Even if the slow attrition of the known and familiar does not dull the edge of his ardour, he will certainly be cast after a time for some defined role, to which he will find it hard not to adapt himself. It may be that apparently liberating, in fact most constricting of roles, the professional Bohemian; or he may become a thoughtful critic of contemporary society, a rising novelist of the younger school, a scholar or teacher—whatever it may be, the mere fact that he is among his own kind, in an organised society where willy-nilly he has always had a place, will mean that sooner or later he is pinned down in some way. Byron would have found it very hard to avoid becoming a Liberal peer: Lawrence could very easily have become a university extension lecturer. I have often thought that Byron's refusal to read the criticisms from England, Lawrence's resentment when he did, spring less from a natural objection to incomprehension and abuse than from a hatred of being categorised at all. The only safe way to avoid falling into any category is to live among strangers, to whose families you do not belong, in whose society you have no place, in whose politics you have no obligatory role to fulfil. Such was the course that both Byron and Lawrence pursued; and by this voluntary exile they were able to ensure that all their acts were gratuitous ones, the unforced products of inner necessity alone.

And it is their exile that lends a special quality to their criticism of their own country. One of the functions that Byron and Lawrence have in common is that of penetrating satirists of the English scene. Lawrence's satire is often reasoned, theoretical, part of a programme; Byron's is more impulsive, personal and petulant, but none the less powerful. Anyone of any nationality who has lived much among foreigners becomes aware after a time that they do not accept his culture at the valuation to which he has been accustomed. At first perhaps he is annoyed, then he begins to explain it all away, to make excuses for them; after all they are only foreigners and they don't really understand. It is unlikely that this criticism from outside will profoundly modify his views. And perhaps rightly so. It is probable that the English critic of America, for example, never does fully understand what makes America tick; and the same is probably true for the Frenchman writing on England, or any of them writing on Germany. But the native critic who had adopted and understood a foreign point of view is in a very different position. It is not merely that he knows the object of his criticism from within, but that it is a part of himself—his irritation is mingled with loyalty, his contempt with respect, his hatred with love. Heine's satire on Germany is of this kind, and so are both Byron's and Lawrence's on England. We can say of these critics of their homelands what Byron says about women:

> And their revenge is as the tiger's spring
> Deadly, and quick, and crushing; yet as real
> Torture is theirs—what they inflict they feel.

Both Byron and Lawrence played at times with the idea that Europe is finished; and Byron's travels in the Near East (virtually outside the orbit of European civilisation), Lawrence's sojourn in the American south-west, are the practical expressions of this belief. But I am not sure that there is anything particularly characteristic of their individual minds in that. It is simply a feeling that has been endemic in Europe, ever since there has been a new world to set against the old one. Did not even Goethe write:

> Amerika, du hast es besser—
> America, you are better off than our old continent, you have no ruined castles, . . . and are not inwardly disturbed by useless manœuvres and vain struggles. . . . And when your own young come to write poetry, take care to keep them from knight-and-robber and ghost stories.

So, when we find Byron writing "There is no freedom in Europe—that's certain; it is besides a worn-out portion of the globe", and planning in consequence to go out to Venezuela; when we find Somers, the undisguised Lawrence-figure in

IMAGE AND EXPERIENCE

Kangaroo, almost echoing Byron's words, "In Europe he had made up his mind that everything was done for, played-out, finished, and he must go to a new country", we are encountering only a modern European habit of establishing a cloud-cuckoo-land beyond the seas. What is peculiarly characteristic of Byron and Lawrence is to use standards derived from know-ledge of another country to reflect upon their own. They re-received passing illuminations in various parts of the world; but with both of them it is Italy that provides the most constant point of comparison. At first it is the superficial obvious con-trasts that are recorded—weather, scenery and manners. And here I cannot forbear quoting at length the delightful stanzas of *Beppo* on this theme, both for their immediate relevance, and as an admirable example of Byron's later easy good-humoured manner.

XLI

With all its sinful doings I must say
This Italy's a pleasant place to me,
Who love to see the sun shine every day,
And vines (not nailed to walls) from tree to tree
Festooned, much like the back scene of a play,
Or melodrame, which people flock to see,
When the first act is ended by a dance
In vineyards copied from the south of France.

XLII

I like on Autumn evenings to ride out,
Without being forced to bid my groom be sure
My cloak is round his middle strapped about,
Because the skies are not the most secure;
I know, too, that if stopped upon my route,
Where the green alleys windingly allure,
Reeling with *grapes* red wagons choke the way,—
In England 'twould be dung, dust, or a dray.

XLIII

I also like to dine on beccaficas,
To see the sun set, sure he'll rise to-morrow,
Not through a misty morning twinkling weak as
A drunken man's dead eye in maudlin sorrow,
But with all Heaven t'himself; the day will break as
Beauteous as cloudless, nor be forced to borrow
That sort of farthing candlelight which glimmers
Where reeking London's smoky cauldron simmers.

BYRON AND LAWRENCE

XLIV

I love the language, that soft bastard Latin,
Which melts like kisses from a female mouth,
And sounds as if it should be writ on satin,
With syllables which breathe of the sweet South,
And gentle liquids gliding all so pat in,
That not a single accent seems uncouth,
Like our harsh northern whistling, grunting, guttural,
Which we're obliged to hiss and spit and sputter all.

XLV

I like the women too (forgive my folly),
From the rich peasant cheek of ruddy bronze,
And large black eyes that flash on you a volley
Of rays that say a thousand things at once,
To the high Dama's brow, more melancholy,
But clear, and with a wild and liquid glance,
Heart on her lips, and soul within her eyes,
Soft as her clime, and sunny as her skies.

Given the differences of temperament and circumstance the
sentiment corresponds closely to that of the letters Lawrence
wrote shortly after he first left England. While he and Frieda
were living on Lake Garda Lawrence read Bennett's *Anna of
the Five Towns* and hated it, hated all that it brought back to his
memory.

> I hate England and its hopelessness. I hate Bennett's resigna-
> tion. . . . I want to wash again quickly, wash off England, the
> oldness and grubbiness and despair. . . . No, I don't believe
> England need be so grubby. . . . One can have the necessary
> things, life, and love, and clean warmth. Why is England so
> shabby?
> The Italians here sing. They are very poor, they buy two
> penn'orth of butter and a penn'orth of cheese. But they are
> healthy and they lounge about in the little square where the boats
> come up and nets are mended, like kings. And they go by the
> window proudly, and they don't hurry or fret. And the women
> walk straight and look calm. And the men adore children.

But at the back of these sensuous and aesthetic contrasts (contrasts that are real enough—for Lawrence the fundamental
problem of England was the problem of ugliness, and I daresay
he was right) it is a moral difference that is felt. Byron writes
to Murray: "Their moral is not your moral; their life is not

your life; you would not understand it; it is not English nor French nor German, which you would all understand." And Lawrence's comments to A. W. Macleod, nearly a hundred years later, simply make the difference rather more precise.

> One must love Italy, if one has lived there. It is so non-moral. It leaves the soul so free. Over these countries, Germany and England, like the grey skies, lies the gloom of the dark moral judgment and reservation and condemnation of the people. Italy does not judge.

"Italy does not judge." In a lighter vein, this is precisely the point of Byron's *Beppo*—that a situation which in England would infallibly have led to a duel, divorce and damages leads in Venice to a good-humoured acceptance of the facts as they are. In the prolonged absence of her lawful spouse. Laura the heroine

> thought it prudent to connect her
> With a vice-husband, chiefly to protect her.

And when the real husband returns neither he nor anyone else sees much to blame in the matter. I am not suggesting, of course, that Lawrence could for a moment have approved this easy-going morality of the married woman and the *cavaliere servente*. Its surface manifestations would have been most displeasing to him; but scratch a little way below the surface, and the position is not far from his; a natural response has been made to authentic human needs, and the results are accepted without shame or loss of dignity by anyone. On the level of light comedy, what *Beppo* celebrates is the virtue of integrity. A longer celebration of the same virtue (using the word virtue in a Blakean, Marriage-of-Heaven-and-Hell sense) is Byron's account of his Venetian mistress Margarita Cogni, La Fornarina, the baker's wife, "wild as a witch and fierce as a demon". Her story is told in a long and brilliant letter (too long to quote) written to John Murray from Ravenna on the first of August 1819. Quite clearly Byron was never in love with her. What appealed to him in this ferocious young woman who strode into his house, dismissed his other female retainers, and for a few months managed his life in her own way is that, to use Law-

rence's words, she answers to her blood direct, "without frib-
bling intervention of mind, or moral, or what not". She
is living, in fact, from her own centre. And so too is that very
different Italian woman that Lawrence met by Lake Garda,
and described in *Twilight in Italy*, the old spinning woman who
took so little notice of him and went on babbling of her own
affairs.

> She was talking to me of a sheep that had died, but I could not
> understand because of her dialect. It never occurred to her that I
> could not understand. She only thought me different, stupid. And
> she talked on. The ewes had lived under the house, and a part was
> divided off for the he-goat, because the other people brought their
> she-goats to be covered by the he-goat. But how the ewe came to
> die I could not make out. . . .

And Lawrence reflects about the old woman:

> She was herself the core and centre to the world, the sun, and
> the single firmament. She knew that I was an inhabitant of lands
> which she had never seen. But what of that! There were parts of
> her own body which she had never seen, which physiologically
> she never could see. They were none the less her own because
> she had never seen them. The lands she had not seen were cor-
> porate parts of her own living body, the knowledge she had not
> attained was only the hidden knowledge of her own self. . . .
> There was nothing that was not herself, ultimately. . . . It was
> this which gave the wonderful clear unconsciousness to her eyes.
> How could she be conscious of herself when all was herself?

It does not matter that Byron's Fornarina was a fierce virago,
and that he is describing a disreputable adventure; and that
Lawrence's spinning woman is a gentle old soul and he is
describing a chance encounter; the quality ultimately celebrated is the same in both cases—integrity, in the strict etymo-
logical sense, wholeness, living from the fullness of one's own
being, not by some reach-me-down standard accepted from
another. This is what both Byron and Lawrence find in Italy,
and do not find in England. It does not matter for my purpose
whether this quality is really to be found in Italy and not in
England—I am not concerned with national differences, only
with a vision of England inspired in both Byron and Lawrence
by the experience of another civilisation. It is a vision of

England as a country preoccupied with the commercial and the second-hand. Byron's satire in the closing cantos of *Don Juan* is directed at a land of marketable virtues, vices assessed at so many thousand pounds damages in the courts, love-making conducted, as Juan himself saw it, in a fashion "half-commercial, half-pedantic". Lawrence's similar but deeper satire, in his own late work *Lady Chatterley*, is similarly directed against a society in which all human values are sacrificed to money and the retention of empty intellectual and social forms.

The particular objects of Byron's satire are long obsolete; those of Lawrence's less so. But I am hardly concerned with their skill at hitting their chosen target. I do in fact believe that a good deal of Byron's criticism is still to the point, Lawrence's the most dangerously penetrating that we have; but leaving aside its aptness to the spiritual condition of our native land, the point I wish to make now is that this kind of criticism could be made of almost any society—by a man who had once belonged to it and now chooses to take up his stand outside. It is an attack not so much on a particular society as on society itself. Byron and Lawrence are engaged in the same campaign; it is a campaign against social man, undertaken in the name of—man, man simply as himself, standing on the ground of bare human dignity. It is perhaps no accident that neither Byron nor Lawrence was an egalitarian. The price of equality is constant vigilance—whole lifetimes spent in keeping the machinery in order. And Byron and Lawrence are not machine-minders. Their criticism of society is not designed to make the wheels run more smoothly, or at a different speed. It is directed to preventing us running our lives by machinery at all.

That at least is their ultimate ground. But it was not arrived at all at once. Both for a time had their dreams of working through the normal social channels. Anyone who has read Byron's three youthful speeches in the House of Lords must recognise not only their sincerity and their power, but their straightforward parliamentary effectiveness. An attentive reader is not likely however to see them as the heralds of a Whig political career. As Professor Pinto and Mr. Wilson Knight have both pointed out, Byron is attacking not a party but a class, and doing it almost single-handed. I should go a step farther and say that these are speeches that are rapidly and inevitably taking him out of politics altogether. And sure enough, his brief parliamentary début was succeeded by a deep invincible disgust for all ordinary political action. He came to believe that England could only be saved by violent revolution; and though he was willing if the need arose, in that he was not anxious to participate. Byron was not the man to find joy in laying violent hands on his motherland. As for his later revolutionary actions in Italy and Greece, they were undertaken in a mood that is perhaps best described as high-spirited despair—a clear-sighted disillusion, with little hope for an immediate result, redeemed from irresponsibility by a total commitment of his own life to the issue. Lawrence's political record is far less impressive; but he too, round about World War I, has his hopes of changing the political face of England, by impressing his ideas on persons of public influence. There was never of course the slightest chance of his being effective—indeed the whole story is an almost grotesque comedy—but far more of Lawrence's work than is commonly realised is spent on drawing up more or less serious plans for the future organisation of English society. As a fantasy the thought of political power continued to haunt him through the periods of *Kangaroo* and *The Plumed Serpent*. And then he turns against it all. "The leader of men is a back number," he wrote—God save the mark —in 1928. And indeed it had never been at the root of his thought. It is not so much that our two exiles become disgusted with social action, as that their authentic life is lived on a plane where it becomes irrelevant.

Exiles therefore they must become. But it is hard for a man to be a separate atom, to be joined to nothing. It was indeed Lawrence's particular detestation. And where organised society fails it is often the natural world that must take its place. Mr. Eliot has remarked that no man would "join himself to the universe" who had anything better to join himself to. Perhaps I think rather better of the universe than Mr. Eliot does; but I am willing to admit that the freedom with which both Byron and Lawrence identify themselves with natural forces is in part a compensation for the frustration of their social instincts. They find in it a religious substitute for that which society and socialised religion has denied them, and in doing so reach some of their most ecstatic moments. The magnificent vision of the ranch in Taos with which that otherwise inferior story *St. Mawr* concludes is Lou Carrington's compensation for the pettiness of civilised life, just as the Alps are for Childe Harold.

> Are not the mountains, waves and skies, a part
> Of me and of my soul, as I of them?

Byron says, just as Lawrence says at the end of *Apocalypse*, "That I am part of the earth my feet know perfectly, and my blood is part of the sea." And that kind of self-identification with a non-human, non-moral, non-social power is what makes them both so much more than critics or satirists of any kind of human society; and it is also the ultimate ground on which these two exiles from their several epochs meet, beyond history altogether.

But now I wish to return to history; and to return to it by way of a gulf, a large and yawning gulf, between Byron's imaginative productions and those of Lawrence. Both present real states of the human soul—often very similar ones; but the depth and penetration of Lawrence's explorations are of a different order altogether from Byron's. Time and again, in his overtly serious, non-satiric works, Byron begins what looks like an extensive foray into unknown regions of the mind; yet after a brief reconnaissance he returns with a few odd souvenirs, and nothing accomplished. Canto III of *Childe Harold* is a good example—apart from the objective and historical parts, which are always excellent. This third canto announces itself as a study of the state of mind of a man who by his own faults and the hardness of society has cut himself off from communion with his kind and seeks for a new life of communion with the energies of nature. Yet the promise is simply not fulfilled. We are put off with a few rhetorical passages—some splendid, some rather meretricious, but none in the slightest degree profound; none, I might almost say, that tell us anything that we might not very well have made up for ourselves. Yet Byron was a man of great general mental powers, and at the time of writing in a state of profound and genuine emotional excitement—learning perhaps for the first time really to come to terms with his own nature. In his letters he covers up the inadequacy of his report by making fun of it.

> I tremble to think of the magnificence which you attribute to the new Childe Harold, I am glad you like it; it is a fine indistinct piece of poetical desolation and my favourite. I was half-mad during the time of its composition, between metaphysics, lakes, love unextinguishable, thoughts unutterable, and the nightmare of my own delinquencies. I should, many a good day, have blown my brains out, but for the recollection that it would have given pleasure to my mother-in-law.

He writes of his drama *Manfred*, composed about the same time, in much the same way.

> I forgot to mention to you that a kind of Poem in dialogue or drama . . . is finished; it is in three acts; but of a very wild, metaphysical, and inexplicable kind. Almost all the persons—but two or three—are spirits of the earth and air, or the waters; the scene is in the Alps; the hero is a kind of magician, who is tormented by a species of remorse, the cause of which is left half unexplained. He wanders about invoking these spirits, which appear to him, and are of no use; he at last goes to the very abode of the Evil principle *in propria persona*, to evocate a ghost, which appears, and gives him an ambiguous and disagreeable answer; and in the third act he is found by his attendants dying in a tower where he studies his art. You may perceive by this outline that I have no great opinion of this piece of fantasy.

Three or four years ago, when I was writing a chapter on Byron in a little book on the Romantic poets, I was taken in by these throw-away lines. I mean that I took them at their face value, inferred that Byron set little store by his attempts to explore the darker recesses of his nature, and was in fact adopting the very prevalent view that the most authentic Byron is to be found in the man-of-the-world persona of the late satires. I should now go some way to modify that view. Of course Byron meant all and more than he said in *Manfred* and the third canto of *Childe Harold*. The feelings of guilt and madness are as much a part of the real Byron as the cool irony of Juan. All

Byron is doing in these self-mocking letters is making a half-rueful, half-comic acknowledgment that not much of this complex of emotions had managed to get itself expressed. "It is a fine *indistinct* piece of poetical desolation," he says of the *Childe Harold* canto. And Byron is decidedly not a man for the indistinct. He normally inhabits a world of clear outlines; and when he leaves something half-unexplained it does not, as he apparently hopes, suggest further mysterious depths; it simply looks as though he has left something out. Yet I cannot for myself doubt that Childe Harold's sense of isolation from his fellows, of kinship with vast natural forces, Manfred's sense of guilt and moral exhaustion, are authentic and are Byron's own. He is in fact in the midst of a complex psychological crisis that he does not understand; and he is not good at presenting what he does not understand. He has not the power of giving an adequate equivalent for these dark fantasies in myth and fable. Some quite second-rate writers—E. T. A. Hoffmann, for instance—have this power; but Byron can only really confront us with what he knows; he has no machinery at all for exploring an unknown situation.

When Lawrence is faced with a similar problem, his reaction is quite different. At the time he wrote *The Woman Who Rode Away* I should say he was quite as nearly mad as Byron when he wrote the third canto of *Childe Harold*. He was half-way through *The Plumed Serpent*, that vast novel where he is making a strained, terrible effort to evoke a latent religious consciousness which obstinately refuses to come to the surface. Reading between the lines of the memoirs of that period I should say that the effort drove him to the limits of his mental endurance. Yet in *The Woman Who Rode Away* he produces a truthful, lucid, aesthetically beautiful indication of where his current religious quest is actually leading. It is not where he wants to go, it is not the answer that he hopes for; but he has the tools to force his way through this particular patch of psychic jungle, and he has the integrity to use them.

To return to Manfred for a moment. Byron's mocking account of it is not wholly inadequate. What Manfred really evokes the spirits of nature for is to beg them for oblivion—

forgetfulness of some sin or crime in his past that continues to prey upon him. The sin remains obscure, but it seems to be linked to a quasi-incestuous relation with someone who is probably a sister. Whether this sin has really been committed, or whether it is a figment of the hero's diseased imagination, we do not know; nor do we know how or to what extent his partner has been injured by it. We are equally in the dark about Manfred's sense of guilt. Is it a sense of moral guilt—that is, a full, rational acceptance by the total personality of responsibility for a wrong done? Or is it rather an irrational, inexpugnable, unaccepted haunting? We do not know about these things because Byron himself does not know; and Byron does not know because he has no means of finding out. We do not know either what to think about Manfred's death. Is it the solution of his torments; or is it the beginning of an eternity of inexpiable remorse? Byron does not know what he thinks about that either. I need perhaps hardly add that the question of the incest-imbroglio in Byron's own life has never been wholly cleared up. That some such entanglement with his half-sister there was seems clear enough. But what happened and what Byron really felt about it we do not know. It may be that that too was one of the things that Byron did not know himself.

Now consider the conduct of Lawrence when faced with a potential incest situation in actuality. The situation, I mean, that is presented in *Sons and Lovers*, where love for the mother prevents the normal development of love for a girl. What Lawrence does is to use the novel for a tireless, exhaustive exploration of the entanglement that is present in his own life— an exploration so thorough and so successful as far as he personally is concerned, however cruelly tragic for others, that he is able to exorcise the ghost for ever, and pass on freely to new experience. Consider what Lawrence does in *The Woman Who Rode Away*. His attempt to summon up the religion of Ancient Mexico is bogged down, as was almost inevitable. So he temporarily abandons that large unmanageable theme and takes a small type case—that of a white woman who, sick of her own constricted existence, literally and physically rides away to a remote Indian tribe, to learn their ways and to know their gods. She reaches her destination; but what she finds, of course, is death. Her only way of knowing the Indian gods is to be sacrificed to them—and so she is, half-willingly too, in the last lines of the story. It is the death of the woman, and it is the death of the whole white consciousness as well—the whole mode of being of the white western world, weary of its self, willingly going down before an older way of life. Lawrence has found his answer; he was to stare at it appalled for a short time longer, and then to retrace his steps. But an unknown area of his mind has been explored.

We are faced, then, with a striking difference in the reactions of Lawrence and Byron to the unknown. Byron can record its presence, in declamatory or ironical vein; and he can do no more. Lawrence can conquer it, can turn the unknown into the known. How are we to account for the contrast? A great deal of weight must be given, no doubt, to a difference in temperament; Lawrence's psychological insight and tenacity are simply greater. But this is only a part of the explanation. Lawrence succeeds not only by his personal qualities, but because the necessary weapons have been put into his hands. He has been given the key to the potentially incestuous situation in *Sons and Lovers*—he was given it, as a matter of fact, by his wife, who was an ardent if uncritical student of Freud when they first met. He recognises his own emotional entanglement as a case of the classic Oedipus situation as psychoanalysis has revealed it. And thus not only is a quasi-scientific and publicly recognised seal set upon his own insights, but the method of further investigation is also made plain. This is not the place to explain at length what happens in *The Woman Who Rode Away*; but there again, without the illumination provided by the clinical psychologists—particularly, in this case, Jung—Lawrence could never have perceived so clearly the exhaustion of the life of the conscious ego, unfertilised from below; and the catastrophic consequences of this sterile self-sufficiency, preserved too long and lost too suddenly.

And this brings me back to the point from which I started—Byron, the exile of the nineteenth century, Lawrence the exile of the twentieth. We have seen as we went along that they were both exiles in a more than geographical sense; in leaving England they left the organised social community altogether, and each embarked on the solitary adventure of responsibility for his own soul, without the support given by membership of a nation or a defined social rôle. We now see that they started on their adventures very differently equipped. Byron has not only little self-knowledge; he has no technique at all for acquiring any. The spiritual disciplines of religion are closed to him, and he is not a man to sit passively watching the motions of his own mind. Faced with elements within himself that he does not understand he can neither remain content with mystery nor pursue the work of self-exploration. The result of this is the curiously shallow rhetorical nature of Byron's presentation of his own conflicts, what is often called his insincerity. It is not insincerity. "Of the quarrel with others we make rhetoric; of the quarrel with ourselves we make poetry," as Yeats has said. Byron's quarrel is emphatically with himself; but he knows himself so little that it might almost be another person. So that his characteristic mode is neither objective nor subjective poetry, but the production of endless fancy portraits of himself, half objectified as fictitious characters. The more superficial aspects appear in the tales; those deeper layers of his nature that he least understood in *Childe Harold*; and the highly successful persona that he evolved in later years in *Don Juan*. The mark of this kind of writing is energy, not comprehension; it infects us with its own enthusiasm, without leading to any new understanding.

Now I doubt if any writer of the twentieth century could do Byron over again. I do not hold the simple faith that modern analytical psychology has installed street-lighting through all the dark places of the soul; but I do believe that it has laid bare the genesis of many of the Romantic conflicts; and that the mere exhibition of their effects can never be sufficient, is hardly even possible again. So Lawrence, with his improved equipment, is going on to a different kind of journey—not merely to seek adventure, like a knight-errant in a romance, but to make of his adventures a purposeful mission, and to bring back reliable reports. And his characteristic function is not the mere rhetorical presentation of his strange encounters; it is the attempt to re-live them in order that they may be understood, and become the stepping-stones to new experience. He can perform it because he has the tools.

So that when it is said, as it sometimes is, that the new psychologically inspired fantasies of modern literature are simply a continuation of the old romantic mode, that is in a sense true. Both pursue the destiny of the individual soul where the outer restraints of society and socially orientated religion are removed. But the modern has a map and a compass to assist him in the quest, while the earlier Romantic had none. To know that the subjective sense of guilt is something different from objective moral evil; to know of the tension between the conscious and unconscious areas of the mind, to know that the emotional consequences of events that occur in one field may be displaced and reappear in another field that has no apparent connection with the first—to know these and similar things as to-day we almost all do know, is to make the old kind of romantic spiritual adventure impossible; it implies that the spiritual adventurer of to-day is summoned to a different task.

I should regard Lawrence as the supreme example of this new kind of mental traveller—the explorer equipped with admirable apparatus, and determined to bring back results. How much longer that kind of exploration will be possible I do not know. For Lawrence and others of his generation it was all new—the power of the unconscious, the illumination given by dreams and symbols, the mechanism of free association and all the rest of it. They had all the excitement of working with a new, fascinating and effective set of tools. But from the literary point of view they may be tools that after a short time destroy the very material they work on. Let me illustrate. We are agreed, I suppose, that something happened to the sensibility of Europe towards the end of the eighteenth century—individual genius was discovered, the morality of the heart succeeded the morality of prescription, emotion rather than craftsmanship becomes the distinguishing mark of poetry—and so forth. That was the first phase of Romanticism; and it gave rise to innumerable outflowings of feeling, which were valued for their own sake, neither the genesis nor the direction of the feelings being particularly clearly understood, or particularly inquired into. A second phase comes in the later nineteenth century, with the deliberate exploitation of these discoveries; for the symbolists and decadents, the odder and more eccentric these emotional experiences, the more valuable they were. There is still no attempt to subject them to explanation. The third phase is that of our own day. The emotional adventures are still undertaken, and still undertaken with something of the old romantic *panache*. (Think of the motto Freud prefixed to *The Interpretation of Dreams: Flectere si nequeo superos, Acheronta movebo*.) But there is a new motive—the motive to understand and to explain—and new possibilities of fulfilling it. And once the genesis and mechanism of an emotional adventure have been understood, how long can it continue to be an adventure? The answer is, I think, not very long; it soons turns into something else, it turns into a problem, and a problem which is in principle capable of solution. When every educational psychologist knows the solution to the great romantic conflicts, their time as generators of poetic creation has not very long to run. The *enfant du siècle* becomes just a mixed-up kid whose difficulties could have been avoided by better training in the nursery school. The problems that obsess Byron are relegated to group therapy, those that obsess Lawrence to the marriage guidance council. The turmoils of Romanticism, at first exciting because uncomprehended, then exciting because provided with new and fascinating explanations, finally become stereotyped, become predictable, become in the end a bore. When that ultimately occurs, literature will have to turn, until there is some new revolution of the heart and the mind of Europe, to that inexhaustible reservoir of novelty and variety—the outer world.

V

RUSKIN AND ROGER FRY:
TWO AESTHETIC THEORIES

Il y a des gens qui s'émerveillent devant l'ordre miraculeux régis-
sant la nature, qui s'étonnent de la beauté qu'on peut y eprouver.
Je dois dire: c'est au fond ces gens-là qui m'étonnent. Serions-nous
d'un autre monde posséderions-nous une âme non terrestre, il y
aurait lieu de s'étonner de ce que nous comprenions quoi que ce soit
des choses de ce monde. Mais puisque nous sommes de cet univers,
puisque nous faisons partie de ses contingences, il est absolument
naturel que notre entendement s' "entend" avec le reste de cet
univers; et le mot de naturel prend ici son entirère valeur.

Axel Stern.

IT is characteristic of the early part of this century that the most
significant movements in arts were separatist movements.
The current was setting strongly towards a literary man's
literature, consciously concerned with vocabulary and rhythm;
an artist's art, concerned with purely formal values. We can
see its English origins in Whistler's Ten O'Clock lecture and
the literary attitudes of the nineties. Later, we have the appearance of significant form and the pure aesthetic emotion; it becomes a gaffe, not a metaphor, to talk of poetry with the
Platonic and Shelleyan sense of imaginative expression in
general; poetry is what is written in verse, and its function
is to amuse decent people, not to legislate unacknowledged for
the world; and we begin to look at the novel as no ordinary
novel-reader had ever looked upon it, from the point of view
of structure or of texture. Parenthetically, we may note the
preoccupation of philosophy with verbal and logical analysis.
As far as the arts are concerned there are diverse expressions
of this tendency. Sometimes it takes the form of a rather
arty irresponsibility, sometimes of a demand for order and
subordination. But the moves are all actually in the same

direction—they are all part of a movement towards disintegration. They either put the arts into a cloud-cuckoo-land, from which the ordinary preoccupations of mankind are excluded; or into a pigeon-hole where there is no danger of their spilling over into religion, or contaminating ethics. Whatever they may say they are, these are both operations against a unified sensibility. A flower cut and put in water is easier to look at than when it is on the tree, but it has no longer any organic connection with the processes of nature; there is more order and subordination in a regiment than in a family, but there is less organic unity. The main social effect of this movement has been a gradual divorce between the original artist and the public; its literary aspect has been discussed by Edmund Wilson as a wide extension of Symbolism. By now many of its productions have added a permanent enrichment to our experience but are no longer, perhaps, immediately active. Historically speaking, the most obvious thing is that this was all necessary. It was necessary to stop the short-circuiting of the special functions of the arts by a premature recourse to ethical and social considerations. Poetry may be a criticism of life, but it is other things first. In the visual arts especially, and in England above all, this isolation and purgation was needed. In mid-Victorian England the visual sensibilities had reached their lowest ebb, and had left on the foreshore a miscellaneous collection of *objets d'art*, whose most striking characteristic is that they can hardly even have been intended to be looked at. One is reminded of Roger Fry's railway-station restaurant.

> If I were to go on to tell of the legs of the tables, of the electric-light fittings, of the chairs into the wooden seats of which some tremendous mechanical force has deeply impressed a large distorted anthemion—if I were to tell of all these things, my reader and I might both begin to realise with painful acuteness something of the horrible toil involved in all this display. Display is indeed the end and explanation of it all. Not one of these things has been made because the maker enjoyed the making; not one has been bought because its contemplation would give anyone pleasure, but solely because each of these things is accepted as a symbol of a particular social status.

This was written in 1912: the curious thing about it is that it might have been written forty years earlier, by Ruskin or William Morris. The attempt to educate the visual sensibilities that it implies was begun in *Modern Painters* in 1849. Since then it has been more or less continuous: Ruskin and Roger Fry were both engaged on the same enterprise; but their different climates of opinion led them along steadily divergent roads. Perhaps it is because there has been so little English art-criticism that what there is is so expressive of the age in which it was composed. Reynolds, Ruskin and Roger Fry might very well stand as representatives of the eighteenth, nineteenth and twentieth centuries. But Reynolds's *Discourses* are after all the expression of a school doctrine; he is training students in an already established tradition. Ruskin and Roger Fry were more independent: "cussedness" is the word Fry uses about himself, and it would do for Ruskin too: and this pertinacious cussedness enabled them not only to express, but to mould the sensibilities of their times. Both were concerned with the education of the visual sense, concerned to make people experience visual satisfactions that they would never have discovered for themselves; and in this respect both have had a large measure of success. Botticelli's angels would not now hang on thousands of English walls if it had not been for Ruskin; nor Van Gogh's sunflowers if it had not been for Roger Fry. Both men, too, were deeply concerned with the relation of aesthetic experience to the rest of life; and here they are in a field where success or failure is more difficult to determine: they reached very different conclusions and each at any rate found one that was highly significant to his own age. This is a not uninteresting bit of cultural history, but it is also something more. The question of how aesthetic experience is related to the rest of life must concern anyone who cares about the arts; indeed it must concern anyone who tries to look at the rest of life at all comprehensively. The works of Ruskin and Roger Fry provide two typical answers to this question, and in this light, each assumes a symbolic importance beyond himself. To both aesthetic experience was a necessity: Ruskin represents all those to whom it is so necessary that it must be related to all his other deep experiences, religious and ethical: Roger Fry represents those to whom it is so necessary that it must be kept in isolation, pure and unspotted from the world.

Collingwood has suggested that the underlying principle from which all Ruskin's practical thinking springs is the unity and indivisibility of the human spirit, and that this involves a comprehensive belief about the mind, "the belief, namely, that each form of human activity springs not from a special faculty—an organ of the mind, so to speak—but from the whole nature of the person concerned; so that art is not the product of a special part of the mind called the 'aesthetic faculty', nor morality the product of a special 'moral faculty', but each alike is the expression of the whole self". This is of course the result of a philosopher's analysis; Ruskin nowhere says this in so many words. The underlying conviction of unity in any case is liable to find expression in a number of different forms; when it is only half-consciously realised it is apt to be expressed in a series of fragmentary identifications between things usually considered diverse; "the strongest part of our religion is its unconscious poetry"; "all art aspires to the condition of music"; "life is a ritual"; there are a good many of these statements in the air of the later nineteenth century. The particular content of the statement will depend on the particular interests of its author. Ruskin's particular interests being in art, his aim is to show that art is the expression of man's nature as a whole, and cannot be justified by a partial appeal such as that to utility or a special aesthetic sense. As the arts with which he is concerned depend on visual sensibility, it is his business first to show the connection of visual sensibility with the rest of the psychic life.

Ruskin's work is not quite so much of a muddle as is sometimes supposed. The first two volumes of *Modern Painters* attempt a more or less philosophical exposition of his theory; and *The Seven Lamps* and *The Stones of Venice* show it in operation. He starts from the belief that the uneducated senses do not really see what is around them, that it is only after an arduous course of training that we can really be said to see at all. He makes a rather unhappy attempt to connect this with Locke's distinction between sensation and perception; but Locke is distinguishing between the physical fact and its psychic result, Ruskin between attentive and inattentive perception. Actually Locke does not suit his purpose at all well, and he would have been happier with the German idealists, of whom he apparently knew little. By the time he comes to the main exposition of his view, the section of *Modern Painters* on the Theoretic Faculty, he has forgotten all about Locke and taken up with Aristotle, if any-one. He has already, by introspection, come to the conclusion that "bodily sensibility to colour and form is intimately con-nected with that higher sensibility which we revere as one of the chief attributes of all noble minds, and as the chief spring of real poetry". He now decides that the exercise of this sensibility, the intense contemplation of sense impressions, can be identified with the Greek Theoria.

> The Theoretic faculty is concerned with the moral perception and appreciation of ideas of beauty. And the error respecting it is, the considering and calling it Aesthetic, degrading it to a mere operation of sense, or perhaps worse, of custom.

Here Ruskin is making, I believe, essentially the same dis-tinction as Roger Fry makes in his early *Essay in Aesthetics* between the apprehension of beauty as sensuous charm and the apprehension of beauty as a satisfying emotional order. "Beauty in the former sense belongs to works of art where only the perceptual aspect of the imaginative life is exercised, beauty in the second sense becomes as it were supersensual, and is concerned with the appropriateness and intensity of the emotions aroused." But Ruskin's statement would include the works of nature as well as works of art; and he uses the key word "moral" to which we will return in a moment.

He next proceeds to argue that Theoria is produced by the systematic training of the senses, and gives an illustration from the sense of taste. When we first experience two different tastes our preference between them seems entirely outside our control. But by repeated experience and careful attention to the same two tastes we come to perceive qualities in both at first unnoticed: as a result we may ultimately reach a settled pre-ference different from the first which is yet regarded by ourselves, and accepted by others, as more correct. As an account of the way in which most people who have had the opportunity ultimately come to prefer Stilton to Australian cheddar, this seems adequate. But from the nutritive point of view there is nothing to choose between them; the faculty which discriminates between these two cheeses performs no biological function. Ruskin proceeds, then, to distinguish between the purely instrumental uses of the senses and those which are ends in themselves. The lower senses of touch and taste are mainly instrumental, mainly subservient to the purposes of life; though Ruskin believed, as Dr. Summerskill does not, that even they can to a limited degree become ends in themselves without detriment to the total organisation of our nature. But sight and hearing are manifestly more than instrumental.

> They answer not any purpose of mere existence; for the distinction of all that is useful or dangerous to us might be made, and often is made, by the eye, without its receiving the slightest pleasure of sight. We might have learned to distinguish fruits and grains from flowers, without having any superior pleasure in the aspect of the latter; and the ear might have learned to distinguish the sounds that communicate ideas, or to receive intimations of elemental danger, without perceiving either melody in the voice, or majesty in the thunder. And as these pleasures have no function to perform, so there is no limit to their continuance in the accomplishment of their end, for they are an end in themselves, and so may be perpetual with all of us; being in no way destructive, but rather increasing in exquisiteness by repetition.

But when we experience the pleasures of sense we also experience in them a feeling of purpose and adaptation to our desires. The pleasures of sense are not scattered and chance-distributed, but form part of an order which training and practice enable us to perceive. We become conscious, not only of isolated pleasing forms, but of a whole formal order in nature. The experience of this formal order is accompanied by an intense sense of the power that has given rise to it. Like the natural theologians of the eighteenth century Ruskin finds that the study of the order of Nature leads to God; though he studies it under a different aspect, and it is revealed to him in beauty of design rather than in practical adaptation. Art is one mode of the

M

study and exhibition of that order. Ruskin does not distinguish clearly between aesthetic satisfaction received from Nature and that received from art. Both are perceptions of a formal order, and the order is in both cases designed and purposive. Nature he regards as the direct agent of a personal God, and he often speaks as though Nature were a conscious artist, aiming deliberately at beauty of form. The human artist abstracts and reproduces fragments of the design he has perceived in nature. He may employ any degree of abstraction in doing so, but however far he departs from representational accidents, it is still from the perception of a formal order in nature that his work has started. Out of which perception, Ruskin says, still speaking theistically, arise joy, admiration and gratitude. (But those who are not theists would equally admit that some emotions of this kind are the inseparable accompaniments of the perception of formal order in nature, or the exhibition of it in art.) Thus we cannot go far in the cultivation of the senses without going beyond the purely sensual. Aesthesis, or the "mere animal consciousness of the pleasantness", passes into Theoria, or "the exulting, reverent and grateful perception of it". And this perception Ruskin calls moral.

It is perhaps easier to say what Ruskin does not mean by this than what he does. He does not mean, for example, that the value of a work of art corresponds to the moral value of the emotions expressed: nor is he using the word moral in any private sense of his own: he is using it in the quite common sense of "pertaining to character and conduct". He means in the first place that the perception of beauty or formal order is not isolated from the rest of life; secondly, that it is not an affair of the intellect, or purely of the senses, but of the moral life in the widest sense, the life of the emotions and the will. He does not mean, either, that the artist uses a sense of form to reproduce the previously existent emotions of actual life, love, sympathy, terror and what not, inspired by other than formal occurrences. The emotion from which the work of art springs is derived directly from the perception of formal order. But these emotions are a part of the general emotional life. The feelings aroused in us by space, by masses at rest, by unity and variety of form, are in fact the emotions of ordinary life, not a special category of their own. All sensitive natures experience these emotions on perceiving certain aspects of form and colour.

> One, however, of these child instincts, I believe that few forget, the emotion, namely, caused by all open ground, or lines of any spacious kind against the sky, behind which there might be conceived the sea. It is an emotion more pure than that caused by the sea itself, for I recollect distinctly running down behind the banks of a high beach to get their land line cutting against the sky, and receiving a more strange delight from this than from the sight of the ocean.

It is from experiences of this kind, though they may later become infinitely more complex, that all our delight in form arises. Ruskin's exposition of this point of view is scattered throughout his work; *Modern Painters* especially is devoted to it. It has been less clearly apprehended than it might have been because it is diffuse and elaborate, and also because it has constantly been expressed in theistic terms. To be talked to about God when he wants to look at pictures is apt to make the twentieth-century reader feel apprehensive. I believe that the alarm is unjustified. To Ruskin the formal attributes that delight us do so because they are a type of the Divine attributes: but without using theistic terminology at all the matter can still be explained. In experiencing the pleasures of sense, Ruskin says, we experience also the feeling of purpose and adaptation to our desires. Let us admit that the feeling of purpose may be illusory, and that Ruskin is often absurd in talking as though a personified Nature had made things beautiful merely for our satisfaction. The feeling, however, is still there; the pleasures of sense do seem adapted to our desires: and this is so because the world of forms and colours that we apprehend is an aspect of nature, of which we ourselves, our purposes and our desires, are also a part. Masses and space affect us emotionally because we are, among other things, masses extended in space. The perception of an order in nature affects us because it corresponds to a similar order in our own minds. It is possible of course to say that it is only our own minds that import this order into nature: in either case the satisfaction we experience is a recognition of our immersion in the natural world, a perception of our share in the order of nature. The extent to which we are capable of this depends partly on acuteness of sense-perception; but it depends still more on the quality of our general response to the world, what Ruskin would call the moral quality of our lives. Like Wordsworth, Ruskin could describe himself as

> well-pleased to recognise
> In nature and the language of the sense
> The anchor of my purest thoughts, the nurse,
> The guide, the guardian of my heart, and soul
> Of all my moral being.

The emotions aroused by the world of form and colour perpetually overflow and mingle with the whole complex of emotions that make up our moral life. Hence it is without metaphor that Ruskin can speak of nobility in a natural scene or in the ornament of a Venetian capital.

In his best writing Ruskin does not use this idea as a means of by-passing the special functions of the arts and getting on to moral ground where he feels more secure. An appendix to *The Stones of Venice* is devoted to the thesis "that the business of a painter is to paint": he goes on to reprove the purists who, out of admiration for Fra Angelico and the moral and "expressional" qualities of art, would altogether "despise those men, Veronese and Rubens, for instance, who were painters par excellence, and in whom the expressional qualities were subordinate". Rubens's "masculine and universal sympathy" is as much an expression of man's moral nature as the delicate devotion of Angelico. The connection of art with morality is not that it expresses any particular kind of morality; but it does inevitably express not merely the technical skill, but the whole ethos of the artist and of the civilisation that produced him. *The Seven Lamps* and *The Stones of Venice* provide continual illustrations of this, some of them brilliant, like the chapter on the Nature of Gothic, some of them absurd, like the vagaries on Popery and Protestantism in cornices. The absurdities call attention to themselves, but they do not invalidate the general aim and method. Much of Ruskin's most illuminating criticism is done in moments of transition between technicalities and preaching; and whatever it is in less comprehensive minds, the continual tendency in him to pass from description and analysis of form to sociology, ethics or religion is a sign of strength, not of weakness. Indeed I believe that Ruskin is only doing continuously and on principle what all critics of art do more or less. You cannot say very much about the formal qualities of a design without going beyond purely formal terms; and Roger Fry, in his early work, continually makes this transition; as in this passage from his edition of Reynolds's *Discourses*:

> In all that concerns the building up of a composition by the adjustment and balance of lighted and shaded planes Guercino must be accounted a scientific, if not an inspired master. . . . Guercino was in a double sense an eclectic, since he learned his design from Lodovico Caracci, and combined with that the strong light and shade of the Naturalistic school. . . . For all that, there is a virility and force about this St. Bruno which the Caracci would have considered vulgar and wanting in ideality.

The formal, the historical and the emotional estimates are all at work here: but the terms in which this last is discussed—virility, force, vulgarity, ideality—are moral terms, in the sense in which Ruskin uses the word when he says that "the characteristic or moral elements of Gothic" are savageness, grotesqueness, rigidity and so forth. The passage from Roger Fry, as we have said, is an early one. We must now trace the process by which he came in his later writings to consider this apparently natural mode of expression illegitimate. He has himself summarised it with his customary lucidity in the *Retrospect*, written in 1920, at the end of *Vision and Design*.

He here sums up the view of his early *Essay in Aesthetics* (1909) by saying that he conceived the form of the work of art to be its most essential quality, but believed this form to be the direct outcome of an apprehension of some emotion of actual life by the artist. By an emotion of actual life he means what we might call a dramatic emotion derived from some aspect of human relationships: the forms of the angels in Giotto's *Pietà* are the outcome of "a raging frenzy of compassion". Fry's early writing is so haunted by this question of the relation between the dramatic emotion and the formal qualities of works of art, that it is curious to note how little, by comparison, it troubled Ruskin. Ruskin finds that what he calls the "expressional" and the "artistical" qualities are in fact always combined in a work of art, and there he is content to leave it. No doubt a good deal of this difference between the two is due to the difference of their early interests. Ruskin's early work is almost all on landscape, where the dramatic emotion can hardly be said to exist, while Fry's was particularly on paintings of religious themes, where the question of the dramatic representation of human emotion is continually brought to the fore. It was fortunate for Ruskin that this was so: in his age and with his lights he could hardly have said much that was useful about Roger Fry's problem: indeed when he does touch upon it he is particularly unilluminating. As it was, his energies were directed to a train of thought that he was exceptionally fitted to pursue—the elaborate analysis of the visual appearance of nature. Roger Fry on the other hand, in a long essay of 1901, wrestles with the task of explaining the frescoes of Giotto in a way which will do justice to both their formal and their dramatic qualities.

> In the *Pietà* a more epic conception is realised, for the impression conveyed is of a universal and cosmic disaster: the air is rent with the shrieks of desperate angels whose bodies are contorted in a raging frenzy of compassion. And the effect is due in part to the increased command, which the Paduan frescoes show, of simplicity and logical directness of design. These massive boulder-like forms, these draperies cut only by a few large sweeping folds, which suffice to give the general movement of the figure with unerring precision, all show this new tendency in Giotto's art as compared with the more varied detail, the more individual characterisation of his early works.

Here, as he says himself in the *Retrospect*, he seems to regard the dramatic emotion and the formal expression of it as completely fused. But even here he is doubtful and rather on the defensive about this point of view.

> It is true that in speaking of these frescoes one is led inevitably to talk of elements in the work which modern criticism is apt to regard as lying outside the domain of pictorial art. It is custo-

mary to dismiss all that concerns the dramatic presentation of the
subject as literature or illustration, which is to be sharply distinguished from the qualities of design. But can this clear distinction be drawn in fact?

Yet he continues to develop this attitude, with its implied
opposition to Whistlerian impressionism, up to the time of the
Essay in Aesthetics, and from it arises what is perhaps Fry's
most illuminating piece of theorising, the attempt to show how
purely formal and sensuous qualities come to affect our emotions.

> The first element is that of the rhythm of the line with which
> the forms are delineated.
> The drawn line is the record of a gesture, and that gesture is
> modified by the artist's feeling which is thus communicated to
> us directly.
> The second element is mass. When an object is so repre-
> sented that we recognise it as having inertia, we feel its power of
> resisting movement, or communicating its own movement to
> other bodies, and our imaginative reaction to such an image is
> governed by our experience of mass in actual life.
> The third element is space. The same-sized square on two
> pieces of paper can be made by very simple means to appear
> to represent either a cube two or three inches high, or a cube
> of hundreds of feet, and our reaction to it is proportionately
> changed.
> . . . Now it will be noticed that nearly all these emotional
> elements of design are connected with essential conditions of
> our physical existence: rhythm appeals to all the sensations
> which accompany muscular activity; mass to all the infinite
> adaptations to the force of gravity which we are forced to make;
> the spatial judgment is equally profound and universal in its
> application to life.

The passage is too long to quote in full, but it is a brilliant
contribution to what is perhaps the basic question in all the
arts—the connection between their complex and dynamic emotional effects, and the relatively simple and inert material
means by which they are produced. It is incomparably more
compressed and lucid than anything in Ruskin, but it belongs
to the same order of ideas as many passages in *The Seven Lamps
of Architecture* and *The Stones of Venice*.

Unhappily he does not proceed with it, but goes on to sum up
his views on the relation of art to nature from another point of

view. He admits "that there is beauty in Nature: that is to say that certain objects constantly do, perhaps any object may, compel us to regard it with that intense disinterested contemplation that belongs to the imaginative life": but that in objects created to arouse the aesthetic emotion, we have the added consciousness of purpose, that the artist "made it on purpose, not to be used but to be regarded and enjoyed, and that this feeling is characteristic of the aesthetic judgment proper". He feels too at this stage that pure formal elements, not allied to representation, are relatively weak in their effect on our emotions. When the artist wishes to arouse our emotions, he represents natural objects which are in themselves emotive, and uses them in such a way that the forms themselves, abstracted from that which they represent, generate in us emotional states, based on the physiological necessities which he has attempted to analyse above. Thus he reached two conclusions which were not necessary to Ruskin—that natural forms themselves cannot arouse powerful aesthetic emotions because they are not purposively designed: and that the artist's purpose must be fulfilled by representing objects which are in themselves emotive. Ruskin escapes from both these conclusions because he believes in the first place that natural forms *are* purposively designed, are made on purpose to be regarded and enjoyed as well as used; and secondly that they can arouse a powerful aesthetic emotion, apart from representation, because the main element of the aesthetic, or in his terms theoretic, emotion is the admiring and grateful sense of this purpose.

Fry's view, then, depends on his implicit denial of purpose in nature, and his extreme preoccupation with the expression of dramatic emotion. It was not likely that he would long remain satisfied with this. The dramatic emotion is clearly of great importance with some artists—Giotto for instance; with others —Cézanne, landscape painters in general—it seems hardly to occur at all. It cannot therefore be used to explain art in general. But the question of the dramatic emotion has so obsessed Fry's thinking, that when he is forced to give it up he feels bound to give up altogether the connection of the aesthetic experience with the rest of the emotional life. Instead of seeking a solution along the lines, for instance, that he himself had already in-dicated—the connection of our experience of form with the necessary conditions of our physical existence, and thus with the source of some of our deepest emotions—he now begins the attempt to isolate the experience of formal relations from every other kind of experience.

The turning-point in Fry's thought occurred when he be-came acquainted with the work of Cézanne; this was followed by the study of other post-Impressionists, and resulted in the organisation of the post-Impressionist exhibition in 1911. As a consequence of this study Fry discovered first "that art had begun to recover once more the language of design"; secondly (this must have been the result of conversations with post-Impressionist artists themselves) that artists who were ex-tremely sensitive to formal relations often had almost no sense of the emotions he supposed them to convey. He considers the case of Raphael's "Transfiguration" and finds that the means used to convey the dramatic emotion have become so out of date that they no longer succeed in conveying it at all. Yet the formal relations still stand, and still constitute a great picture. He concludes that people have formerly supposed themselves to be moved by the dramatic emotions when they were really moved by purely formal considerations. He suggests that when Goethe explains the unity of this composition by saying "Below, the suffering and the needy; above, the powerful and helpful—mutually dependent, mutually illustrative", he was really moved by the coherence of the design, but mistook the source of his emotion and gave an explanation in moral terms.

Faced with this difficulty Fry concludes that the only solution is to abandon, along with the dramatic emotion, all attempt to relate the formal experience to the emotions of the rest of life, and to isolate "this purely aesthetic quality to which Mr. Clive Bell gives the name of 'significant form'". But he never quite accepts in its entirety this conception, most closely associated with the name of Mr. Clive Bell, of "the pure contemplation of spatial relations . . . independent of all associations from past life". Indeed he hardly could, for he has himself brilliantly shown how our contemplation of spatial relations is inevitably bound up with the physical conditions of our existence, hence with a whole complex of associations from past life. And it is this haunting sense of dissatisfaction with the isolation of pure formal experience that makes Roger Fry's work so interesting.

Yet the gulf between our sense of form in a work of art and our previous experience of form in nature is to him impassable because he cannot feel that there is any purpose in the forms of nature: the formal material that nature provides must therefore always remain an "intractable material which is alien to our spirit". To Ruskin there was no difficulty; his theistic philosophy can easily bridge the gulf; the forms of nature are beautiful to us because God intended them to be so. We are impelled then to ask ourselves whether the attempt to relate aesthetic experiences to the other experiences of life is dependent on a theistic philosophy. It has already been suggested that it is not. Yet it seems probable that it is dependent on some unifying principle, on some attitude in which it is possible to see all our diverse experiences from a single point. The concluding passage of *Vision and Design*, where Fry discussed the value of the aesthetic emotion, indicates that he himself realised this.

> As to the value of the aesthetic emotion—it is clearly infinitely removed from those ethical values to which Tolstoy would have confined it. It seems to be as remote from actual life and its practical utilities as the most useless mathematical theory. One can only say that those who experience it feel it to have a peculiar quality of "reality" which makes it a matter of infinite importance in their lives. Any attempt I might make to explain this would probably land me in the depths of mysticism. On the edge of that gulf I stop.

But why stop? If a train of thought has led to a point where it can only be completed by mysticism, why not complete it nevertheless? It is here that the contemporary climate of opinion, the unrecognised philosophical *ambiente*, becomes important. At the back of Fry's thought, as of that of so many intellectuals in his time, there seems to be an unstated but ever-present belief that any unifying principle must be inadmissible, that any attempt to survey experience comprehensively must be obscurantist and slightly disreputable. Hence Fry's use of the word mysticism, which I think is used here at least partly in the pejorative sense of something cloudy and ill-defined. So Roger Fry's theory must remain incomplete: having gone as far as anyone in the sensitive experience and lucid analysis of the aesthetic emotions, he leaves them cut off, drawing no nourishment from the rest of life, giving none to it. This perhaps is the reason that Fry's writing has had less effect on the general mind than Ruskin's, in spite of its vastly greater clarity. His aesthetic theory remains like a beautiful new motor-car, its lines admirably designed for power and ease of control; the only thing necessary to make it go is that he should put some petrol in it. But faced with that awe-compelling necessity he stops.

He feels that mysticism is a gulf in whicn the intelligence must suffer shipwrecks. There are of course those who would still take the plunge. *E il naufragar m'è dolce in questo mare.* But the kind of mysticism necessary to complete Roger Fry's theory is hardly more mysterious than the existence of a pure aesthetic emotion unrelated to anything else. The pure contemplation of spatial and formal relations gives us a sense of reality because it is an apprehension of one kind of reality—the formal nature of the world of which we are a part. Experiences of space and form are a part of our ordinary experience. Both Ruskin and Roger Fry have been particularly skilful at analysing them and their emotional effects. It is of such experiences that the aesthetic experience is made up. There is nothing particularly rare about them: the only thing that is rare is the education of the sensibilities to a degree at which we become fully conscious of them, become capable of abstracting them from the accidents by which they are attended. By intense contemplation of such experiences of form and space we become conscious of the unity between ourselves and the natural world: the formal material which nature provides is no longer an "intractable material which is alien to our spirit"; our experience of it is a part of the conditions of our existence. It is true that this sense of unity is always being lost; the artist has to recreate it. Often his personal mode of doing so is incomprehensible to his age; then the visual sensibility has to be re-educated, and few men have done more of this than Ruskin and Roger Fry. But Ruskin is clearer about what he is doing: as the wide tracts of Modern Painters begin to open out before him he realises that his business "is not now to distinguish between disputed degrees of ability in individuals, or agreeableness in canvases; it is not now to expose the ignorance or defend the principles of party or person; it is to summon the moral energies of the nation to a forgotten duty, to display the use, force and function of a great body of neglected sympathies and desires".

The words Roger Fry needs to complete his theory are quoted by Ruskin from Linnaeus's *Systema Naturae: Deum sempiternum, immensum, omniscium, omnipotentem expergefactus transeuntem vidi, et obstupui.* "As one awakened out of sleep I saw the Lord passing by—eternal, infinite, omniscient and omnipotent, and I stood as in a trance." That is expressed in theistic terms, but it is a mistake to suppose that what has been expressed in theistic terms is necessarily unavailable to those who are unwilling to use them. We must continue, as Ruskin does, the quotations from Linnaeus. "I saw animals dependent on vegetables, vegetables on things earthly, things earthly on the globe of the earth, then, by never -shaken law, the globe of the earth to revolve around the sun from which it has its loan of life." That is the sort of unified vision of the world attainable by natural science: but it is wholly analogous to the unified vision attainable by art. The vision of Linnaeus did not come by an unrelated intuition, but as a result of years of precise observation of particulars. So the aesthetic vision described by Roger Fry does not come unexplained, unrelated, as the gift of a special aesthetic sense, but as a result of a multitude of experiences of individual forms and relations. It is Roger Fry's special distinction to have shown that the aesthetic experience is not compounded out of pre-existent dramatic emotions, as the literary critic of art would have it. It is Ruskin's special distinction to show how it is abstracted from a multitude of sense-experiences, to have shown how the experience of the senses can lead directly to that unified apprehension of nature, and of ourselves as a part of nature, which can fairly constantly be recognised, under various mythological disguises, not only as that which gives value to aesthetic experience, but also as one of the major consolations of philosophy.

Part Three

VI

GEORGE MOORE AND THE NINETIES

I

I AM not one who oft or much delights in contemplating the division of literary history into periods: at best it is a barren exercise. Nevertheless it has a certain importance; largely a negative importance. No doubt all history is a seamless web, and everything is continuous with everything else, and our subdivisions are imposed and arbitrary schemes. No doubt these schemes have no substantial existence, and we have no real criterion for deciding that one is right and another wrong; the most we can say is that some are appropriate and useful and others less so. The best-laid scheme cannot give us much positive assistance; but regarded simply as a heuristic mechanism an inappropriate scheme can do a good deal to deform our picture of literary history. It has seemed to me for a long time that the concept of "the Victorian age" has had just this effect. The Victorian age presumably extends from somewhere about the accession of that respectable monarch in 1837 to her death in 1901. But the life of the spirit does not coincide very accurately with the vicissitudes of the temporal power, and as a division of literary history this slice of time makes very little sense. It has presented us with the picture of an age of patient moral and social fervour on the one hand, of the slow decline of the Romantic impulse on the other, both fading into a sort of penumbra after the Victorian heyday. This is succeeded by a short space of total eclipse, until the darkness is dispelled by the sudden emergence of the light of Eliot and Pound. What we have here is plainly not a very complete or accurate account of what went on, so we have been persuaded to intercalate a short period called the nineties, just to signalise our recognition of the fact that various changes were taking place. As an alternative I should like to propose for consideration a period extending from about 1880 to 1914, a period distinct in spirit from what we usually think of as Victorianism, a period in which all the foundations of modern literature were being laid, but recognisably distinct from modern literature too. I am not quite sure about 1880; a case might be made for putting the beginning of our period back into the seventies, perhaps to the publication of Pater's *Renaissance* in 1873; but on balance 1880 is probably about right. It is not until the late seventies that the influence of Pater becomes decisive on style and feeling, or that the influence of French realism begins to make itself felt in the novel. And as for 1914—perhaps it ought to be 1910; but 1914 is such a landmark in cultural as well as political history that it seems the most appropriate point to choose.

A paper on the nineties should not ideally begin by abolishing the nineties, or by merging them in a larger unit; and one may well concede that it is in the nineties that the tendencies of the period find their fullest expression. It is the decade of the one serious poetical cenacle, the Rhymer's Club; of the two most characteristic literary magazines, *The Yellow Book* and *The Savoy*; of what is probably the best of the English realist novels, Moore's *Esther Waters*; and of the great social-literary scandal, the Oscar Wilde trial. But a decade is an embarrassing unit in literary history; in general it is far too short to be useful, and there is not a writer of any weight in the nineties whose significant work does not extend outside them. One has only to cite the names of James, Hardy, Conrad, Moore, Gissing and Yeats. It is sometimes said that the nineties were not an attitude but a state of mind—a state whose peculiar colour has been variously described as mauve and greenery-yallery. This is a good enough starting-point for period nostalgia, a vision of the poppies and the lilies, the green nightgowns, the blue china, the gaslamps reflected in a Whistlerian Thames, the Sickert music-halls, and Sherlock Holmes's Inverness cape. One may become an addict to these historic stimulants, but they do not really tell us very much. And the trouble about the actual achievements of the nineties in their most characteristic forms is that they are so minuscule. The poetry of Dowson and Lionel Johnson, Cracken-thorpe's stories and Henry Harland's, will not bear very much weight. Yeats's ninetyish phase is largely proleptic—it looks forward to a much greater achievement of a different kind later on. And Wilde, except as a personality and a portent, seems to me a greatly overrated figure. So if we insist on looking at the nineties by themselves we are presented with a decade where many forces are stirring but not to any very complete purpose.

Having proposed a longer period as the appropriate unit I should like just to suggest its general characteristics; but only in a very summary fashion, since the bare existence of these twenty-five years as a literary concept has not yet been generally recognised, still less examined. I see three principal develop-ments. First, a greatly increased range and a new freedom in the choice of subjects from actual life; all that we ordinarily call realism. I shall not make any distinction between realism and naturalism, for though in French literary history they are always carefully distinguished, this has no particular relevance to English, and in the controversy of the eighties the word realism is the one that always seems to have been used. Leaving aside the shocked indignation, of which of course there was much, we can get an idea of the cautious welcome extended to realism, and the recognition both of its novelty and its foreign origin, from Henry James's remarks on Zola:

A novelist with a system, a passionate conviction, a great plan—incontestable attributes of M. Zola—is not now easily to be found in England or the United States, where the story-teller's art is almost exclusively feminine, is mainly in the hands of timid (even when very accomplished) women, whose acquaintance with life is severely restricted, and who are not conspicuous for general views. The novel, moreover, among ourselves, is almost always addressed to young unmarried ladies, or at least always assumes them to be a large part of the novelist's public.

This fact, to a French story-teller, appears, of course, a damnable restriction. . . . Half of life is a sealed book to young unmarried ladies, and how can a novel be worth anything that deals with only half of life? These objections are perfectly valid, and it may be said that our English system is a good thing for virgins and boys, and a bad thing for the novel itself, when the novel is regarded as something more than a simple *jeu d'esprit*,

N   181

and considered as a composition that treats of life at large and helps us to *know*.

I take this quotation from an advertisement for the series of translations of Zola published by Vizetelly from 1884 onwards. Vizetelly was of course the publisher who was most closely associated with the realist movement; he was prosecuted for his publications and eventually imprisoned, in 1888. In subsequent comment on the affair he is generally represented as a sort of martyr for culture, but a further perusal of the advertisement pages I am speaking of leads one to take this with just a small pinch of salt. It may be that Vizetelly was filled only with a pure desire to serve modern letters and to show contemporary society the realities on which it was based, but it is also fairly evident that Vizetelly's Realistic Novels are advertised with half an eye towards a possibly scandalous success; and I mention this because the suggestion that "This is not for young ladies" (or the alternative suggestion that "This will certainly be read by young ladies but their parents ought not to know"), made seriously, or defiantly, or with a behind-the-hand snigger, is a very recognisable element in the literature of this time, quite as recognisable as the high Victorian attitude of Tennyson—

> The prudent partner of his blood
> Lean'd on him, faithful, gentle, good,
> Wearing the rose of womanhood—

—and so forth. The advertisement of George Moore's *A Mummer's Wife*, for example, begins by announcing, "This book has been placed in the Index Expurgatorius of the Select Circulating Libraries of Messrs. Mudie and W. H. Smith and Son."

Second, a confused set of tendencies that cluster round the notion of "art for art's sake". These never amount to a formal doctrine in England, and hold together in a loose synthesis a number of different ideas, mostly derived from France. Parnassians, Symbolists, Decadents—these school labels have a tolerably plain meaning in French literary history, but English literary ideas are much less clearly analysed. "Art for art's sake", for what the phrase is worth, goes back to Gautier, and

Gautier had been an influence on Swinburne in the sixties. Transposed into a moral, rather than a literary code, it reappears in the conclusion to Pater's *Renaissance*; and the cult of exquisite sensations, expressed in the languid Paterian rhythms, haunts the production of the nineties and extends some considerable distance into this century. But the strictly literary ideals to which it gave rise remain shifting and uncertain. On the one hand we are constantly hearing echoes of "L'Art", the last poem in *Emaux et Camées*, with its praise of a hard-chiselled perfection of form.

> Lutte avec le carrare,
> Avec le paros dur
>   Et rare,
> Gardiens du contour pur;
>
> Peintre, fuis l'aquarelle,
> Et fixe la couleur
>   Trop frêle
> Au four de l'emailleur.

On the other hand, the quite contrary doctrine of Verlaine's "Art Poètique":

> Il faut aussi que tu n'ailles point
> Chosir tes mots sans quelque méprise:
> Rien de plus cher que la chanson grise
> Ou l'Indécis au Précis se joint.
>
> Car nous voulons la Nuance encore,
> Pas la Couleur, rien que la Nuance!

So that we are left uncertain whether the prevalent ideal is an intaglio cut in the hardest stone or a misty Whistler nocturne. But what these ideals have in common is an insistence on the claims of the artist as artificer against those of the artist as interpreter of life. "The Yellow Dwarf", the pseudonymous book reviewer of *The Yellow Book* (his name, by the way, is borrowed from *Le Nain Jaune*, a Parnassian periodical of the sixties) makes a great point of the purely aesthetic nature of his criticism, and is greatly disturbed when he suspects that a work of fiction might have a moral, or be intended as a tract for the times. And, as in France, this lightweight aestheticism passes over into Symbolism. Whether there is anything in English letters that can be called a Symbolist movement I am not sure; but the word seems inevitable, and is not without its uses. Symbolism can be said to occur when the cult of the exquisite, particular sensation, embodied in the perfect form, begins to acquire transcendental overtones, begins to be seen as a means of access to a more authentic world underlying the world of appearances. As a half-sentimental literary idea we see this floating around in a good many places. As a serious conviction, involving the whole moral and literary personality, we see it in the early essays of Yeats.

Now these two tendencies, the realist and the symbolist-aesthetic, are inveterately opposed in France. But in England they show a curious tendency to fuse together. This is because moral ideas in England are commonly clearer and more strongly held than literary ones; a literary controversy tends to shift itself to the moral plane. And morally the two different schools are in fact moving in the same direction. Both place the demands of art outside and above moral exigencies, and the need for a moral emancipation is so much more pressing in England that it obscures other differences. The movement may be towards fantasy and dream, or it may be towards the recognition of the most sordid social actualities; but these do not feel themselves to be vitally opposed, for they are both expressions of the same need. Moral and psychological adventurousness and the pursuit of an exquisite and refined form go hand in hand in England, and even tend to be seen as much the same thing. George Eliot, we may notice, comes in for equally heavy knocks on both counts —for lumbering bluntness of style and form, and for the ever-present moral superintendence under which her work is seen to labour.

The third very marked feature of the time is a conscious re-action against the English literary tradition. This is something relatively new, at any rate since neo-classical times. It formed no part of the Romantic upheaval, though I suppose a foretaste of it may be found in Matthew Arnold's exhortations against English provincialism and complacency. But the reaction I am speaking of has a new flavour, and it continues into the most formative literature of our time. It is the beginning of that chronic Francophilia that affects many of the Anglo-American intelligentsia even to our own day. The manifestations that first leap to the mind are the slightly absurd ones—Pater murmuring that Poe was so coarse, he could only read him in Baudelaire's translation; Wilde writing *Salome* in not very good French; the scraps of French idiom that interlard the pages of Henry James—down to the still current illusions that French coffee is good and the architecture of Paris beautiful. Of course the influence of France was necessary, it was the only one possible, it was an example of that perpetual process of fruitful interchange of which the history of European letters is composed. But there was in this particular wave of French influence an element of affectation. Yeats's use of Mallarmé—whom he cannot possibly have understood—as a name to conjure with provides us with one instance. There went with it a slightly perverse determination to throw overboard some of the most characteristic achievements of the English genius—Moore's dismissal of Shakespeare and the traditional English novel for example. Without the slightest leaning to that absurdest of attitudes, a literary nationalism, it remains true that the actual achieved body of work in a given language is an inescapable condition for future work. The nineties show signs of wishing to make an escape; and, though this is another subject, and complicated by Anglo-American literary relations, the tendency persisted into the *avant-garde* of the twentieth century.

II

In a period where many of the representative writings are on a very small scale it is difficult to find a typical figure to stand for the central movement of the time. I have a candidate to propose for this office; it is George Moore. There is no particular virtue in being typical; but even if it is the portrait of an age that we are trying to draw there are advantages in examining an individual man, an actual writer, rather than tendencies exhibited in fragments. George Moore has qualifications that will be particularly useful to us in this respect. In the first place he exists. He is discernible with the naked eye, which can hardly be said for Crackenthorpe or Dowson. Never quite in the centre of the picture, he nevertheless played a real part in the literary history of the *fin-de-siècle*, and in his vivid outrageous autobiography he has played a considerable part in chronicling it. He has a large body of work to his credit, uneven, it is true, but some of it of undeniable excellence, and much of it of peculiar interest. And although his career extends far into this century he remained remarkably faithful to the intuitions of his earlier years. Even his defects are for our present purpose a recommendation. Moore was not Prince Hamlet, nor was meant to be; almost at times the fool. He was incapable of what in any ordinary acceptation of the term would be called thought. He picks up ideas from everywhere, never understands them quite thoroughly or thinks them out, mixes them up to make a miscellaneous stew and often pretends to knowledge that he does not really possess. As an informant on matters of fact he is unreliable in the extreme. To anyone attempting a critical examination of Moore, particularly to anyone who is sensible of his merits, these are highly embarrassing qualities. But if we want to feel the shape and pressure of the time they are extremely useful ones. He wrote of himself:

> My soul, so far as I understand it, has very kindly taken colour and form from the many various modes of life that self-will and an impetuous temperament have forced me to indulge in. Therefore I may say that I am free from original qualities, defects, tastes, etc. . . . I came into the world apparently with a nature like a smooth sheet of wax, bearing no impress but capable of receiving any; of being moulded into all shapes.

And it is so with his literary development too; he picks up like a magpie all the notions and influences that were at large in the world around him, spills them out with an air of proud discovery—in fact, as Oscar Wilde said of him, conducts his education in public. If we want to find out what the literary scene looked like to a young man of advanced tastes in the eighties and nineties we can hardly do better than look at his early works. Greater literary personalities will tell us less. The tireless spiritual energy of Yeats, the quick-witted positiveness of Shaw, are too idiosyncratic to tell us much except about their possessors.

The document I wish to look at is the *Confessions of a Young Man*. It was written in 1886; it refers to a period between 1873, when Moore first went to Paris, and 1883, when his first novel appeared; and as we now have it, it was annotated by its author at two later dates. I remember abominating it when I first read it, years ago; and it does indeed give the picture of an intolerable young coxcomb. But I entirely failed to see its significance. It is an account of Moore's literary education, and pretty well the complete account, since he was almost illiterate when he first went to France. It is an education picked up in cafés and studios, the editorial offices of magazines, and the Gaiety bar. We need not stickle for the factual accuracy of the story. The apartment with the red drawing-room, the Buddha, the python and the Turkish couches is unlikely to have been as Moore describes it in the mid-seventies. It seems to owe far too much to Huysmans' *A Rebours*. And *A Rebours* did not come out till 1884. What we are contemplating in fact is a panoramic view of the formation of a taste and an attitude, of all the varied aesthetic and social influences that went to make it, from the standpoint of 1886. It is a view that still seemed valid to Moore in 1904, and even beyond the limits of our period, in 1916.

The inevitable first reaction to the book is to find it an appalling muddle. Enthusiasms and recantations seem to follow each other in no sort of order. Every opinion is contradicted by its opposite a few pages farther on. There are no dates, and no possibility of making the story into an intelligible chronological sequence. Then one realises that Moore is perfectly well aware of this, and has even made his capriciousness into a sort of principle. "Never could I interest myself in a book", he writes, "if it were not the exact diet my mind required at the time, or in the very immediate future." And later, in excusing himself for lack of sensibility to Shakespeare, "There are affinities in literature corresponding to, and very analogous to, sexual affinities—the same unreasoned attractions, the same pleasures, the same lassitudes. Those we have loved most we are most indifferent to. Shelley, Gautier, Zola, Flaubert, Goncourt!

187

how I have loved you all; and now I could not, would not, read you again." But there are other ways of revealing a sensibility and an attitude than the ordered chronological *Bildungsroman*. This pell-mell jumble of passions and revulsions spreads out, as it were, the contents of Moore's imagination for our inspection; and we can see that the objects displayed, apparently a mere chance assortment, actually fall into two groups. One group is composed of fantasies and dreams, often slightly perverse fantasies and dreams, unchecked by bourgeois ethics of ordinary social reality. The other group consists of equally passionate aspirations after the actualities of life, the tangible realities of contemporary experience and modern urban living. These two enthusiasms sometimes clash violently. Each at times tries to deny the existence of the other, yet both continue to exist—and even in the end come to a kind of reconciliation. They are united, not only as the most staring opposites may be, by the accident of inhering in the same personality, but by a real common factor. The common element is the purely literary one, the need that each passion has to find its fullest and justest verbal expression. Starting with a notable ignorance of both English grammar and the English vocabulary, Moore ultimately finds the ruling passion of his life in the desire to write well.

Fantasy and dream came first, and came even at first in a verbal embodiment. His first literary passion was for the mere name of a novel he heard his parents discussing—*Lady Audley's Secret*. This was followed by the revelation of Shelley, also turned to initially for the same reason. "Lady Audley! What a beautiful name! . . . Shelley! That crystal name, and his poetry also crystalline." Most of the English lyric poets were read soon after. But from Shelley the young Moore had learnt atheism, and he followed this up by a course of the rationalist classics, Lecky and Buckle. It is noticeable that George Eliot comes in with these. She appears as the great agnostic, not as an artist; and the only one of the classic English novelists that Moore mentions with any enthusiasm is Dickens. Then to France, to study painting; not that he had any talent, but France and art became the objects of a romantic devotion, like the names of Lady Audley and Shelley. There were some flirtations with

188

Hugo and Musset; but the first real revelation came from Gautier from reading *Mademoiselle de Maupin*. I have come to the conclusion that it would be hard to exaggerate the influence of this work on the sensibility of the *fin-de-siècle* in England. It is constantly cited and referred to; and still more often its situations and its spirit are echoed without open acknowledgment. Later scholarship has shown how decisive was the influence of Gautier on Swinburne; and Moore was sufficiently acute to notice it himself. "The 'Hymn to Proserpine' and 'Dolores' are wonderful lyrical versions of Mlle de Maupin," he writes. The frank sensuality, the delight in visible and tangible beauty, combined with the unquiet romantic *Sehnsucht*, the longing for an ideal satisfaction, was a combination of ingredients that the more decorous English romanticism had never supplied. Above all there was the hint of perversity brought in by the epicene nature of the hero-heroine; a double delight, for it was at once a new source of erotic stimulation and a new means to *épater le bourgeois*. Moore expresses the spirit in which it was accepted with uncommon clarity:

> I read "Mlle de Maupin" at a moment when I was weary of spiritual passion, and this great exaltation of the visible above the invisible at once conquered and led me captive. This plain scorn of a world exemplified in lacerated saints and a crucified Redeemer opened up a prospect of new beliefs and new joys in things and new revolts against all that had come to form part and parcel of the commonalty of mankind. Shelley's teaching had been, while accepting the body, to dream of the soul as a star, and so preserve our ideal; but now I saw suddenly, with delightful clearness and intoxicating conviction, that by looking without shame and accepting with love the flesh, I might raise it to as high a place within as divine a light as ever the soul had been set in.

It was above all the tone of *Mademoiselle de Maupin* that Moore picked up, and it is a tone that is to echo through much of the literature of the nineties and to give it much of its peculiar flavour. It is a young man's tone, and that of a young man whom our elders would certainly have called a cad. It is rather light-heartedly erotic, and quite openly predatory. It is haunted by sexuality and makes a great deal of its "paganism";

yet it does not for a moment suggest the antique world; rather a setting of *deuxième empire* frou-frou, tea-roses, Parma violets, the minor pleasures of an elegant nineteenth-century Bohemianism. Yet beneath this worldly assurance the note of romantic idealism is never quite absent; the young social and sexual buccaneer is haunted by the ghost of a sad Pierrot sighing after an impossible love. Let us look at a few examples.

> Why should I undertake to keep a woman by me for the entire space of her life, watching her grow fat, grey, wrinkled and foolish? Think of the annoyance of perpetually looking after any one, especially a woman! Besides, marriage is antagonistic to my ideal.
>
> (Moore, *Confessions*.)

> If I were to be the lover of one of these ladies like a pale narcissus, moist with a tepid dew of tears, and bending with willowy languor over the new marble tomb of a spouse, happily and recently defunct, I should be as wretched as the dear departed was in his lifetime.
>
> (Gautier, *Maupin*.)

> He can read through the slim woman whose black hair, a-glitter with diamonds, contrasts with her white satin; an old man is talking to her, she dances with him, and she refused a young man a moment before. This is a bad sign, our Lovelace knows it; there is a stout woman of thirty-five, who is looking at him, red satin bodice, doubtful taste. He looks away; a little blonde woman fixes her eyes on him, she looks as innocent as a child; instinctively our Lovelace turns to his host. "Who is that little blonde woman over there, the right-hand corner?" he asks. "Ah, that is Lady —." "Will you introduce me?" "Certainly." Lovelace has made up his mind.
>
> (Moore, *Confessions*.)

> All this does not prevent me from positively wanting a mistress. I do not know who she will be, but among the women of my acquaintance I see nobody who could suitably fill this dignified position. Those who may be regarded as young enough are wanting in beauty or intellectual charm; those who are beautiful and young are basely and forbiddingly virtuous, or lack the necessary freedom; and then there is always some husband, some brother, a mother or an aunt, somebody or other, with prying eyes and large ears, who must either be cajoled or given short shrift.
>
> (Gautier, *Maupin*.)

GEORGE MOORE AND THE NINETIES

I was absorbed in the life of woman—the mystery of petticoats, so different from the staidness of trousers! the rolls of hair entwined with so much art, and suggesting so much colour and perfume, so different from the bare crop; the unnaturalness of the waist in stays! plenitude and slenderness of silk. . . . A world of calm colour with phantoms moving, floating past and changing in dim light—an averted face with abundant hair, the gleam of a perfect bust or the poise of a neck turning slowly round, the gaze of deep translucid eyes. I loved women too much to give myself wholly to one.

(Moore, *Confessions*.)

It makes me have a low opinion of women when I see how infatuated they often are with blackguards who despise and deceive them, instead of taking a lover—some staunch and sincere young man who would consider himself very lucky, and would simply worship them; I myself, for example, am such a one. It is true that men of the former kind abound in the drawing-rooms, where they preen themselves for all to behold, and are always lounging on the back of some settee, while I remain at home, my forehead pressed against the window-pane, watching the river shroud itself in haze and the mists rising, while silently setting up in my heart the scented shrine, the peerless temple, in which I am to install the future idol of my soul.

(Gautier, *Maupin*.)

I have two points to make in setting these extracts side by side. One is how extraordinarily closely Moore echoes Gautier's tone, and how easy it is to recognise that tone as particularly characteristic of the nineties. We find it again and again in Wilde, in *The Yellow Book* and *The Savoy*, and even, though decorously veiled, and entirely without the connivance of the author, in some of the characters of Henry James. The second point is that the attitudes implied here are entirely social and sexual. But *Mademoiselle de Maupin* had a preface—the famous preface which was the manifesto of the "art for art's sake" movement. Moore does not mention it, but we can hardly suppose that he did not read it. And we later find, by a curious linkage, that he associates *Mademoiselle de Maupin* with Pater's *Marius the Epicurean*. There seems to be little in common between the aesthetic sensuality of Gautier and the spiritualised hedonism of Pater. It may of course be that the one is simply the Oxford version of the other, and Moore partly makes the

191

association on those grounds—with a certain rude psychological insight and a good deal of injustice to what Pater supposed himself to be saying.

Mr. Pater can join hands with Gautier in saying:

> *Je trouve la terre aussi belle que le ciel, et je pense que la correction de la forme est la vertu.*

"I think that correctness of form is virtue"; that is the real link that Moore makes between Gautier and Pater. The social and sexual antinomianism is only the correlative of a general pursuit of formal beauty, which can manifest itself as much in the sphere of verbal arrangement as in the sphere of conduct.

> But *Marius the Epicurean* was more to me than a mere emotional influence, precious and rare though that may be, for this book was the first in English prose I had come across that procured for me any genuine pleasure in the language itself, in the combination of words for silver or gold chime, and unconventional cadence, and for all those lurking half-meanings, and that evanescent suggestion, like the odour of dead roses, that words retain to the last of other times and elder usage. . . . "Marius" was the stepping-stone that carried me across the channel into the genius of my own tongue.

I said before that psychological adventurousness and the search for perfection of form go hand in hand. Here we see the process in action. Gautier suggests a style of life; Pater extends it; and at the same time he suggests a style of writing. The cultivation of a mannered exquisiteness of sensation leads directly into the cultivation of prose as a deliberate aesthetic instrument.

After the reading of *Maupin* Moore plunged deep into the waters of aestheticism. Other tales of Gautier followed, and the delicately chiselled nostalgias of *Emaux et Camées*. The inevitable next step was Baudelaire.

> No longer is it the grand barbaric face of Gautier; now it is the clean-shaven face of the mock priest, the slow, cold eye, and the sharp, cunning sneer of the cynical libertine who will be tempted that he may better know the worthlessness of temptation. "Les Fleurs du Mal", beautiful flowers, beautiful in sublime decay. What a great record is yours, and were Hell a reality how many souls would we find wreathed with your poisonous blossoms.

GEORGE MOORE AND THE NINETIES

(There is no need to suppose that Moore in 1886 wrote these lines without a tinge of irony.) Bertrand's *Gaspard de la Nuit*; Villiers de l'Isle Adam, whom Moore used to meet at the Nouvelle Athènes; Verlaine; Gustave Kahn's experiments in *vers libre* and faint evocative vocabulary; Ghil's theory of coloured vowels, a development of the doctrine of Rimbaud's sonnet, which gave rise to an often quoted passage in *Muslin*; Mallarmé, whose conversation Moore enjoyed, while confessing that he was quite unable to understand either the poetry or the Symbolist theory. Excited by this heady brew, it is not surprising that Moore was unable to appreciate the contemporary experiments in the poetry of common life. When he came to read Coppée he was able to enjoy only his early Parnassian poems.

> But the exquisite perceptivity Coppée showed in his modern poems, the certainty with which he raised the commonest subject, investing it with sufficient dignity for his purpose, escaped me wholly, and I could not but turn with horror from such poems as "La Nourrice" and "Le Petit Epicier". I could not understand how anybody could bring himself to acknowledge the vulgar details of our vulgar age.

But a new force was piling up behind the aesthetic screen, and it was soon to burst out. Moore was busy trying to write short stories apparently in the manner of Villiers' *Contes Cruels*, and poems, "Roses of Midnight", in what he believed to be the manner of Baudelaire. One day by chance he read in a magazine an article by Zola. (Presumably *Le Roman Experimental*.) The words *naturalisme, la verité, la science* affronted his eyes. He learnt that one should write with as little imagination as possible, that contrived plot in a novel or a play was illiterate and puerile. It all struck him like a revelation, and he realised the sterile eccentricity of his own aestheticism. He had read a few chapters of *L'Assommoir* when it had appeared in serial form, but like others of his tastes had dismissed it as an absurdity. Now he began to buy up the back numbers of the *Voltaire*, the weekly in which Zola was making propaganda for the naturalist cause.

The idea of a new art based on science, in opposition to the art of the old world that was based on the imagination, an art that should explain all things and embrace modern life in its entirety, in its endless ramifications, be, as it were, a new creed in a new civilisation, filled me with wonder, and I stood dumb before the vastness of the conception, and the towering height of the ambition.

This mood of enraptured stupefaction did not last; at the time of writing the *Confessions*, in 1886, he is able to look back at the Zola articles and say, "Only the simple crude statements of a man of powerful mind, but singularly narrow vision." And a few pages farther on from the account of the naturalist revelation is a thoroughgoing attack on Zola's limitations, an attack whose consequences are amusingly described in the essay "A visit to Medan". But it is not my purpose to write the history of Moore's literary opinions in detail. The point is that from now on the ideal of a distinctively modern art, grounding itself on the realities of the contemporary world, lies side by side with aesthetic fantasy in Moore's mind. It is surprising how easily they came to lie side by side. On a later page of the *Confessions*, *Mademoiselle de Maupin* and *L'Assommoir* are cited together as the two books above all from which the respectable circulating-library young lady must turn away; they are mentioned almost as though they were the twin pillars of modern letters, in spite of the fact that *Maupin* had appeared in 1836, and that the two works had nothing whatever in common, except that neither is exactly the thing *à mettre entre les mains de toute jeune fille*. And the fact is that naturalism did not drive out aestheticism, it substituted a new aestheticism of an extended kind. The immediate effect of the Zola discovery was to send Moore back to Coppée's modern poems, and to persuade him to modernise his "Roses of Midnight". But this soon proved to be a hopeless enterprise, and he turns to reflect, not at all on the social and descriptive implications of naturalism, but on its purely literary qualities. He re-reads *L'Assommoir*, and is impressed by its "strength, height and decorative grandeur", by the "immense harmonic development of the idea, and the fugal treatment of the different scenes", by "the lordly, river-like roll of the narrative". In short, it was "the idea of the new aestheticism—the new art corresponding to modern, as ancient art corresponded to ancient life" that captivated him, and was to compel his imagination for many years to come.

The later history of Zola's reputation has borne out Moore's intuition. Towards the end of the *Confessions* he writes:

> One thing that cannot be denied to the realists: a constant and intense desire to write well, to write artistically. When I think of what they have done in the matter of the use of words, of the myriad verbal effects they have discovered, of the thousand forms of composition they have created, how they have remodelled and refashioned the language in their untiring striving for intensity of expression, for the very osmazome of art, I am lost in ultimate wonder and admiration. What Hugo did for French verse, Flaubert, Goncourt, Zola, and Huysmans have done for French prose.

It would once have seemed eccentric to talk of Zola in this way, perhaps did even when Moore was writing. But in later years nobody has been very interested in Zola the reporter and sociologist; and complaints about the supposed coarseness and crudity of his style have given way, and justly, to admiration for his impressionist painting and the organisation of his large set pieces. The massive symbolism in his writing has not passed unnoticed, and the flat opposition between naturalist and symbolist has been much played down. By now, when the professed "scientific" pretensions of *Le Roman Expérimental* can no longer be taken seriously, the real nature of Zola's achievement can be seen more clearly, and it is seen much as Moore saw it. In making the transition from Zola's untenable naturalist theory to his far more interesting and comprehensive practice Moore is taking the line that both criticism and fiction itself were to take in the years to come.

But Moore's discipleship to Zola was brief. He soon saw something nearer to his real aim in Flaubert, where the demands of a scrupulous realism are united with an equal scrupulosity of rhythm and phrasing. However great the difference between their achievements, Flaubert's strict attachment to the truth, to be sought only through formal perfection, probably came nearest to embodying Moore's artistic ideal. *A Mummer's Wife* is his only Zolaesque novel; he was annoyed if one did not recognise that *Esther Waters* was in inspiration "pure Flaubert". But strangely, even Flaubert was not the object of Moore's lasting devotion. Talking of his own literary infidelities he says, "even a light of love is constant, if not faithful, to her *amant de cœur*"; and the most enduring of his literary passions was for Balzac. "Upon that rock I built my church, and his great and valid talent saved me from the shoaling waters of new aestheticisms, the putrid mud of naturalism, and the faint and sickly surf of the symbolists." It is only in Balzac that he can find an unrestricted romantic imagination united with a complete engagement in the involved turmoil of contemporary life. Essentially a spectator on the sidelines, Moore is fascinated by that colossal vitality; and if for Alisander he is more than a little o'erparted, we can at least recognise in the totality of his work something of his master's passion for the diversity of human experience.

Disorderly and capricious as Moore's expression of his enthusiasms is, it can still tell us something, and something that is of importance beyond his own career. He was more completely involved in French literature than any other writer of the nineties—more even than Symons; and we can see in him a complete microcosm of the French influences that were then reshaping English literature. His experience tells us of the opening of a new chapter in the history of English fiction. Three steady preoccupations can be discerned among his shifting allegiances: one is with telling the truth about experience instead of merely devising an agreeable story; the second is with imaginative freedom in spite of the circulating libraries and the young ladies; the third is with formal justness and beauty, in expression and organisation, instead of the laboured or slapdash approximations to which the English novel in all but its highest moments had been prone. Together they make a break with many of the traditions of English fiction—with the traditions of picaresque adventure, indiscriminate humour, genial satire and reforming zeal. A severer artistic ideal takes their place. And this break is not merely a matter of Moore's own work. We are not considering his intrinsic quality at the moment, though my own conviction is that it is far higher than has been generally recognised; we are using him simply as a convenient periscope to survey the literary scene of his time. And the lessons he was learning were also being learnt, wholly or in part, by Hardy, Conrad and Henry James.

James is a far greater, Hardy and Conrad more central writers than Moore. It is relatively easy to fit them into a "great tradition" of English fiction. Moore has always his own marked idiosyncrasy, and the criticism of our time, in its preoccupation with prevalent trends and successful revolutions rather than with individual quality, has been inclined to see it as a dead end. This is not, I think, true; and if it is necessary to justify Moore to the trend-mongers one may do so by showing that he was leading, if not up the main road, into an area where the greatest prose experiment of our time has its beginning. We have seen Moore oscillating between aesthetic reverie and naturalism, and if we were to follow the development of his art we should find him in the end arriving at a style that was to harmonise the two. He manages in his best work to present in all their uncompromising contingency the actualities of common experience, and yet to preserve the inevitability of impression, the delicate rightness of diction and rhythm that he had learnt from the high priests of a scrupulous art. At the end of our period, when Moore was past the threshold of old age, another Irish writer brought out his youthful confessions; and in it he defined the function of the poet, the literary artist, as it appeared to his eyes. It is to be "the mediator between the world of reality and the world of dreams". No writer in the world has carried farther than James Joyce a dual allegiance to an exhaustive naturalism on the one hand and a complex aesthetic symbolism on the other; and I think it is likely that neither the title nor the content of Joyce's *Portrait of the Artist as a Young Man* would have been quite the same in 1916 if it had not been for the prior existence of Moore's *Confessions of a Young Man* in 1886. And there are other resemblances more strongly marked. Critics have often spoken about the absolute originality of Joyce's *Dubliners*; and that is a curious instance of how far George Moore's achievements have dropped out of sight— itself perhaps a curious instance of the general failure to recognise the importance of the *fin-de-siècle* as a formative power in modern literature. For *Dubliners* has an obvious ancestor in Moore's stories in *The Untilled Field*. Joyce's stories have an urban instead of a rural setting, and make far more use of the romantic-ironical contrast. But it is surprising that the closeness of his manner to Moore's has not been observed. Part of it no doubt is a matter of a common discipleship. Moore's debt to Pater's prose has always been acknowledged; and Joyce's use of the same master is obvious, especially in *Portrait of the Artist*. It would be too long to illustrate in detail, but the echoed cadences sometimes reveal themselves in a sentence.

> From without as from within the waters had flowed over his barriers: their tides once more began to jostle fiercely above the crumbled mole.
>
> (Joyce, *Portrait of the Artist*.)

> I could see that he believed the story, and for the moment I, too, believed in an outcast Venus becoming the evil spirit of a village that would not accept her as divine.
>
> (Moore, *The Untilled Field*.)

Neither of these dying falls would be quite as they are if they had not echoed so often already through Pater's prose. In feeling and treatment too we can see common obligations. "The Window" in *The Untilled Field* and "Clay" in *Dubliners* are both stories about humble old women; and I doubt whether either of them would exist if Flaubert had not written "Un Cœur Simple". But the similarities between the two volumes are so marked and pervasive that I am persuaded the debt is more direct. Moore said later that he began *The Untilled Field* "with the hope of furnishing the young Irish of the future with models"; and reading *Dubliners* beside the earlier book we can hardly doubt that for Joyce he achieved just that. He also said that as the work progressed "the first stories begot a desire to paint the portrait of my country"; almost the words in which Joyce described to his publisher the purpose of *Dubliners*: "to write a chapter of the moral history of my country". One could go on to speak of the last story in *Dubliners*, "The Dead", and of how extraordinarily close it is in feeling to, say,

"The Exile" and "Home Sickness" in Moore's collection. But to do justice to the charity, the gentleness, the centrality of feeling that these two lonely antinomian writers achieve in these beautiful tales would be to desert periods and influences, and would demand quite other tools and another manner. I end on this note just to give a small illustration of what is still often forgotten—how intimate the connection is between the writing of the late nineteenth century and what is most new and living in the twentieth.

VII

GEORGE MOORE AND THE NOVEL

GEORGE MOORE was born just over a hundred years ago, and in just this lapse of time it often happens that a writer has dropped out of the immediate literary consciousness without yet acquiring a place in history. This appears to be Moore's present situation. Though he went on writing until 1928, he lies under the cloud that obscures the *fin-de-siècle*. But Moore's period (which in this context means his state of mind as much as his chronological span) is the period when the English imagination was being profoundly influenced by the literary experiments of France. It is emerging from a long imputation of ninetyish triviality; whatever we come to think of its actual achievement it can only be seen now as an important chapter of literary history—the introductory chapter, in fact, to the history that is still being enacted; and with it George Moore himself is bound to emerge from his obscurity. Perhaps too there is a feeling that George Moore, the hero of a hundred anecdotes, is not wholly serious. There have indeed been enough stories about him, and rather than adding to their number it would be worth while to inquire why a writer with such a massive achievement behind him should up to now never quite have made his mark. Most of the reasons will turn out to be poor ones; but on the way it should be possible to discover something about what his achievement really was. For this is by no means easy to determine.

Of course he himself made it difficult. He issued his work in limited editions, produced endless revised versions, treated himself as the author of a sacred scripture, admitting some works to the canon, and casting others out into the apocryphal darkness. All this has made it very hard for the common reader, that final arbiter of literary reputation, to form any clear image of him. In England especially we like our writers to have well-defined personalities that can be recognised in their work, like those of Dr. Johnson, Charles Lamb or Bernard Shaw. But George Moore let fall the truth about himself in these words from *Confessions of a Young Man*:

> I came into the world apparently with a nature like a smooth sheet of wax, bearing no impress, but capable of receiving any. Nor am I exaggerating when I say I think I might equally have been a Pharaoh, an ostler, a pimp, an archbishop; and that in the fulfilment of the duties of each a certain measure of success would have been mine.

Moore did as much deliberate self-exhibition as any writer since Rousseau; yet he remains fluid, without outlines, just as he looks in his portrait by Sickert. We can learn something of him by thinking of the diversity of his ambitions; to ride the winner of the National; to paint like Manet; to write like Zola; to be a great lover; to write like Flaubert, Balzac; to be a man of the world; to be an Irish patriot; to write like Landor; to write like Pater. . . . Most of these aspirations represent full-time jobs, quite incompatible with each other. Steeplechasing and painting disappeared pretty early: love and the world hung around rather longer: gradually, writing emerged as the main stream of his life. Merely writing, literature; not founding a school, or disseminating ideas, or influencing society. So that in his old age we see a galaxy of creations—and if we try to look through them to their creator, we see only a ghost; perhaps a mocking, perhaps an embittered, perhaps a contented ghost; surely rather a lonely one, at all events one who has long ago given his flesh and his substance to his works. This waif, this wisp, this near-absurdity that confronts us is what is left of a man whose authentic life was given to the asceticism of the arts. This kind of asceticism has never been much appreciated in English civilisation.

Rather than looking for the man behind the work it would be useful to look at the historical situation. What actually were the possibilities for a young novelist in the latter years of the nineteenth century? We must look at France as well as England to explain Moore: but as it happens the answer is the same for both. He could continue the tradition of realism—the rich accumulation of factual particulars, with a strong bias towards social, even sociological interpretation. What had lately become a method and a dogma in France had in an unselfconscious way always been a large component of English fiction in the eighteenth and nineteenth centuries. Or he could begin to develop an almost untried form, the novel of sensibility which neglects the outer definition for the inner, and instead of aiming at objectivity and information, sees the whole through the coloured medium of the author's temperament or through the temperament of some character in the work who becomes for the time being the author's aesthetic representative.

Moore chose realism; very Zolaesque and bedevilled by heredity and environment in *A Mummer's Wife*; infinitely more human and generous in that great novel *Esther Waters*. But a great French novel rather than a great English novel. Although it is about servants' halls, racing stables, lodging houses and pubs, it has little of the smell of English literature. English social portraiture has been strongly tinged with a sort of bourgeois romanticism. Moore complained that the English novelists refused to learn that life is neither jocular nor melodramatic. The world of *Esther Waters* is neither; and it has a sober fidelity to facts as they are that brings it nearer to Flaubert than to the typical English figures, Fielding and Dickens. Fidelity to some of the facts, at least; for English life is really rather jocular; and when it consents to be dramatic at all, it is as likely as not to be melodramatic. But Moore, as an Irishman trained in France, would hardly realise this. He reserves his humour for the practical purpose of annoying his friends, and disdains to put it in his novels, where it could only spoil the texture.

The autobiographies—*Confessions of a Young Man, Hail and Farewell, Memoirs of my Dead Life*—have probably been most read. Gossip is always popular, and if it is malicious gossip, so much the better. Moore lost many friends by it, and hurt some delicate sensibilities: but there is not really much vice in him, and there is no doubt that he elevated this rather dubious form to the level of a work of art—a work of art whose nature has perhaps not been very well understood. He boasts, for instance, of his amorous successes; in some societies this is fairly normal, but not in ours; and we are at once impelled to ask, Ought he to have said these things? and, irresistibly, I fear, Are they true? The answer to the first question is that by ordinary standards of decency he certainly ought not; the answer to the second is wrapped in mystery; but it rather appears that they were not as true as all that. However, it does not matter much. What he is really doing is writing a sparkling, desultory chronicle whose central figure happens to be called George Moore; and for his other characters he makes free with other actual persons. As a historical record it is probably wrong; as a way of treating one's friends it is certainly shabby; aesthetically it is a success. Since the reader is not implicated, and it is only the social and historical personality of the author that is blamed, perhaps we should anticipate the verdict of posterity and forget these misdemeanours. Some of his victims, anyway, gave as good as they got; Yeats, in the course of a brilliant satirical portrait, revealed that Moore was so unpractical that he had never even discovered how to keep his underpants from slipping down.

This damaging revelation from a fellow-Irishman is satisfactory to lovers of poetic justice, for Moore owed a great deal to Yeats. *Evelyn Innes,* that fine novel which was later expunged from the canon, is dedicated to Yeats; and I have always supposed that the figure of Ulick Dean the musician is partly drawn from him. And when the possibilities of realism seemed to be exhausted, Yeats carried Moore off to Ireland and involved him in the Irish literary movement. Moore was very little of a crusader, but he was intensely sensitive to any breeze that stirred the literary air. For years he had been a Parisian or a Londoner; Ireland, with its sad empty spaces, was almost a new country to him; its moving simplicities recalled the stories of Turgeneff; and association with Yeats recalled another part of his French experience, hitherto unused—what he had learned from the symbolists.

What he had learnt from the symbolists was no doubt only a fragment of that mass of poetic theorising at which he must have assisted. Moore's capacity for dealing with ideas was always conspicuously limited. But he had at least absorbed the concept of the work of art as a self-subsistent entity, explicable in its own terms, responsible to its own being, rather than to some reality outside itself. It would seem that the Irish-Yeatsian reactivation of symbolist discussions was the turning-point in Moore's literary life. The stories in *The Untilled Field*, the short novel *The Lake*, are indeed a portrait of Ireland, intimate because he had been born and bred there, fresh because he was a returned traveller; but they are also a movement into an entirely new literary territory—new to Moore and new to English fiction—where the beauty, harmony and integrity of the words on the page are a more important consideration than their efficacy in representing an outer reality. A transference, in fact, from what Mallarmé had called *l'état brut de la parole* to *l'état essentiel*.

For the most notable aspect of these Irish tales is a linguistic one. Moore claimed that his handling of the Irish idiom in *The Untilled Field* served as a model for J. M. Synge; and this may be true. The tales were written to be translated into Gaelic, as part of a programme for supplying literature in the vernacular. And since they were to appear in another tongue, it was no use to attempt variety, sharp contrasts of style, the setting off of one character's speech against another, all the tricks of "characterisation" that the great Victorian novelists had employed so lavishly. Moore had never been very successful in this (he had no real command of common English speech); and here it would be useless; translation obliterates these distinctions.

Instead he looks for a neutral harmony, a style where all will be in keeping. Among his former friends the painters the greatest crime had been a passage that was out of tone: he now begins to apply the same lesson to literature. What most upsets the harmony in a work of fiction? Natural dialogue, surely. Characters who insist on talking in Cockney, in society slang, in the dialect of an anomalous class or time; whose style refuses to relate itself to that of the author's own reflections. Some of the more self-conscious novelists had been half aware of this problem already, and kept the servants and the rustics from speaking on that account.

Henry James did not formulate the matter in these terms, but there can be little doubt that it was real to him. The fine intelligence that he requires at the centre of his novels is no doubt there primarily as a moral discriminator; but the restriction of his principal characters to persons of unusual sensibility and perception represents ultimately a stylistic demand—a demand that all shall be in keeping. When the essential dramatis personae make this realistically impossible, he has recourse to a frank convention. The infants in *The Turn of the Screw* talk like Henry James.

All this could hardly have appeared as a problem at any earlier period in the history of fiction. When previous novels had attained the status of works of art it had rarely been in virtue of their texture, and when they had reached the kind of harmony and integrity that a symbolist aesthetic would have approved it had been because of some quite unsymbolist notion of social or literary decorum. After Flaubert, after the aesthetic doctrine of the succeeding generation, the requirement that a novel should not only represent something, but should be something, reaches the level of deliberate awareness. It becomes difficult for the scrupulous novelist to remain content with using language in a mainly referential way, to be satisfied if he points to the right things, no matter by what verbal instrumentality the pointing is done. We are already within sight of the dual allegiance of the early Joyce—the allegiance at once to "realism" and to "beauty". And the great obstacle to the *claritas* and *consonantia* that go to constitute beauty, was the novel's inevitably mixed form. I put this in the past tense, for manifestly the technical situation has now changed; but as the novel stood at the end of the nineteenth century it was always a mixed form—a mixture of narrative for which the author makes himself directly responsible, and dialogue, for which he delegates responsibility to his characters. The situation is not new—it prevails in the epic, as Plato was the first to remark. But the epic was always controlled by a standard of heroic decorum, assimilating all things to its own stylistic level. The

205

novel alone, a bastard new-come form, with no demonstrable noble antecedents, had no such imposed standard of literary manners. And it remained for some refined aesthetic to impose one, to wrestle with the difficulty of a form where the deepest and subtlest considerations, made on the author's own terms, may have to rub shoulders with, or express themselves through, the crudest and most incondite dialect in the mouths of the characters. The narrative and the dramatic methods are always potentially at war. We have glanced at James's solution in passing, and this is not the place even to touch on the varied experiments of the last forty years. Moore's solution is different, and to see it in its developed form we have to look at the last group of novels: *The Brook Kerith* and *Héloise and Abelard* are the chief.

The first thing one notices about these books is the enormously long unbroken paragraphs, giving a repellently solid appearance to the page. However, they are not what they appear, stretches of unbroken narrative. They are interspersed with conversations, sometimes between two, sometimes between several people; but the indentations and the inverted commas have been suppressed. This is not a mere typographical device, for with a little further investigation we notice that an unbroken rhythm runs through the whole paragraph, narrative and dialogue alike. That is, the peculiarities of individual utterance have been sacrificed to the harmony of the whole. Just the slightest of gestures is made in the direction of naturalism and characterisation; the characters do not all speak alike, there are suggestions of colloquialism and dialect—but only so much as will allow the musical line to run continuously through a whole passage, as it does, for instance, in the enchanting opening of *The Brook Kerith.*

> It was at the end of a summer evening, long after his usual bedtime, that Joseph, sitting on his grandmother's knee, heard her tell that Kish having lost his asses sent Saul, his son, to seek them in the land of the Benjamites and the land of Shalisha, whither they might have strayed. But they were not in these lands, Son, she continued, nor in Zulp, whither Saul went afterwards, and being then tired out with looking for them, he said to the servant: We shall do well to forget the asses, lest my father

should ask what has become of us. But the servant, being of a mind that Kish would not care to see them without the asses, said to young Saul: Let us go up into yon city, for a great seer lives there and he will be able to put us in the right way to come upon the asses.

Though the date of *The Brook Kerith* is 1916, that is not a modern prose style; far less so than that of *A Mummer's Wife* or the *Confessions* of thirty years before. And *The Brook Kerith* and *Heloise and Abelard* are remarkably unlike most modern novels. It is natural to begin by talking of George Moore's subject, but one continues by talking of his manner of presentation; for in the later books the manner of presentation has become the subject in a way that the novel previously had hardly known. Of course certain areas of human experience are inevitably represented—in *The Brook Kerith* a notoriously challenging one; the life of Jesus treated as a purely natural and human chronicle. The carpenter's son does not die on the cross, but lives on in hiding. And the tremendous climax comes when, years later, Paul, preaching Christ crucified, is confronted by the still living Jesus. Now if Moore had still been thinking on the lines of the conventional novel the whole plot would have been concentrated on this point; but it is not. It wanders through the Syrian landscape, follows the fortunes of Joseph of Arimathea, lingers among the rival sects and faiths of Palestine. *Héloise and Abelard* makes the same sort of varied leisurely progress through twelfth-century France. Moore has no historical axe to grind; he shows people behaving as they do behave; alike, in his view, in the first century as in the twelfth, or the nineteenth. There are startling anachronisms, there are digressions and inserted show-pieces, but they hardly matter, the true object of attention throughout is the sustained, slightly soporific texture of the prose, capable of absorbing into itself all the diversities of experience with which it deals.

Moore acknowledged Landor and Pater as his masters, and the writing does remind us of both. But he has given himself a harder task than theirs, for Pater's people do not converse, they only reflect or make set speeches; and Landor's do not act and only occasionally feel. George Moore's triumph is to have combined vividness of presentation with a prose whose rhythm and texture is itself beautiful to contemplate. At this point it will almost certainly be objected that whatever this achievement is worth it has not much to do with the novel. Serious criticism of the novel of late has been so inveterately moralistic that we have been hectored into discussing all works of fiction almost exclusively in terms of just moral discrimination—even if little has been done to show by what standards the justice is assessed. What has been said about Moore's most characteristic achievement has plainly nothing to do with this line of approach. Yet the conscientious contemplator of the novel must give a great deal of weight to this moral approach, not as a moralist himself, for he may make no such pretensions, but because the sphere of the novel is in part the same as that of the moralist—it is the sphere of human conduct, particularly conduct in its social relations. This is true of the novel in a sense that it is not of other forms—of the lyric for instance, whose characteristic material is the moment of apprehension, given, unanalysed, immediate, and therefore morally neutral; of tragedy, whose philosophic analogue is not ethics but metaphysics. There is a general sense in which everything man makes is implicated with his moral experience; but the novel is implicated with it in a special sense as well. And our account of George Moore so far has not touched on this aspect of his work at all, has hardly even suggested that it is there to be touched on. If this were all that is to be said it could well be argued that Moore was an interesting minor experimenter in certain narrative techniques, and that as a novelist he had hardly started.

But of course this is not the whole story about Moore. He tried to choose subjects almost as a decorative painter might try to choose suitable architectural sites for the exhibition of his craft; but whether he would or not, his subjects involved him with life, with an immense variety of human experience. And here we begin to perceive a divergence, a divergence which we might expect, but in Moore's case it is a particularly wide one, between the social personality and the artist. In spite of his exhibitionism, in spite of his faults in taste, in spite, it would appear, of a personal lack of any adequate philosophy, there is in his work a great moral integrity. One doubts if he ever thought about it, and in his best novels it becomes apparent in a singularly effortless and unforced way. We demand a justness of moral perception from the novel, and believe that a good novel could not exist without it any more than a beautiful woman could exist without a backbone. But it is not in virtue of her backbone that she is beautiful; nor is it necessary that she or those who appreciate her beauty should call constant attention to the possession of this indispensable ‚piece of equipment. Moore's work has a moral backbone; it is not in virtue of this that it achieves its peculiar kind of success, but it is nevertheless there, and it is as well to end by insisting on it, for it is in this matter (through the combined skill as caricaturists of himself and his friends) that he is commonly thought to be deficient.

This moral integrity of his work is one that owes much to his early realist training, and, strangely enough, owes something to the insouciance and irresponsibility that puzzles us in his life. Moore has none of the twentieth-century maladies; he does not suffer from anxiety, or a sense of guilt, or the plight of modern man. (I doubt if he knew we were in one.) So his characters are not coloured by any overwhelming emotional tincture of his own. This makes him very unlike most modern novelists; but it also means that he can see people simply as they are. The spectacles through which he looks at the world neither magnify nor diminish, and they are made of uncoloured glass. So that he becomes a superb recorder, quite irrespective of his own sentiments and opinions. We have the paradox that this renegade Catholic, who had rejected all the forms and all the philosophy of the Church, gives in *Evelyn Innes* the superbly understanding study of a woman irresistibly drawn to the religious life; that the callous young arriviste of the *Confessions*, who called pity the vilest of the virtues, can show the grave sympathy for the common lot that runs through *Esther Waters*: that the hero of all the facile sexual success stories should give, in *Héloïse and Abelard*, the infinitely touching story of a love that ends, on this side of the grave, in emptiness and frustration. On the one hand, Moore is the incomparable painter of the

209

world before the deluge; love, sunshine, Paris in the spring; the simple sensual happiness that seems to have vanished from our hag-ridden age; the verbal counterpart of a painting by Renoir. On the other, he can turn a steady gaze on the dramas of asceticism and renunciation. It is hard to believe that *Sister Teresa* and *The Lovers of Orelay* were written by the same man; and it is only possible because the author stands aside; he is not committed; he simply observes and understands. Objective, impersonal comprehension of this kind becomes at its highest pitch a kind of charity. Moore the artist possessed this gift; what he did with it when he was off duty I do not know; but I believe that its presence in his works will be more perceived as the personal legend about him begins to fade.

VIII

CHANCE AND JOSEPH CONRAD

L ET me begin by quoting a scrap of dialogue:

> "I should call it the peace of the sea," said Mr. Charles
> Powell in an earnest tone, but looking at us as though he expected
> to be met by a laugh of derision.
> "A very good name," said Marlow looking at him approvingly.
> "A sailor finds a deep feeling of security in the exercise of his
> calling. The exacting life of the sea has this advantage over the
> life of the earth, that its claims are simple and cannot be evaded."
> "Gospel truth," assented Mr. Powell. "No! they cannot be
> evaded."

This comes from the opening pages of *Chance*. Mr. Powell
is of course a retired sailor, and so is Marlow, and they are
paving the way to acquaintanceship by uttering sentiments on
which both are agreed. But coming as it does early in the first
chapter, with its suggestion of simple, large-scale ethical
statement, one rather expects this conversation to strike a
note that will echo throughout the book. Why otherwise
should it be there? However, the note is not sustained. The
narrator who reports this dialogue is on a cruising holiday with
Marlow. They meet Mr. Powell by chance at a small Thames-
side inn. Mr. Powell tells them the story of his first voyage as
second officer. By chance Marlow had heard of the ship
Ferndale and its master, Captain Anthony, under whose command Powell sailed. Marlow in fact had known Captain
Anthony's sister and brother-in-law, a couple called Fyne, and
had become transiently involved in their affairs. From this
point the tale deserts Mr. Powell and the Thames-side setting,
which turns out to have been only an introduction, and follows

the Fyne household—not even the Fynes themselves, but the fortunes of a girl who happened to be staying with them at the time Marlow knew them. *Chance* is in fact her story and that of Captain Anthony—Captain Anthony, the sailor brother of Mrs. Fyne, who runs off with the girl from the Fynes' house, and marries her.

Conrad's manner of winding his way into his story is always an extraordinarily indirect one, and in this introduction we have, as it seems to me, three false trails. The first is the title itself —*Chance*. There is, it is true, a good deal of chance about the meeting with Mr. Powell, his mention of the *Ferndale*, the fact that Marlow knew something of the story of Captain Anthony, and so forth. But after that, when the tale really gets under way, there is no more chance about it than about the plots of most novels. The suggestion of some fated coincidence is hardly more than a preliminary flourish. Secondly, this intricate introduction with multiple narrations (very skilfully managed, by the way) seems to promise a more complex and many-sided mode of apprehension than the book actually affords. It is not for instance the prelude to a complex way of presenting character and situation through several different visions, as it might be in Henry James. The plot, when it unfolds, though strikingly original (I know nothing else remotely like it) is in fact seen in a fairly simple light, in spite of the elaboration of the machinery. Third, the passage about the simple and inescapable claims of the sea turns out to have no particular relevance to the plot of this book, though it is of course a theme that keeps recurring in Conrad, more markedly in other books.

It is for reasons of this kind that Conrad the novelist still seems to leave us with a number of puzzling questions. An elaborate array of narrative and suggestive devices does not lead quite where we expected. What sort of writer is he, where is the centre of his work, what is the key to his sensibility? But key is not the right word, for it suggests something that could be opened like a piece of mechanism, while the mystery of Conrad is rather something that needs illuminating, like a scene in deep shadow. Mr. Forster has spoken of a central obscurity in Conrad, inspiring half a dozen great books, appearing to promise some philosophic statement about the universe, but never making it. Ought we to go on trying to make deductions about this cryptic and unspoken pronouncement; or are we to conclude, as Mr. Forster does, that it is not really there, even implicitly; and try to approach Conrad in another way? Are we for example to accept the popular view? In the popular view there is no mystery about Conrad at all; he is simply the great novelist of the sea and the exotic—"the coral isle, the lion-coloured sand". He himself disliked and repudiated this sort of reputation; he hated to be thought a writer of sea stories. But the popular view of any writer, though it may be right or wrong, adequate or inadequate, is always worth looking at. It always points to something important; and here I think it points to a good deal more than the fact that many of Conrad's characters are sailors and many of his stories set on ships. The sea setting goes very deep into his sensibility, and so does the element of exoticism and romantic adventure. It is an essential part of the experience of reading Conrad that we are moving in strange, remote, only half-understood regions, and in an element where intrigue, violence and physical danger are always present or threatening. The more sophisticated alternative view is to play down this side of the novels, to see only the moral and spiritual perils, to see Conrad as the analyst of obscure psychological compulsions, difficult and tormented decisions. The sea and the exotic settings then become only accidental; the heart of Conrad is in much the same place as that of many another novelist.

I do not think that this last attitude represents our spontaneous, immediate reaction to Conrad. His work is not quite easy to assimilate to the central tradition of the novel, and, if we are not bullied about it, we are apt to feel that he is in some ways a special case. Let me mention some of the obvious ways. In the first place, his is largely a male world. Of course, he has many women characters, and in some of the books they are meant to carry a great deal of the weight. But they are seldom among his most successful creations. (I would make an exception of Mrs. Verloc in *The Secret Agent*.) They are usually seen more indirectly and remotely than the male characters, and are studied less for their own sakes than for their effect in evoking special loyalties and devotions in men. One might add that Conrad has a largely male public too. In my experience very few women really enjoy Conrad, and this is not only because the feminine sensibility so often ceases to function at the mere mention of a topsail halyard, but because the characteristic concerns and occupations of the woman's world play such a very small part in Conrad's work. Again, Conrad writes as a foreigner in a language not his own. This is always mentioned, but after some thought I have come to the conclusion that it had no very fundamental effect on his style. It does, of course, produce a good many surface peculiarities. Conrad learnt French before he knew English, and he remained always addicted to some curious Gallicisms. I read in *Nostromo*, "Three men were arrested on the road"; only to discover a few lines later that they had not been arrested at all, since they are galloping away on their horses. It then dawned on me that what Conrad had intended to convey was not that they were arrested, but merely that they had stopped. These are surface matters, however, and apart from occasional strangenesses of idiom the general run of Conrad's prose remains convincingly and splendidly English, based, as we know it was, on a long study of the English classics. But the fact that he writes as a foreigner does nevertheless mean something else of great importance. It means that he is never dealing with a society where he is completely at home, where he has a natural, instinctive, inbred knowledge of background, manners and relationships. It means that he hardly ever writes of the primary and universal social organism, the family. He had no particular fixation on his own youth, and he left Poland too early to bring with him any wide knowledge of its life; a sailor sees the world, but his glimpses of it are notoriously transitory and superficial; and Conrad's later years in England were so much devoted to the mysteries of his craft that they brought him very little into relation with the normal fabric of English society. This means that almost all settings have for him an element of the exotic; many of them are strange to his readers, but all are in some degree strange to him; and in this respect the popular view of his work as a series of travels among unknown men is more than a superficial one.

This is a heavy handicap for a novelist to bear. One legitimate reason for reading a novel is for the insight it gives into a particular way of life—the terms on which life was actually lived in a particular place at a particular time.

This motive has been unfashionable of late years, but it will come back into its own for it is an essential part of the pleasure of the novel. Some of the greatest triumphs of the novel have been in the portrayal of an organic society, intimately known, felt by the writer in his bones before the operation of conscious thought begins—Tolstoy's Russia, Flaubert's France, Dickens's England. That immense source of strength is denied to Conrad, and he has to find something to replace it. His most typical, central solution to the problem is to turn to the study of solitude. All his great characters are solitaries. It has often been said, and he has virtually said it himself: he is preeminently the novelist of isolation—the appalling moral isolation of Razumov, the different isolation of the ship's captain, alone with his responsibility, the literal isolation of Heyst on his island, Heyst who is isolated anyway, with or without companions, by the spiritual regimen he has imposed upon himself. Some variant of this situation is central to all Conrad's novels. But the novelist cannot work in this mode alone. Of all writers he is the most implicated with society and the social bonds. And there is only one kind of society that Conrad had ever known intimately, had fully participated in as an adult human being—the society of a ship at sea. I do not think that we can find anywhere in Conrad a group of people, bound together by the normal customary bonds into a living community, except in the stories of the sea—*The Nigger of the Narcissus, The Shadow Line, Typhoon, Youth* and the latter part of *Chance.* So when the common reader persists in thinking of Conrad as a writer of sea stories it is for a very good reason: it is because it is only in the sea stories that he finds the sense of an organised nexus of social relations, to which he is accustomed, both in the novel and in life.

IMAGE AND EXPERIENCE

Those who are unpersuaded by this argument will at once want to point to *Nostromo*, that splendid panorama of a whole country, with all its variety of ranks, races and trades, its numerous groups of private lives entagled in a great intricate net of political intrigue. *Nostromo* is often held to be Conrad's masterpiece, and certainly it merits all the tributes that have been paid to its magnificent orchestration, its complexity and breadth, and its moving close. But I am unwilling to see it as Conrad's greatest success. I cannot avoid the feeling that the whole thing is something of a *tour-de-force*, that Sulaco, the turbulent South American state, is mainly a splendid piece of scene-painting. We are dazzled by its atmosphere and its colour, but we are not soaked in it, impregnated by it, as we are by the settings of some of the great large-scale novels by other writers with which *Nostromo* has tacitly been equated. We do not live in Sulaco as we live in Tolstoy's St. Petersburg, Flaubert's Normandy, or Lawrence's Eastwood. Nor can I feel that, until the very end, we care for what happens to the characters—the Goulds, the Avellanos, Decoud, Nostromo himself—with anything like the intensity that we feel for some of Conrad's other personages—for Lord Jim, for Captain Mac-Whirr, for Heyst and Lena, or for Flora de Barral. And if anyone wishes to raise an eyebrow at this concern with a living scene and characters with whom we feel emotionally engaged, if anyone wishes to suggest that these are naive criteria for the novel, I shall remain wholly unimpressed, for I believe they are of its essence.

And now to return to *Chance*. Marlow relates the story of his brief connection with the Fynes and their unlucky girl-friend· Marlow meets the girl herself, and most of her past life is related to him by Fyne. But I do not think that these several narrations really allow us to see her in varied lights. They are frameworks round the tale, not authentically separate viewpoints. Flora de Barral is the unhappy daughter of a fraudulent financier. She has been brought up in a luxurious physical and moral loneliness, by a cold and treacherous governess. This woman, when the father's fantastic affairs finally crash, subjects her to a hideously cruel and sudden attack, denounces her father to her as a swindler and a criminal, pours out on the child all her revenge, hatred and disappointed scheming. At this critical point the Fynes befriend her; and for years afterwards; but she has been so deeply wounded that she has lost all confidence in herself and others, and has withdrawn into silence and inaccessibility.

The Fynes are an extremely lively piece of characterisation——he a good, solemn and responsible civil servant, she an equally solid and solemn professional feminist. There is absolutely nothing wrong with the placing of these characters. Conrad has observed, understood, and portrayed by an excellent method. Yet the absence of real intimacy of which I have spoken is always felt; the Fyne household lives in the mind with only a far-away and intangible reality. Perhaps this is appropriate, for all is subordinated to a single moral effect—the appalling isolation, the unbearable loneliness of Flora, emotionally ravished in adolescence and never able to emerge from her state of dumb shock. The picture of her desolation and her humiliations is built up with fragments of narrative by Fyne and Mrs. Fyne, observations and surmises by Marlow, scenes, fragments of scenes, glimpses, guesses, all contributing to the establishment in the reader's mind of the figure of Flora as a being whose feelings "had been trampled in the dirt out of all shape". It is handled, as far as the sheer machinery is concerned, with immense technical assurance; yet there is a slightly disturbing sense of being kept at a remove, or rather several removes, from the actuality. A reconstruction by Marlow of a scene described to him by Mrs. Fyne, who herself has only had a report of it from Flora's uncle, is not the same thing as a direct vision of Flora as an acting and suffering being. The requirement is to present Flora's life after the crash, in the house of a family of odious relations; and I believe that this elaborate series of outworks is necessary simply because Conrad has not the specific, intimate knowledge of the cross-currents in a dreary lower-middle-class family to portray it direct; and being the scrupulous artist that he is, he sets his subject at a distance, and relates it through a medium which he knows how to handle.

IMAGE AND EXPERIENCE

This part of the story reaches its climax at the point where de Barral, the disgraced father, is due to be released from his term of penal servitude, and the hopelessness of Flora's situation is at its most intense. At this point Captain Anthony, Mrs. Fyne's sailor brother, makes his appearance, falls in love with the girl and carries her off. I put this briefly in a sentence, because in fact we never see this process taking place. We are made very clearly aware of the emotional essence of the situation. It is that Flora, after years of cruelty, indifference or impersonal kindness, suddenly finds herself loved, and, hardly able to believe it, finds an escape from her intolerable loneliness. From the little we have heard of Captain Anthony up to now, and from all we know of Flora, this is a sufficiently astonishing development; yet we learn of it all in a curiously hypothetical way—largely through speculations of Marlow's about what must have happened, on the basis of one conversation with Flora after she has gone away. Such are the elaborate indirections of the method that this great central episode cannot be presented at first hand. This is often so in Conrad; for all Marlow's ubiquity there are many, and many of the most important, scenes at which he could not possibly have been present. We are convinced, touched, impressed, as we may well be by the report and interpretation of a thoughtful intermediary; but we do not *see*. In Henry James's sense the thing is hardly "rendered", any more than the scene with the governess was "rendered" in the earlier part of the book. And I believe this to reflect the fact that Conrad's knowledge of what would occur in such circumstances, indeed in many of the relations between man and man and man and woman, is curiously external and remote. Not, of course, his psychological knowledge, his understanding of an emotional reality; it is simply that his knowledge of circumstantial detail, detail of speech and social relationships, is not intimate enough to allow some of these critical scenes to be presented otherwise than deviously and indirectly. Where we need a scene in clear daylight we have a dissolving vista of hints and suggestions. This I believe is the main cause of the obscurity in Conrad that has worried Mr. Forster.

But *Chance* is a tale in two parts; and the second part is set on the sea, on board the *Ferndale*. This second part pursues the fortunes of Captain Anthony, Flora, by now his wife, and the repulsive, broken de Barral whom they have taken to sea with them on his release from prison. Captain Anthony, with characteristic single-mindedness, has taken de Barral at Flora's valuation and offered him sanctuary on his own ship. The situation is one of agonising strain. Flora is obliged to devote herself to the service of her repulsive father, who is virtually insane, filled with suspicion against Captain Anthony, and wholly ignorant of his true position. Captain Anthony, who loves the girl and has taken in the father from an impulse of pure devotion, has also been injured in youth. He finds it hard to believe that he is loved, and Fyne has blunderingly told him that Flora can only have turned to him in desperation. He accepts this view, places himself simply as Flora's protector, and refuses to press his claims upon her any further. And Flora—remains an enigma; even less than before are we allowed inside her consciousness.

As before, we follow the narrative through the eyes of others. But the others are now different. The mechanics of the transition are ingenious enough. Marlow persists in keeping in touch with Mr. Powell, the retired sailor of the introductory scene, and get from him the story of his first voyage on the *Ferndale*—which was also the second voyage of Captain Anthony as a married man. This part of the tale is told by Marlow, freely elaborating and interpreting the account of Mr. Powell. No different in narrative method, then, from the earlier part of the book. Nor is the essential material offered by the situation very different, except that it is multiplied by three— there are three lonelinesses to be portrayed. But somehow the quality of the novel seems to have changed. We cease to remember the intermediaries through whose consciousness the material has passed. We live on board the *Ferndale* as we never lived in the Fynes' house. And the reason I think is simple—we are now on board a ship. Not only Marlow and Mr. Powell but Conrad himself understands every detail of the *Ferndale*, not only physical and operational, but social as well. Conrad knows how a first officer is related to his ship and its captain, how that relation is upset by the introduction of a captain's wife; what a steward and a steward's wife might be able to see of it all; how a young second officer, newly joined, might impinge on the situation. The moral imagination of a great novelist Conrad always has; if he had not we should hardly be discussing him now. But his moral imagination often works, not exactly in a void, but in a world insufficiently realised, insufficiently dense, without all the manifold small pressures that go to make up life as it is lived. Here in the *Ferndale* the density, the actuality, the sense of living in a physical and social world with its own peculiar quality and flavour is triumphantly present. And so the true greatness of the latter half of the book is able to realise itself more fully; a greatness which consists in the piled-up sense of emotional incomprehension, of solitude and strain; in the splendid peripeteia, almost melodramatic, by which the strain is resolved; and the immense flooding current of generous release, far more than a conventional happy ending, in which even Mr. Powell comes ultimately to be included.

And here I wish to return to a slightly more sophisticated version of the common judgment that Conrad is a great novelist of the sea and the exotic. This denouement could only have been fully realised by him on a ship, for this was the only social order in which he was fully at home. The alternative would have been a setting up some Malayan river, on some tropical island, or in some extraordinary revolutionary or conspiratorial group—at any rate in some environment where he is released from the necessity of portraying the detailed pressures of a normal shore-based social life which he did not deeply understand and was not deeply interested in. And here we can perhaps find a place after all for the pronouncement about the simple claims of the sea. It expresses a need for simplification that was vital to Conrad. The complexities of his narrative method are, as it were, layers of protecting covering to an essentially simple heroic vision. This fits Captain Anthony well enough; he is primarily a man of such simple and absolute loyalties; it is his dilemma, almost his tragedy, that he is in a situation where integrity of this kind seems bound to be insufficient. But it does turn out to be sufficient after all. Straightforward obedience to what seems to him a simple and inescapable demand does manage to cut through the hateful tangle in which he and his wife are involved. It is characteristic of Conrad that he should see this kind of integrity most plainly in the form of fidelity to a craft—the demands that seamanship makes extended to the whole of life. Kipling does the same sort of thing, and if it seems inappropriate to introduce Kipling at this point I will add at once that Conrad does it with infinitely greater subtlety. Both see fidelity as a matter of personal honour, but personal honour incarnated in the exigencies of a profession or a craft. The second part of *Chance* is called "The Knight"; Captain Anthony's absolute seamanlike devotion is an analogy to the code of chivalry. Working as Conrad was without deep national or social roots his adoption of the code of the sea was natural for him. He sometimes extends it, and it becomes the code of any sensitive man of action. But it is never, I think, the code of a whole society, and rarely obedience to a deep instinctive pattern of behaviour. The loyalty of Conrad's heroes is almost always to something they have chosen, either as one chooses a profession, or as one adopts a deliberate and conscious attitude. For the world of Conrad's later readers, a world where customary social roots have become more and more ill-nourished, this purposeful adoption of a code has a peculiar importance. Off the ship his characters are lonely souls, and Conrad becomes the great student of isolation; but not, like some later writers, of total isolation. It is not as a natural force that the sea is of most importance to Conrad; he found in its discipline and its loyalties a bond which was able to link both him and his work with the common interests of humanity.

Chance is not a bad title for one of his greatest books. If it has no peculiar aptness to this particular novel, it does suggest something about his work as a whole, and his relation to it; a fortuitousness in the choice of his material, unlike the inevitability with which the Russian must write of the Russian soul, or the Englishman of the English class system. It was not chance that gave Conrad his imaginative penetration, his simplicity, his nobility of vision; but it was chance that made him a master-mariner, that cast his lot among East Indian islands, that gave him so many opportunities of insight into lonely souls in strange environments. And this chance made him the great novelist of a whole tract of experience that no other writer of his stature has ever attempted to explore.

INDEX

INDEX

INDEX

225

INDEX

INDEX

INDEX

A NOTE ABOUT THE AUTHOR

GRAHAM HOUGH was born in England in 1908 and educated at the University of Liverpool and Queen's College, Cambridge. He traveled widely in the Far East and taught for many years in Singapore. He has also held visiting professorships at the Johns Hopkins University and at Cornell University. Since 1951 Mr. Hough has been a University Lecturer and Fellow at Christ's College, Cambridge. His previous books include *The Last Romantics* (1949), *The English Romantics* (1953), and *The Dark Sun* (1957), an analysis of the thought and feeling governing the work of D. H. Lawrence.